Home
Almanac

Edited by ALICE WONG *and* LENA TABORI

Designed by TIMOTHY SHANER *and* CHRISTOPHER MEASOM

welcome
BOOKS

NEW YORK • SAN FRANCISCO

CONTENTS

Chapter 3
Design & Improvements

Chapter 4
Repairs & Maintenance

Chapter 5
Entertaining & Etiquette

Chapter 6
Resources 226

Before I was eight, I lived in seven homes. After that, I lived in just one until I married, and then moved from apartment to apartment four times in seven years (and bought a ramshackle country house in the midst of it all—with a down payment borrowed from my children's nanny!). I finally bought one four-story house in the city where I worked. (I borrowed that down payment, too.) I did renovate it from top to bottom before I moved in, but then I lived there, doing normal repair and maintenance and raising my children, Katrina and Natasha, while I ran up and down the stairs and created systems to keep everything in the right place on the right floor.

Many, many friends stayed there over the years and many parties took place there—family rituals like Christmas, small dinner parties, an engagement party, a wedding, and lots of author publication celebrations. We cooked for ourselves and for our many guests. When I was renovating, I found some beautiful kitchen appliances for my very open kitchen from an Italian company (featured in the wonderful book *Attention to Detail*). When I first turned on the gas oven to roast a chicken, the oven blew up—something to do with the Italian/American gas connection. Oils from the griddle leaked into my cutlery drawer, and the fan wasn't strong enough to remove the smoke from my aesthetically exquisite indoor grill. The charming Italian I had bought it all from came in a taxi and took it away. I had the carpenter give me drawers where the oven had been, and a cutting board replaced the grill. I spent the next twenty-five years going downstairs to the little kitchen in the office if I needed an oven (which I often did, especially when we were baking Christmas gingerbread cookies).

Now I am finally renovating my little ramshackle house in the country. My daughter Katrina was married there. I have a real architect and a real contractor (for a little shingled, multi-paned old-fashioned cozy house). I am buying American appliances and spending too much time thinking about closets and speaker wires and hardware, about where the washer and dryer should go and how to do it all without any chemicals for me to do battle with the rest of my life. I also spend half my time in San Francisco living in a house that feels like a spa overlooking Mt. Diablo. No children, just a dear man (who is brilliant with laundry and infrastructure) and orchid orphans always waiting by the door (left by friends once they have stopped flowering). A place where we have rugs that need cleaning and gutters that need repair and parties that need organizing. I need this book!

None of us learned how to deal with any of this in college, just as no one taught us how to diaper our firstborns. But somehow, over the years, we cope. This book is intended to help—help clarify what needs to be paid attention to, provide advice to make it all less daunting, simplify and organize the tasks at hand so that you enjoy your apartment or your home, whether you own or rent it.

And it is a great gift to anyone who moves into their first place. We've tried to cover everything—maybe too much. Let us know what we have missed.

—LENA TABORI

For the past six years, my husband and I have been living in our gracious three-bedroom apartment in Brooklyn with our three young daughters. We made six months of renovations on the apartment before we could move in. I waddled around in front of our contractor, huge with my second pregnancy, threatening to give birth any minute and constantly telling him that he absolutely must be on time with completion. He delivered the apartment almost finished, less stove installation, in the beginning of May; my baby was born May 6.

The apartment we purchased for our growing family was a fixer-upper. In fact, we turned it down when we first saw it. It was dark, smelly, and covered in moldy-green carpeting. The previous owners had been in there for more than thirty years and it seemed like they didn't do anything after they first moved in. Our real estate agent convinced us of the apartment's great potential. So we tore down walls, put up a new kitchen, renovated the bathrooms, redid the floors and the electricity, sanded, stripped, painted. . . it is still amazing to me all the work needed to make an apartment someone else just moved out of livable to us. I must admit, my husband is the decorator in our family. He was in his element finding the perfect silver knobs for the kitchen cabinets, choosing the pedestal sinks for the bathrooms, and duplicating the hanging dining table light from something he saw in a magazine. Me, I obsessed about the schedule of course, and about storage space: from lots of kitchen cabinets to built-in storage for hiding toys in the living and children's rooms.

The apartment is very lived-in now. Even though we have someone come clean once a week, every evening is maintenance. . . toys and books in the bins, dishes in the dishwasher, dirty clothes in the hamper, stray remotes back in their spots. The walls need repainting, but it will have to wait a little longer until my youngest is less dangerous with pens. We will need to rearrange the children's bedrooms soon to accommodate new sleeping arrangements and furniture now that the baby is growing out of her crib. We are thinking about making the storage room into an office/private space. And frankly, I'm getting a little tired of the curtain treatments and couch covers. Time for a bit of sprucing up.

There are simply so many areas of the home that you can spend forever perfecting. What is important to you? Do you take joy in changing the look of your living room with every season? Do you insist upon a perfectly made bed and a well-organized closet? Do you take pride in your well-stocked and well-used toolbox? Do you always have an improvement project in the works? Do you love to share your home with friends? Your home is uniquely yours, suited to your needs and what you like. *Home Almanac* contains a wealth of information and ideas for all your interests. Whatever balance of decorating, cleaning, organizing, repairing, improving, and entertaining is right for you and your home, *Home Almanac* helps and inspires. And like your home, *Home Almanac* is meant to be enjoyed. So curl up, learn a little, dream a little, and continue the process of perfecting your home.

—ALICE WONG

Chapter 1
Room by Room

GRACE

Entryways

Everyone coming into your home, whether an old friend stopping by, family members gathering for a celebration, or you yourself returning from errands, deserves a warm welcome. What lies just within your front door should encourage everyone to relax, to feel comfortable, to make a smooth transition from the cares of the world outside. When it's time to leave, a well-designed entry will give you a feeling of being pulled together, knowing that you haven't forgotten your keys and that your hair looks neat. Though the "entrance agenda" might seem daunting, you actually can accomplish it all in very little space.

A versatile, stylish entry will include:

■ COLOR Offer a clue to what lies beyond by extending the color palette of the living room right to the front door, or splash out with bold color choices. Experiment in the entry; if you wonder how crown moldings or a chair rail would look in your home, install them first in the entry to judge the effect.

■ FLATTERING LIGHT Soft halogen or low-wattage bulbs in a ceiling fixture or table lamp will not jolt someone coming in from the outdoors.

■ A MIRROR Whether you're rushing in or rushing out, a generous mirror will let you check your hair and your coat as you breeze by. What's more, a mirror will reflect the opposite wall, making the entry seem more spacious.

■ A SIDE CHAIR Sit down to remove wet boots comfortably. Packages, book bags, and attaché cases will fit nicely on a simple chair. Anything bigger will invite an accumulation of household junk.

■ A TABLE To keep your days running smoothly, make a habit of storing your bag and keys on a slender table. It will bring peace of mind—and save plenty of time.

■ A CONTAINER Place a basket or a bowl on the table and everyone in the family will stop to check for mail, the daily newspaper, messages and reminders.

■ NATURE Fresh-cut flowers are a luxury, but a single bloom in a bud vase gets the point across just as well. Another practical way to include the outdoors in the entry is with a bowl of lemons, apples, or richly colored pears.

■ PLAN AHEAD Decide beforehand where to store coats, hats, and umbrellas. When a visitor calls, you can quickly dispose of this business, then offer an invitation to sit down and be comfortable.

The Living Room

Relaxation. Think of your dream living room, and relaxation is surely a big part of the fantasy. Whether it's vast or cozy, sunny or intimately dim, vintage or modern, cluttered or spare, messy or immaculate, what matters most is that you surround yourself with comfortable furniture— the couch!—and collections of favorite objects. You want the walls painted a color you adore, the floors finished perfectly, the window treatments to provide just enough light from dawn to dusk. The successful living room lowers your blood pressure; it soothes and invigorates, it charms your guests and embraces your family.

In the last century, a matching "three-piece living-room suite" was the hallmark of a well-decorated living room. The three-seat sofa and two chairs with matching upholstery took pride of place; the look was completed with a coffee table and a couple of end tables. Everything matched, and "Does it go with the rest of the room?" was the first hurdle to clear.

Today, we make our own rules. If you want a leather sofa and brocade chairs, go for it. A pair of couches, a pair of loveseats, wicker recruited from the front porch: If it pleases you, it's right. One joy of furniture is that it's not nailed down: Push the couch here, shove it over there, plop it in the middle of the room. If your room has some outstanding architectural features—French windows, a fireplace, built-in bookcases—position major furniture pieces to play them up. If your room has an eyesore or another drawback—it's awkwardly shaped, has an ugly window, or doesn't receive enough daylight—camouflage the problem with your arrangement of furniture and lighting.

The Four Seasons Need More than Vivaldi

The key to designing seasonally appropriate living-room décor lies in the small touches.

■ In spring, pull back heavy draperies, trade paisley for polished cotton cushions, keep a vase of tulips or daffodils.

■ For summer, roll up the wool carpet and throw down sisal or rag rugs; fill that vase with daisies or dahlias.

■ As the light changes with the advent of autumn, the wool carpet returns and the warm colors of the harvest—crimson, burgundy, russet—appear on lampshades and comfy throws. Put out big bowls of baby pumpkins and gourds and baskets of Indian corn.

■ In the snowy cold of winter, pull the drapes and cover those throw pillows with luxurious cashmere or fine wool that's been cut from some clothing you've outgrown.

■ Pay special attention when the holiday festivities have passed and the dreary months of January, February and March loom. A flowering bulb, a spray of forsythia or cherry blossoms, or a wreath of eucalyptus will keep the room cheerful.

If you're renting a home and plan to move in the next few years, invest in high-quality furniture and accessories that will move with you. Once you've bought the house of your dreams, spend on architectural improvements like custom millwork and energy-efficient windows that will increase your property's value.

No Room Is Too Small, Honest

The living room does not have space for a three-cushion sofa, much less a sprawling sectional. Move down the scale until you reach the piece that will work for you, then design around it:

1. Three-seat sofa
2. Love seat
3. Mission bench with cushion
4. Garden loveseat
5. Porch swing hung from the ceiling.

What Is That?

Think about featuring a conversation piece in your decorating to help guests relax. What is a conversation piece? It's anything that piques one's curiosity and has a good story, such as a marble sculpture your mother crafted or a clay ashtray you made in kindergarten.

For Rooms With a View

Answer these questions, then treat your windows accordingly.

■ *What is the view?* OCEAN—Plan daylight viewing, with window treatments that flood your room with sky and sea. Once it is dark, substantial coverings eliminate "the black hole" and make rooms feel cozy. CITY—Plan twenty-four-hour viewing, with sheer curtains that can be pulled aside to act as a frame for your beautiful, glittering cityscape.

■ *Which direction?* North light is cool; east sun is morning; south is sunny most of the day; west exposure gives great sunsets. Most designers look for a warm palette for northern room. Rooms that are blessed with lots of sunshine do better without repeating the heat in the palette.

■ *How are the windows?* Will you need to disguise worn aluminum frames, or do you want to show off pristine arts and crafts woodwork?

■ *Is privacy an issue?* If you can see others, you can be seen too!

The six most versatile accent pieces:

Folding screens

Ottomans

Area rugs

Mirrors

Small tables

Pedestals

Conventional Wisdom for Upholstered Furniture

When it's time to choose the fabric for the upholstery of your sofa, loveseats, and chairs, many interior designers will tell you that neutral colors and designs work best. What they mean is that bright, intense colors and bold designs can become tiring after a year or so. That's not true with basic solids like ivory, beige, putty, taupe, sage, and café au lait, because they are more adaptable to design updates, even from season to season. Indulge your passion for the bold with lavish use of fringes, tassels, and lampshades. If solid-color fabrics bore you, look for soft patterns like stripes based on mattress ticking, a chalk stripe, or a tone-on-tone damask. A versatile pairing of colors (classics include the blue-and-white combo inspired by Scandinavian design and the camel-and-black often preferred by male members of the household) can be the springboard for any number of rich accents. Imagine that blue-and-white with intense lemon, or camel-and-black with firehouse red. A primary palette of two colors gets extra dimension from textured or patterned accents: toile, stripes, gingham checks. There is always room for paisley, floral prints, plaids and animal patterns; it would be a boring world indeed without them.

Home Entertainment Checklist

■ Television ■ Radio Receiver ■ CD Player ■ DVD Player ■ VCR ■ Computer Hardware, such as CD Burners ■ Video Game Accessories ■ Video Camera Accessories ■ Digital Camera Accessories ■ Extra Cords, Cables, and Power Strips

Entertainment Systems

Shopping for entertainment systems can be as simple as a trip to the drugstore or as ambitious as acquiring a new car. At the beginning of the twenty-first century, traditional video systems are being supplanted by digital ones, and home entertainment technology will become bigger, brighter, and better.

Interior design professionals are charged as television snobs, but it is more likely our attitude toward television that creates the problem. We contemplate every element in the room for its aesthetic value—colors, fabrics, and artwork. Then, when everything coordinates perfectly, a television is plopped in the mix. Thinking about the television presence in the home, beforehand, can help resolve the situation.

■ What will be the main television of the house? Which room will it reside in? What support equipment will it have?

You can buy items at major online auctions, such as eBay. Make sure the item is new in the box (NIB), still under warranty, and less expensive than buying it new from the store. Often times, although the auction starts out at a good price, bidding drives the price up. Don't forget to factor in the cost of shipping the item (which many major department stores include for free).

■ Where will the television that is watched during task work like cooking and ironing be?

■ Will there be a television in the bedroom dedicated to private relaxation after the day's activities? If you have frequent visitors, definately place one in the guest room.

Plan an entertainment system that can be in place for three to five years. Include separate storage for individual family members' personal DVDs and CDs. Provide a way station where stray accessories, such as phone chargers, video game accessories, headphones, spare wires, and video recorders and tapes, can gather. If you intend to upgrade your equipment, allow enough space for the newer model.

Cable or broadcast TV? The TV antenna, a whimsical configuration of metal rods and wires poised on every rooftop, has just about vanished from view. "Rabbit ears," antennas that attached directly to the television, are gone, too. In its day, the antenna was used to improve the reception of broadcast television from local stations. The antenna's heir, the satellite dish, was popular for a few years, but some say that the days of the satellite dish are numbered. The national networks are still broadcast free, but more than 85 percent of households have cable access.

The Dining Room

> If you own a beautiful but fragile carpet, a spot under the dining room table will keep it pretty safe from the to-and-fro of everyday activities. If you still have concerns about keeping the carpet on the floor, consider mounting it as a wall hanging.

America is divided into two types of people. One camp treasures their most valuable possessions and keeps them carefully and safely stored between holidays. The rest of us treasure our valuables too, and we make them part of our daily lives. If it were possible to apply this theory to rooms, the dining room would qualify as one often saved for special occasions. Perhaps formal dining rooms need to be reconsidered. Think of the dining room as a family nourishment center, where the "good" china and silver are laid for each meal and everyone gathers around the table to feed body and soul.

The Furnishings

The focal point of the dining room is its table and chairs— arguably not the most comfortable seating in the home, but just right for encouraging conversation. Other standard furnishings include a sideboard, which holds the table linens, and a buffet, which provides storage for crystal and china. Many people like to hang a chandelier over the center of the table, which is a nice gesture when there is a generous mirror over the sideboard to reflect the light.

Lighting for Drama

The design possibilities of this room are as exciting as they are unexplored. As the stage for limited amounts of time, the room is ideal for more adventurous design approaches to the walls, floors, and ceilings. Because the furniture arrangement is rarely adjusted, fragile wall treatments, such as wallpaper and fabric, are safer here. Design lighting to be adjustable, so that you can read the newspaper at breakfast and enjoy glittery candlelight at night.

Double Duty

Home design experts, and the furniture makers who pay close attention to the designers' clients, confirm that the dining room is most likely to serve more than one purpose—also functioning as a home office, a sewing room, or a computer room. Many recent designs for dining room furniture have featured flexible pieces: a sideboard that can accommodate computer equipment or a buffet roomy enough for the sewing machine. If you know that your dining room will have multiple functions, let that guide your choice of furniture. Sleek lines for the table and comfortable straight-back chairs will be more adaptable.

Essential China Set

China sets come in many different styles, including porcelain, fine bone, earthenware, and stoneware. Make sure to pick a style that you find attractive, but if you're using it on a daily basis, pick one that you won't be too heartbroken to replace if damaged.

Most sets contain eight place settings consisting of a: Bread plate ■ Cup and saucer ■ Dessert plate ■ Dinner plate ■ Salad plate ■ Soup bowl

These serving dishes can be china or silver: Cream pitcher ■ Gravy boat ■ Pitcher ■ Platters (large and small) ■ Serving bowls (three should be adequate) ■ Sugar bowl ■ Teapot

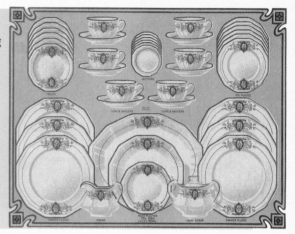

Everyday Centerpieces

Most dining room tables beg for a centerpiece, but supplying fresh flowers everyday is going to be extravagant. Think in layers and you will be able to accommodate endless changes. Try this arrangement for starters.

1. Begin with a tapestry, a length of vintage textile, or another substantial fabric. It's not necessary to cover the entire tabletop; treat the material as a runner.

2. Place finely embroidered linen or lace on the base.

3. Choose a tray and fill with silver, wood, or pottery objects. Think in terms of shape and texture so the three elements work well together.

4. Snuggle in a candelabra, a tea service, beaded fruit, or some crystal.

Change the arrangement as whim dictates to keep the dining room fresh and intriguing. It will please you.

Essential Glassware

An ideal glassware collection contains eight pieces of each glassware listed, but you can get by with a simplified set containing all-purpose wine, water, and juice glasses.

■ Pilsner tall and thin with heavy base; for beer and ale
■ All-purpose wine glass for informal settings ■ Champagne flute long and slender; for champagnes and sparkling wines
■ Red wine glass large bowl allows red wine to breathe
■ Martini glass triangular-shaped bowls; for martinis, cosmopolitans, and other mixed drinks ■ White wine glass smaller bowl than the red ■ Water glass can also be for highball drinks and beer ■ Old fashioned squat glass; for mixed drinks or drinks with ice ■ Juice glasses ■ Tall beverage glasses for iced drinks ■ Miscellaneous bar glasses brandy, liqueur, sherry

The Essential Silver Set

There are almost as many serving utensils as there are types of food dishes. The key is to start with a basic set, and then slowly add specialized pieces.

The Basic Set

■ Salad fork ■ Dinner fork ■ Dinner knife ■ Soup spoon ■ Teaspoon ■ Butter knife

For a More Formal Setting, add: ■ Dessert fork ■ Dessert spoon ■ Fish fork ■ Fish knife ■ Individual steak knife ■ Round bowl soup spoon

For the Server

■ Carving fork ■ Carving knife ■ Cold meat fork—serves sliced meats and cutlets ■ Flat server—serves fish, large entrée pieces, and desserts ■ Gravy ladle ■ Ice tongs ■ Large serving fork—serves meats and fowl ■ Large and small ladles ■ Master butter knife ■ Pie server ■ Pierced serving spoon—serves juicy entrées and vegetables ■ Salad set—tongs, spoon, fork ■ Serving spoon

For Those Special Meals

■ Asparagus server ■ Bar knife for slicing lemons and limes and opening bottles ■ Butter pick ■ Cheese serving knife ■ Cracker scoop ■ Cream sauce ladle ■ Demitasse spoon for after-dinner coffees and caviar ■ Fruit spoon ■ Ice cream fork for frozen desserts, ice cream cakes ■ Iced beverage spoon for iced coffees and teas ■ Jelly server ■ Lemon fork ■ Macaroni server ■ Melon spoon ■ Mustard ladle ■ Nut spoon for candies and nuts ■ Olive and pickle fork ■ Oyster fork ■ Salt spoon ■ Strawberry fork ■ Sugar spoon

Taking Care of Silver

■ Wash your silver immediately after use with hot soapy water, and dry with a cloth to prevent water spots. This will cut down on the need to polish.

■ To remove tarnish from silver, place aluminum foil, shiny side up, in a cooking pot. Place the item(s) in the pot, and add enough water to cover all pieces. Add a tablespoon of baking soda, and bring to a boil. Boil for around three minutes. Cool water, and remove pieces. Dry thoroughly.

■ Wrap silver in acid-free tissue paper to prevent tarnishing when storing. Don't place pieces in plastic bags (they trap condensation) or fasten with rubber bands (they could discolor metal).

■ Avoid prolonged contact with salt, egg yolk, mustard, fruit juices, cooked vegetables, fish, or vinegar.

■ Dip polishes and silver polish wipes have become increasingly popular, but be warned: they can remove oxidized patterns on silver, and even damage silver if used on a regular basis.

■ Clean fork tarnish with a piece of string dipped in polish. Then "floss" the tines.

■ Use an old toothbrush with white toothpaste containing baking soda to remove old stains.

The Kitchen

Call it the heart of the home or the pulse of the house; the kitchen gets more wear, sees more activity, and works harder than all your other rooms combined. Planning, not the amount of available space, is the key to an efficient kitchen. We have seen restaurants with postage-stamp-size kitchens where the chef has room to prepare magnificent meals. A kitchen that is too big, where the distance between stovetop and refrigerator is more than a few steps, can be less practical.

The first consideration for any kitchen, whether it is inherited, on the drawing board to be designed, or about to be remodeled, is the Essential Triangle: the placement of the sink, refrigerator, and stove, particularly in relation to each other.

Avoid placing the refrigerator and stove side by side; if there is no choice, install extra insulation between them to reduce the lost energy.

Once the sink, refrigerator, and stove are in position, other elements will begin to fall into place.

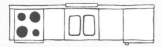

A Galley Kitchen, where all the appliances and cabinets share a wall, is often installed in smaller apartments and as secondary food prep areas in finished basements, poolhouses, or guest houses.

The Kitchen with an Island, whether the island contains the sink or the stove, still needs careful planning for the triangle.

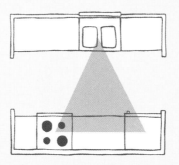

A Symmetrical Kitchen features a triangle that is equal on all three sides.

An L-Shaped Kitchen offers more space, though the triangle should be designed for efficiency.

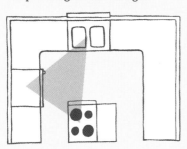

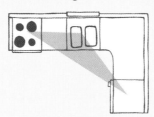

Common Kitchen Layouts

■ The dishwasher is set under the counter, near the sink and the dish cupboards.

■ Countertops and food preparation often do not go hand-in-hand. Non-porous materials, such as Corian© and granite, work for basic counter space; cutting boards and other portable work surfaces can be called to duty as needed.

■ Food cupboards are close to the refrigerator and a food preparation area. A simple system for storing staples is to designate cupboards for sweet or savory products—no more rooting around in the wrong cupboard.

■ Electronic appliances, unless used daily, are best put in closed storage, where they can stay dust-free and not get in the way of food preparation.

■ Good task lighting is essential in the kitchen, to show when lettuce is completely washed, when the eggs are cooked just right, and when ingredients are measured properly.

■ At least one fire extinguisher and one smoke detector are essential.

Kitchen Improvements

Kitchen design is a complex business, and for good reason. Everything dangerous in your home is in here—gas lines, electricity, running water, toxic cleaning agents, you name it. Most kitchens are inherited, remodeled, or custom-designed; whichever category yours fits into, there are improvements available.

■ Once safety and hygiene are accounted for, function is next.

■ Imagine the kitchen throughout the seasons of the year, from one year to another; will it still work for you?

■ Have some fun. The kitchen is a gathering spot; make yours appealing with whimsical collections or an unexpected piece of furniture such as a sofa or an easy chair.

■ Plan to be tidy. An empty cupboard alongside a chair awaits for the day's newspapers and week's magazines.

Open or Closed Storage?

Most kitchens are a combination of the two, an unintentional, inadvertent, by-default collection of food, utensils, cookware, mail, cleaning agents, paper products, and oh-so-much-more. Part of that is the nature of the kitchen: it is a hub of activity. If the fundamentals of your storage plan are right for your needs, you'll carry some degree of order.

■ Open shelves are the most basic form of storage. The advantage is

(continued on page 25)

Essential Kitchen

The Basics

■ Bottle opener ■ Can opener ■ Colander ■ Corkscrew ■ Cutting boards (one for meat/poultry and one for all else) ■ Dry and liquid measuring cups ■ Grater ■ Ice cube trays ■ Kitchen shears ■ Kitchen timer ■ Large stirring spoon ■ Measuring spoons ■ Meat thermometer ■ Nested mixing bowls ■ Pots with lids (small, medium, large) ■ Roaster pan with cover and rack ■ Saucepans (1 quart and 2 to 4 quart) ■ Skillets (8 inch and 12 to 14 inch) ■ Slotted spoon ■ Spatulas (plastic and metal) ■ Teakettle ■ Timer ■ Tongs ■ Tupperware ■ Vegetable peeler ■ Whisk ■ Wooden spoon

Knives

■ **Boning knife** curved; for soft vegetables ■ **Bread knife** serrated edge slices and halves bread ■ **Carving knife** ■ **Chef's knife** for most fruits and vegetables ■ **Cleaver** for large pieces of meat, like shanks and ribs ■ **Paring knife** for fruit and vegetables ■ **Sharpening steel** to keep blades sharp ■ **Slicing knife** cut meat, poultry, and vegetables

For Your Inner Baker

■ Baking pan ■ Baking sheet ■ Bundt pan ■ Casserole dishes (two) ■ Cooling rack ■ Loaf pan ■ Muffin tin ■ Oven thermometer ■ Pie plate ■ Rolling pin ■ Round cake pans (two)

To Round Off Your Kitchen

■ Egg beater ■ Extra-large pot ■ Funnel ■ Juicer ■ Ladle ■ Pasta server ■ Potato masher ■ Sieve ■ Vegetable steamer (can be metal or even bamboo) ■ Vegetable scrub brush ■ Wok

Essential Pantry

Staples

■ Beans, dried and canned: black, chickpeas, lima, kidney, pinto ■ Bouillon cubes and powder ■ Bread crumbs ■ Breakfast cereals ■ Broth, chicken and beef ■ Cinnamon ■ Cocoa ■ Coffee ■ Cornstarch ■ Cream of tartar ■ Dried fruits ■ Fruit Juice ■ Grains: millet, kasha, couscous ■ Honey ■ Meats ■ Milk: condensed and evaporated ■ Nuts: walnuts, almonds, cashews, hazelnuts, pine nuts ■ Oils: olive, vegetable, peanut, corn, sesame ■ Onions ■ Pasta, dried: fettuccine, macaroni, lasagna, penne, spaghetti ■ Peanut butter ■ Popcorn ■ Potatoes ■ Preserves ■ Rice: white and brown ■ Salt ■ Soup, canned and instant: tomato, chicken noodle, vegetable ■ Sugars: white, brown, confectioners' ■ Syrup ■ Tea ■ Tuna ■ Vinegar: red, white, balsamic

Condiments

■ Basil ■ Bay leaves ■ Black pepper ■ Chili powder ■ Garlic ■ Ginger ■ Horseradish ■ Ketchup ■ Marjoram ■ Mayonnaise ■ Mustard, regular and Dijon ■ Oregano ■ Pasta sauce, bottled ■ Peppercorns ■ Relishes ■ Sage ■ Salad dressing ■ Salsas ■ Sesame paste or tahini ■ Soy sauce ■ Tabasco sauce ■ Tomato puree ■ Worcestershire sauce

Baking supplies

■ Baking powder ■ Baking soda ■ Cornmeal ■ Extracts: vanilla, almond, etc. ■ Flour: white, whole wheat ■ Molasses ■ Non-stick cooking spray ■ Rolled oats ■ Wheat germ ■ Yeast

(continued from page 23)

that you can see at a glance what you have and where it is; that is the disadvantage too. And everything collects dust.

■ Wall-hung kitchen cupboards with glass doors are a closed-display for dishes and glassware.

■ Wall-hung and floor-mounted cupboards with solid doors can give the kitchen a more streamlined appearance.

■ Islands offer four sides of storage, good for a combination of open and closed shelves.

■ Hoosier cabinets, which are also known as flour mills, were the first mass-produced freestanding kitchen storage in America. Made of oak, a Hoosier cabinet is a good investment if you are renting and likely to move.

■ A Welsh dresser is the classic open/closed storage combination that is so popular in Europe. The top shelves feature a plate rail for display and underneath closed storage.

How Does Your Garden Grow?

They are fragrant, but that's not the only reason fresh herbs can take your breath away. In supermarkets and specialty food shops, fresh herbs, especially those that are unusual or out-of-season, are costly. Add to that the fact that you have to buy far more than you need and there is waste. A kitchen window box planted with your favorite herbs is an enduring pleasure as well as admirable economy. You pinch or snip only as much tarragon or basil as you need; the harvesting actually encourages growth. Isn't nature grand?

The Can't-Boil-Water Kitchen; The Pro's Kitchen

Most of us fall somewhere between these two extremes, but it's safe to say that we've each been in the can't-boil-water kitchen at some point. The technology of remote cooking and convenience of prepared foods allow cooking to be an elective, rather than an essential, skill. Your kitchen can reflect your place along this chain; a microwave oven and coffeepot ensure basic survival. With a copy of *The Joy of Cooking* at your elbow and versatile cookware such as a $2^1/_2$-quart saucepan, a sauté pan, and a mixing bowl, you can move to the next stage. As you learn and experiment, your personal preferences begin to emerge: a flair for grilling or a penchant for oven-roasting, baking over cooking in general, quick meals or complicated endeavors. Invest in top-quality tools when you know that you will use them seriously; experimenting is more practical with less-expensive basics.

Utensils You Might Be Surprised You Need

PANCAKE TURNER can be used for everything from scrambling eggs to grilling hamburgers; to, of course, flipping pancakes perfectly.

JAR OPENER, or try this neat trick: put thick rubber bands around the body and lid of the jar. Using the rubber bands as grips provides the traction to get a stubborn jar open.

RUBBER SCRAPER used for removing the last bits of batter, icing, or mixtures from jars.

Bedrooms

"*Show me the living room and I'll show you the man*" *may be the cliché, but it is the bedroom that is most revealing about you. Early bedrooms were simple, functional places, often with room for a bed and a wash stand, but without so much as a closet. After all, what was there to do in the bedroom but sleep? Bedrooms have certainly evolved, with each generation placing more importance on them and investing greater attention in their design. A historical bedroom might just fit in one of today's walk-in closets.*

Bedroom design is separated from design in other rooms by emotion: when you put together the bedroom, you are expressing yourself for yourself only. This room is a window into your soul. If you lavish no other room, indulge the bedroom. The time you spend here should supply the emotional nourishment that every happy person consumes. Fantasize about your perfect bedroom; everything you see in the vision should be comforting to you. If it doesn't bring you comfort, it should be somewhere else.

Creating an Atmosphere

To create this atmosphere of "emotional nourishment," toss out the notion of a room that offers just the utilitarian good night's sleep. Our bedrooms are havens, refuges from the pressures of daily life. When that door closes behind you, it should shut out stress (*see The Perfect Bed, page 136*).

. . . And Here We Have A Lovely Matching Six-Piece Suite

Yes, a bedroom can be furnished by pointing a finger. The bed matches the end tables, which match the bureau, which matches the dresser, which matches the mirror hung over it. Our favorite bedrooms are one-of-a-kind collections of beloved pieces and current fascinations. If you're in love with a console table, it may fit alongside the bed. An old piano bench is wonderful at the foot of the bed; its seat no longer stores sheets of music, but sheets of lovely linen.

Got Kids?

Bring an infant into the family and you will want to keep him close, in a bassinet in your room, then into a crib in an adjacent nursery. Always design for safety; as a girl or boy becomes more independent, you will be thankful for your foresight. As they grow into their personalities, children take more active roles in their bedroom design. When they enter the double-digits

You see your reflection in mirrors and windows, in the restroom at work, in a friend's home, or in the fitting room at a store. But the mirror in your bedroom should be the most truthful. A full-length mirror reflects hats and shoes, a cheval mirror is long and has been mounted on a stand so that it can be tilted, and a three-way mirror provides extra views. Self-confidence comes from knowing that you look good, and if your mirror is badly lit, distorted, or too short, you will not enjoy that sense of assurance before you face your public.

(age ten and older), they will want ultimate control, and one day you may come to a door with an emphatic KEEP OUT! sign.

■ New standards have increased the safety of infant and toddler furniture. Cribs manufactured before these standards may not be safe. If you are in doubt about a piece, check with the U.S. Consumer Product Safety Commission (*www.cpsc.gov*).

■ When the crib is replaced by a regular bed, mesh safety sides are recommended.

■ Invest in furniture that will be appealing in years to come; if a piece has good lines, the frame can be painted and refinished in any number of ways.

■ Let older children make design decisions. Color, furniture, and bedding are all up for grabs, and there are many companies that are geared toward selling to children and teens.

The Basics You Must Do Without

Take the television out of your bedroom and you have instantly made the room more serene, secluded, private, and intimate. Though designers have become increasingly clever about disguising the TV in armoires and remotely operated tables, it is the nature of television that should not interfere with the delicate balance in the bedroom. Jack Paar and Johnny Carson were the first emissaries to the bedroom for late-night viewing. Years later, studies have found that the distraction and intrusion television represents outweigh its entertainment value. Ditch the TV and grab a book for late-night relaxation. Set the radio to a music station, so that you do not awaken to the news hour. If you have a treadmill, stairmaster, rowing machine, or another big piece of exercise equipment, move it to another room; whether you use it faithfully or not, it is a hulking reminder of a different part of your life.

Company's Coming

An overnight or weekend visit with relatives or friends is the ultimate test of hospitality. If you have the luxury of space and can designate a single room for guests, take advantage of it. The most sensible bedding for a guest room is twin beds. Longtime couples usually get a kick out of it (they are reminded of Lucy and Ricky Ricardo!) and friends find individual beds more accommodating. Encourage guests to unpack, with good hangers and abundant closet space, and empty drawers. For your visitor, personalize the room with a framed photo of you both at an earlier time (this makes a good souvenir too). Alert guests beforehand of any potential discomforts, like the roar of early morning traffic or a persistent draft. And yes, sleep there yourself one night to performance-test the guest room.

Be sure to provide your guests with additional blankets and pillows. Some other nice comforts include a newly packaged toothbrush, toothpaste, razor, water carafe, and drinking glass. Little luxuries are wonderful as well: flowers, candies, and magazines will keep your guests coming back!

The biggest beds do need a lot of space to set them off. On the other hand, one of our editors has a king size bed that she created by joining her childhood twin beds, and the sentimentality they bring her is worth the sacrifice of space.

The Bathroom

O h, how it has changed! The bathroom, once three pieces of white vitreous porcelain—a sink, a tub, and a toilet—was considered simply a utilitarian room. During the housing boom that followed World War II, someone tipped a bucket of color into the white finish, and those three bathroom pieces re-emerged in a rainbow of dusty pink, mint green, powder blue, and harvest yellow. Toward the end of the century the national perception of the bathroom underwent a seismic shift and the one-time strictly business room emerged from its cocoon as a sparkling spa—a soul-restoring salon devoted to taking care of one's self.

The bathroom has changed in other ways. Houses have more of them: the powder room just inside the front door is a comfort station for those arriving and departing or invited for an evening. The half-bath or mud room off the kitchen is utilitarian clean-up from cooking or gardening. A full bath includes the original sink, tub, and toilet, but often a shower has been added. In the master bedroom, each partner may have a private bathroom and dressing area. Those couples that do share one bathroom often install two sinks and a separate shower and bath. In its own way, the once shunned bathroom has claimed bragging rights and is eagerly shown off to visitors.

At its core, every bathroom is about hygiene and safety, and each element of the room must be carefully and professionally evaluated for them. It is possible to transform the bathroom into an exotic retreat, but only when the fundamental fixtures, electricity, and plumbing have been deemed safe.

Fixtures

Happily for lovers of the new bathroom as luxury space, the fixtures that were made in the late 1800s and early 1900s have kept their appeal, and they function well, too. In fact, it may be more expensive to fit a bathroom with vintage fixtures than with new ones. But cost calculated with space makes the bathroom the most expensive room in the house. Whether your style is vintage or state-of-the-art modern, it is still possible to spend $1,000 for a bathroom faucet, if you desire.

Like the kitchen, the bathroom usually returns any investment in improvements when the house is sold. If new fixtures are to be installed, they should be chosen for timelessness; the freestanding sway-back rollicking red bathtub is not for everyone. With basic fixtures in place, the décor can be taken in any direction.

A Private Room For Personal Collections

Most bathrooms need help navigating from sterile to sublime. If you are to get the most enjoyment from yours, bring in things you love. Hang favorite art, place a sculpture on a pedestal, or display your collection of cookie jars. If you love anything green, bring it all together here. Cats, dogs, birds, and frogs are all popular collectibles, and come in so many different forms that they can appear on wallpaper as well as shelves, on shower curtains and as statues.

Children's Bathrooms

As soon as they are born, we want our children to learn to use the toilet! The bathroom is one of the two most dangerous rooms in the house (along with the kitchen). For children the dangers are even greater, because they are not knowledgeable about electricity and water, about bathtub overflows and, most of all, what is meant to be flushed down the toilet.

When they are just starting out, supervise your children closely. Observe what trouble spots attract their attention. Get down to their eye level and test cabinet doors, turn-off valves, and electric cords. Remove the lock from the door. Provide stepping stools so that they can reach the sink and toilet. Then have fun with decorations, such as rubber duckies and water toys that charm them. Assess the bathroom every year, on the child's birthday perhaps, and adapt it to suit the new wants and needs.

Working with the Space You Have

Most bathrooms are limited in space; working with the space you have may be easier than designing without limitations. Small bathrooms can be taken to new proportions with clever lighting and mirrors, dramatic wall treatments, and the illusion of space. Sometimes simply switching the location of fixtures will reveal extra space. Explore your options; if your home is part of a multiple-unit dwelling, there may be restrictions on where plumbing lines can be installed.

The Greenhouse Effect

Poor ventilation in the bathroom is a problem: steam and moisture will cause wallpaper to peel, paint to curl, and mold to grow. But just enough ventilation will create an environment in which you can indulge your green thumb.

- A sunny, dry bathroom will adore cacti and succulents.
- A sunny, moist room will love flowering plants like African violets.
- A dark, dry room is up to the challenge of sansaveria, or snake plants.
- A dark, moist room will enjoy bromeliads, the tropical plants that take in water from their leaves, not by roots.

For instant drama in a bland bathroom, lug in the biggest potted plant you can find—an arcing banana palm or a maidenhair fern. If you are lucky with ivy, cover the wall of the tub with chicken wire and train ivy around that.

C. COLES PHILLIF

The Home Office

With recent technological advances, such as faster computer lines, more convenient delivery services, and highly accessible Internet tools, many people are finding it easier than ever to maintain an office in their homes. But whether you're head of a stay-at-home business, or need a little space to manage your household, your home can benefit from an office area. With a sturdy desk, supportive chair, computer, telephone, and storage system, you can easily create the kind of atmosphere that will motivate you to get things done.

The Basics

A solid office system should contain:

- Desk and chair
- Computer with Internet access and a printer
- Dependable phone line (separate from your home line) with voicemail or an answering machine. You may want to invest in two phone lines: one for the telephone and one for the Internet or fax.
- Filing/storage system for paperwork and office supplies
- Wastebasket and paper shredder
- Complete your office with a fax machine, copier, or scanner.

Creating a Space

To decide how much space you need, take into account how much privacy and noise reduction you'll desire. People living alone can usually set up anywhere, but for people who live in noisy households, it pays to pick a room with a door that closes. You may want to soundproof the room as well. At-home businesses that deal with clients could benefit from separate entrances that do not go through the rest of the house. If it is impossible to find a separate space, try roping off a section of the kitchen, family room, or bedroom to be used for infrequent office work.

Light & Electricity

Thankfully, many offices now realize that fluorescent bulbs are not the best lighting to utilize in an office space. Your office should have soft, indirect lighting that allows you to see clearly without straining your eyes. Track lighting is a good choice, but you should also have access to spot lighting, like that provided by small office lamps. Natural light will lift your spirits, but don't rely only on the light of your window for illumination.

If you are converting a pre-existing room into an office, make sure that you have enough outlets installed to accommodate your electronic appliances and your lighting needs. If you'll be using your home office heavily, one outlet is

Use your space wisely. Even if you aren't especially pressed for elbow room, it's a great idea to invest in a bulletin board to tack up messages, a calendar, or miscellaneous notices. A pegboard also allows you to hang various office tools on the wall, and metal shelves or bookshelves will free up your office by getting the paperwork off your desk. See our organizing tips on pages 84–87 for more ways to maximize office space.

definitely not going to cover the room and could cause a fire hazard due to outlet overload.

Office Décor

Although it's tempting to simply choose office furniture from a catalogue or pick it up on sale, be cautious: most furniture is designed for large corporate spaces and may not fit your room. Take measurements first to be certain you're buying the right size. Modular furniture is versatile in that you can add to it as your office grows by introducing or removing parts as you see fit.

Even though the main function of your office is productivity, that does not mean you need to work in a setting devoid of personality. After all, one of the perks of working from home is having the benefits of home all day long. Put up pictures, maintain a leafy houseplant, or simply add some personal touches to make your office more inviting to you.

To Your Health

Modern technology has done wonders for the office community, but it can also do a number on your health. Follow these simple steps to reduce the amount of strain put on your body during the workday.

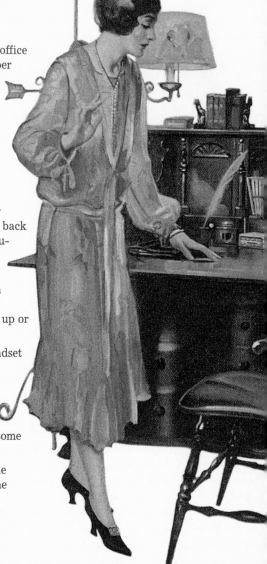

■ Your desk should be approximately 32 inches from the ground, and provide you with enough space to accommodate a computer and some extra elbow room for paperwork. L-shaped desks are optimal for freeing up work space.

■ The computer monitor should be approximately 20 inches away from you.

■ Your chair should be supportive, but also adjustable to your body. A folding chair may look like a cheap solution, but your back will thank you if you invest in a good chair, possibly with pneumatic adjusters and rollers.

■ Your feet should touch the floor solidly, and your knees should be bent at a 90-degree angle. If this isn't possible, get a footrest. Your arms should be parallel to the ground and your elbows should remain at your sides without straining to reach up or down when you type.

■ If you'll be on the telephone a lot, invest in a hands-free headset to get rid of neck pains.

■ Reduce eyestrain by keeping your monitor on eye level, and tilt the bottom up slightly.

■ A window directly facing the monitor can cause a glare at some hours of the day. Work around these hours, or purchase some lightweight curtains to shade your screen from the sun.

■ Use a wrist rest in front of your keyboard to take some of the pressure off your forearms. Don't allow your wrists to lie on the rest when you are typing.

Home Office Reference Center

Complete your home office with a well-rounded set of reference books. A thesaurus, an almanac, a desk reference, concise encyclopedia, grammar guide, and book of quotations can help you in a multitude of office duties. But whether or not you run a business at home, the following books are essentials for any home library:

TELEPHONE BOOK Keeping you connected to your community is only one of its perks. It also has a helpful listing of emergency numbers in your area, and sometimes contains local coupons.

DICTIONARY Make sure to pick one that is the most current, but also best suited to your household. The twenty-five-pound tome you might buy will just sit unused, collecting dust, if all you are really looking for are simple definitions. If you have kids, invest in a children's dictionary as well.

ATLASES A road atlas is excellent for planning road trips. A world atlas can provide helpful geographic data. Rand-McNally is a trustworthy source.

FIRST AID MANUAL This provides fast and accurate reference for common household injuries and disasters. Most of them usually leave a space for you to fill in personal emergency numbers or family medical contacts. Keep this together with your first aid kit.

GENERAL HOME MAINTENANCE BOOK Although we at *Home Almanac* have tried to provide you with enough tips to fix the most basic of repairs, it's a good idea to pick up one of these manuals to assist you in any household situation.

COOKBOOKS Even if you're a die-hard take-out artist, it's always nice to have a cookbook around for those nights when your budget is small but your appetite is big. Start with basic ones like *The Joy of Cooking* or *Better Homes and Gardens' New Cookbook*, and then build from there.

Your home library can also include:

Medical Guides

Religious texts like the Bible, the Talmud, or the Koran

Film/movie guides

Gardening books

Chapter 2 Cleaning & Organizing

Cleaning Basics

A clean house is generally a happy house, but not all of us have the time or money to employ a fully staffed housekeeping unit to keep our home in shape. Thankfully, Home Almanac *provides you with a wealth of guidelines you can use to clean up any mess. Unsure about what you should include in your cleaning arsenal? Here is a handy inventory of tools and products no homemaker should be without. Sometimes simply having a list of what needs to be done can do wonders for focusing on the task at hand.*

General Guidelines

■ In general, clean from the top down. Think about it: you wouldn't want to wash the floor and then have dirt fall on it while dusting the lampshades.

■ Work on one room at a time, one area at a time.

■ Resist the urge to put misplaced items back in their proper locations one at a time, as you find them, which would force you to make many unnecessary trips from the room you are cleaning to all around the house. Instead, gather all misplaced items in a box or basket, and then put them away all at once.

Put your tools and cleaners in a small caddy, so when you do routine cleaning the ones you need most are readily accessible.

Cleaning Tool Kit
Cleaning Products

■ Baking soda ■ Bleach (diluted with water, works to fight mildew) ■ Borax ■ Dishwashing liquid ■ Floor/wall cleaner (usually contains ammonia) ■ Wood furniture polish ■ General-purpose cleaner (kitchen and bath spray) ■ Heavy-duty cleanser like Ajax ■ Household ammonia ■ Lemon juice ■ Metal polish ■ Oil soap (like Murphy's, for wood products) ■ Salt ■ Sanitizer like Lysol ■ Toilet-bowl cleaner ■ White vinegar ■ Window cleaner

See Healthy Cleaning on page 48 to make your own nontoxic, cost-efficient cleansers.

Tools and Utensils

■ Broom ■ Bucket ■ Dust mop ■ Duster (acrylic wand or feather) ■ Dustpan and brush ■ Handheld vacuum ■ Latex or non-allergenic plastic gloves ■ Old newspapers ■ Paper towels ■ Scrub brush ■ Soft cloths (for dusting and polishing; you can use old, white T-shirts) ■ Sponge mop ■ Sponges (keep one handy for dry sponging) ■ Spray bottle (to hold your spritz water) ■ Squeegee ■ Steel-wool pads ■ Toilet brush ■ Toilet plunger ■ Toothbrush

■ A basket can also serve as a catchall in the hallway or kitchen. Make it a daily routine to empty the basket and put accumulated items back in their places.

■ A hamper in every bathroom will cut down on mountains of discarded clothes in the bedrooms.

■ Don't be afraid to delegate chores or split your cleaning time. If you feel overwhelmed by a large cleaning task, instead of tackling it all at once, split it into two manageable time frames.

■ Don't be distracted by the television or telephone. Some music in the background can make the time more enjoyable, but don't forget what your real intent is—to clean your house.

General Cleaning Schedule

DAILY

■ Make the beds. ■ Straighten up. Pick up misplaced items, toys, and dirty clothes. ■ Wash dishes and wipe down kitchen counters. ■ Take out the trash. ■ Wipe bathroom sinks and the shower door.

Dust cloths and sponges should be rinsed thoroughly after each use and washed regularly in a solution of water and vinegar. Kill bacteria in non-plastic sponges by microwaving them on high for one minute.

WEEKLY

■ Clean the kitchen and bathroom more thoroughly. ■ Dust furniture and shelves. ■ Vacuum rugs, wood floors, and high-traffic areas. ■ Mop non-wood floors. ■ Change linens. ■ Buy groceries. Discard spoiled food in fridge. ■ Do laundry (you may have to do this more frequently for more than two people). ■ Empty wastepaper baskets.

MONTHLY

■ Clean windows. ■ Clean the stove and oven. ■ Wipe down cabinets. ■ Clean inside the refrigerator. Empty the drip pan if your refrigerator is equipped with one. ■ Vacuum curtains, blinds, and furniture. ■ Dust, sweep, and vacuum each room. ■ Wash out the kitchen trash container. ■ Polish silver, brass, and other metal pieces. ■ Clean appliances.

SEMI-ANNUALLY

■ Defrost the refrigerator/freezer. Vacuum fridge coils. ■ Shampoo carpets. Wax floors (if necessary). ■ Wash curtains or blinds. ■ Clean behind heavy furniture. ■ Check heating and cooling systems. ■ Organize and store photographs, videos, music collections. ■ Go through "junk drawers." ■ Clean out closets.

Seasonal Cleaning Schedule

SPRING

- Go through clothes. Donate or discard old clothes. Clean and store winter wardrobe. ▪ Flip mattresses. ▪ Wash heavy linens (comforters, quilts, etc.), rugs, and windows. ▪ Clean ceiling fans and vents. ▪ Thoroughly go through and clean bathrooms and kitchen (go through cabinets and drawers). ▪ Bring out garden supplies and outdoor furniture from storage. Service lawn mowers and leaf blowers. ▪ Check smoke and carbon monoxide detectors. ▪ Check for winter damage to roof and yard. ▪ Clean out garage. ▪ Clean out gutters. ▪ Wash and install screens. ▪ Repair porches, decks, or patios. Get barbecue grill ready. ▪ Check and replace air-conditioner filters. ▪ Examine outdoor faucets for winter damage and test hoses and sprinklers. ▪ Clean ashes from fireplaces, and have chimneys inspected.

FALL

- Clean carpets. ▪ Flip mattresses. ▪ Replace or bring out doormats. ▪ Donate or discard old clothes. Wash and store summer wardrobe. Bring out the winter wardrobe. ▪ Clean and store outdoor furniture, tools, and garden hoses. ▪ Wash windows and light fixtures. ▪ Weatherproof your house and check for good insulation. ▪ Remove screens and install storm windows.

Store brooms upside down to maintain them. Dip them in soapy water and dry with a rubber band around the head to keep bristles straight. Rinse sponge mops and then tie plastic bags around the heads so they don't dry out.

The Ten-Minute Tidy

You have a surprise guest coming over in ten minutes, and your home looks like a tornado just came through. Here are a few hints for those times the clock is definitely running:

- Focus on the areas guests will see: the bathroom, the hallway, the kitchen, and the living room. Don't worry about any other rooms—just close the doors.

- Collect all misplaced items in a basket or container. Put the collection in an unused room. You'll deal with it later.

- Do a quick once-over of the bathroom: wipe up the counter, sink, and mirror. Any misplaced items can go in the hamper.

- Dust off any noticeable surfaces, i.e., tops of tables, electronics and chairs. Get rid of any dead flowers or overflowing trash bags.

- Fluff up throw pillows. Straighten rugs and furniture.

- Put away clean dishes in the kitchen. Load dirty dishes in the dishwasher, or in the oven (just don't forget to take them out before turning it on!).

- Make sure you look together—it's amazing what you can get away with if you simply look organized!

Sanitation in the Home

Appearances can be deceiving. What looks clean may not be very sanitary, and sometimes the very act of cleaning improperly can spread germs around even further. Whether it's following our helpful steps for a cleaner kitchen or learning the ingredients of disinfection, there's a lot you can do to make your home a more sanitary place.

General Sanitation

■ Clean up messes (especially food) with dishwashing liquid and water before disinfecting surfaces. It might surprise you to know that some organic spills can actually render the sanitizing agent chemically inactive.

■ Consider how much cleaning power you actually need. Every time you use a cleaning agent in your home, you introduce a foreign substance that hangs around far longer than you think. Gain some perspective on the amount of cleaning you'll actually be doing, and choose a product that best fits your needs. You wouldn't use a bazooka to kill a fly, so don't go overboard when deciding on product strength.

■ Make soap and towels available at every sink in your home. People are more likely to wash up if the tools are readily accessible. Paper towels are great for cleanups and they keep germs from spreading, since you throw them out after one use. But for a more ecologically minded household, use cloths and towels and launder them regularly in hot water.

■ Rinse, dry, and ventilate all areas that have been disinfected before allowing in children or pets.

The Most Dangerous Place in the World (Well, at Least in the Home)

The place most prone to causing sickness is the kitchen. Over 76 million people in the United States contract food-borne illnesses every year; unfortunately, a majority of these infections come from the home. Yet, stopping the spread of germs can be as easy as washing your hands in hot, soapy water for at least twenty seconds after using the bathroom or petting an animal, and before cooking and during cooking. Here are some other suggestions:

■ Once a week, throw out any foods that have gone bad and clean spills inside the fridge. The FDA recommends you maintain your refrigerator at 40° F and your freezer at 0° F for optimum food storage. Don't pack the fridge too full or it will hinder the circulation of cold air. Try not to store foods like vegetables that will be eaten raw underneath raw foods such as meats. Large amounts of leftovers should be divided up among shallow containers, since these will allow foods to cool more quickly and thereby halt the growth of contaminants.

Ingredients for Disinfecting

Alcohol: can be used as a disinfectant, but be warned: it is highly flammable. Rubbing alcohol and wood alcohol are toxic, and should be kept from food areas.

Chlorine bleach: can be used for everything from whitening laundry to extending the life of freshly cut flowers (add a few drops to the vase). A simple solution of 1 tablespoon bleach mixed with a gallon of water is a great general disinfectant.

Hydrogen peroxide: often used as an antiseptic, but can also be diluted and used as a disinfectant or bleach for delicate clothes.

■ Clean fruits and vegetables by holding them under running water and using a vegetable brush if necessary. Don't wash raw meat, as this will only spread bacteria throughout the kitchen. A good way to make sure that you keep utensils free from cross-contamination is to drop utensils in the sink after you use them. This way you'll be sure not to confuse the knife you used on the raw chicken with the one you want to use to chop tomatoes for your salad. Don't defrost food at room temperature. It allows bacteria to grow at an alarming rate. Defrost in refrigerator or in microwave on defrost setting.

■ Scrub the sink and drain before washing produce in it. Wash the fridge door and cabinet handles and sink-faucet knobs to prevent the spread of germs.

■ The appearance of meat can sometimes be misleading. Invest in a good meat thermometer to insure meat is well cooked, which keeps bacteria count low.

■ Cutting boards are a very easy place to spread germs to food. Make sure to wash boards in hot, soapy water before and between each food item you cut. Replace worn-out boards. And finally, invest in two cutting boards: one for raw meats and one for vegetables and fruits.

■ Sanitize brushes, abrasive pads, and sponges in a solution of 1 tablespoon chlorine bleach to 1 gallon of water. Soak for a few minutes, and then remove and air-dry. Or kill bacteria on sponges and dish cloths by microwaving them on high for one minute (even sponges that are only two to three days old can contain millions of bacteria!).

■ Microwaving has become a culinary art in itself, and over 90 percent of American houses have one. But when cooking or reheating food, make sure to cover with a glass or plastic cover, adding a little liquid to create germ-killing steam. After defrosting food, cook it immediately before bacteria has a chance to grow. Also, for those microwaves without revolving trays, turn the dish several times to make sure the food is fully cooked.

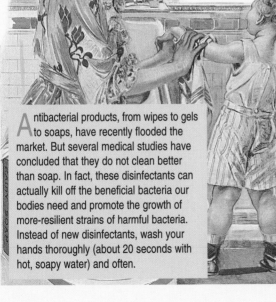

Antibacterial products, from wipes to gels to soaps, have recently flooded the market. But several medical studies have concluded that they do not clean better than soap. In fact, these disinfectants can actually kill off the beneficial bacteria our bodies need and promote the growth of more-resilient strains of harmful bacteria. Instead of new disinfectants, wash your hands thoroughly (about 20 seconds with hot, soapy water) and often.

OTHER AREAS WHERE SANITATION IS NECESSARY: Damp basements, to prevent the spread of mold ■ Changing tables and diaper pails (just make sure children don't come in contact with disinfectant directly after it has been applied) ■ Bathroom: Regularly clean and sanitize the toilet bowl inside and out. Keep showers and tubs free of mold and mildew to prevent the spread of microbes. Don't let water pool on counters. Disinfect sink drains with a bleach solution. ■ Pay special attention to these germ hotspots: front door knob, car steering wheel and door handles, water faucet handles, and infant/toddler seats, cribs and toys.

Cleaning the Bathroom & Kitchen

The bathroom and the kitchen are by far the most-used rooms in your home. They are also the places that need to be cleaned on a daily basis to insure good hygiene for everyone in the house. If you maintain a good cleaning schedule for these rooms, it will actually save you more time and effort than if you let it go for a while and have to tackle a big mess.

The Bathroom

Bathtub/Shower

■ Spray down the area. Using a sponge with a general cleaner or dishwashing liquid, go over the whole tub. If you have an enamel or porcelain tub, make sure you use a nonabrasive cleaner.

■ Use a toothbrush to focus on the areas around faucets and knobs, and to get in cracks in grout. Undiluted vinegar works well on the nooks.

■ If your showerhead is clogged, remove and soak it in a bowl of descaler or undiluted vinegar. Use a toothbrush to clean the holes.

■ When the tub or shower has been cleaned, rinse thoroughly to reduce streaking. Use a cup of water, or your showerhead if you have a flexible one. You might want to finish with a leave-on shower spray.

■ Dry shower curtains completely to eliminate mildew and clean with a disinfectant regularly. Colorfast shower curtains can often be washed in the washing machine on the gentle cycle; just don't put them in the dryer.

■ Clean glass shower doors with a non-abrasive shower/tub cleaner and rinse thoroughly. Use a squeegee to eliminate streaks.

■ One cup bleach to one quart water is a good solution for fighting mildew and tub stains. To prevent fungal growth, keep the room well ventilated and run the vent fan after you shower to eliminate condensation.

■ Get rid of lime and mineral deposits by setting a rag soaked in white vinegar on the spot for about an hour. The deposits should come right off.

A good drain maintenance procedure is to pour in $1/2$ cup baking soda, then follow with a small stream of water. Do it every other week.

45

Sink

■ Follow the same steps as for the bathtub.

■ Remove buildup in a faucet tap by hooking a plastic bag filled with vinegar over the faucet. Secure with a twist tie and let sit for several hours or overnight. Rinse well once buildup has dissolved. Chrome taps can be descaled of mineral deposits by rubbing with a cut lemon.

■ Use a baking-soda paste to get rid of difficult grime spots.

Bathroom Mirror/Medicine Cabinet

■ Take the time to go through and throw out any expired medicines or cosmetics. If necessary, take items out and wipe down each shelf before replacing.

■ Clean the bathroom mirror with a window-cleaning solution. Use newspapers to dry. If you find your mirror fogging up constantly, try rubbing on a little moistened soap and then wiping away. Or rub a small amount of shaving cream into the mirror. Don't rinse.

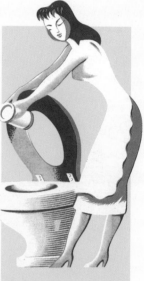

Floor

■ Sweep or vacuum up hair and dust.

■ Ceramic tiles usually only need a very general cleaning. Wipe down with soap and water and let air dry. Don't polish.

■ Bath mats can usually be thrown in the washing machine, but check the label first. Air or tumble dry.

■ Always rinse sponges, cloths, and toilet brushes well after using to prevent them from spreading germs or getting slimy.

Toilet

■ Use a toilet brush and cleaner to clean the bowl. Make sure to clean under the rim of the bowl (especially the holes, which can become clogged). Wipe down the seat and top with a general cleaner, and rinse with a damp cloth.

The Kitchen

General

■ Clear all foods, cookware, and miscellaneous items away.

■ Toss oven mitts and dish towels in the laundry.

Sink

■ Load dishwasher (*opposite*) or put all dirty dishes in sink. For tough stains or cooked-on food, soak pots and pans.

■ Clean dishes: glassware, cutlery, then crockery and pots and pans.

■ Wipe down sink with a dish detergent solution, using vinegar on drain stains.

Countertops/Surfaces

■ Follow instructions on pages 50–51 for cleaning countertops.

■ Disinfect handles.

Defrosting the Freezer

Although no one enjoys it, defrosting can be demystified if you know the tricks. First unplug the refrigerator and move food to a cooler (now is a good time to get rid of spoiled items). Soften up frost in the freezer by putting a bowl of hot water inside and letting it sit for about 10 minutes. This should make the ice soft enough to remove. Don't forget to plug the refrigerator back in when you're done!

■ Wipe down vent hood with hot water and grease-cutting dishwashing liquid.

■ Clean glass and chrome with a solution of 1 tablespoon ammonia to 2 cups water, and wipe down recently used appliances.

Refrigerator/Pantry

■ Go through and throw out all spoiled food items.

■ Wipe up spills.

Floor

■ Sweep and damp-mop floor.

■ Take garbage out frequently to avoid pest and odor problems.

For appliance care, see Cleaning Appliances on page 54.

Dishwasher Loading Tips

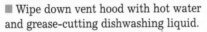

UPPER RACK: Cups and glasses (load between prongs; don't let them touch or they may chip) ■ Tupperware and other lightweight plastic items

LOWER RACK: Pots and pans ■ Plates and bowls (place between prongs) ■ Cookie sheets, oversized serving platters

BASKET: Flatware (alternate with handles down and up to clean fully. Separate silver from stainless steel to avoid damage or discoloration)

THINGS NOT TO PUT IN THE DISHWASHER: Antique or decorated dishware and china ■ Kitchenware with handles of bone, ivory, or wood ■ Sensitive materials: crystal, cast iron, tin, gold, pewter ■ Sharp knives (blades can become dull) ■ Some aluminum (it may darken) ■ Woodenware

Healthy Cleaning

Today there are over 70,000 products on the market, for cleaning almost every surface in your house. But no matter how sparkling they get your tub, think twice before using them, and consider the toll they might take on your health. Chemicals like formaldehyde, phenols, and petroleum can cause respiratory irritation, damage mucous membranes, and harm circulatory systems. Yet these chemicals are all commonly found in floor cleaners, spray deodorizers, and household disinfectants. Thankfully, many environmentally friendly alternatives are effective as cleaning agents. You might need to use a little more elbow grease, but you'll get points for saving money and protecting your health.

The Six Essential Ingredients

BAKING SODA With its alkaline properties, baking soda can be used to neutralize acids. Mix baking soda and water to a pastelike consistency and use it as everything from a juice- and tea-stain remover to a chrome polisher. In addition, the absorbing qualities of baking soda make it useful for neutralizing odors in refrigerators and freezers: simply place an open box or a small bowl of baking soda in the fridge or freezer. Loosen up slow drains by combining $1/2$ cup each of baking soda, salt, and vinegar and pouring it down the drain. Let it sit for 15 minutes and then follow with a quart of boiling water.

HYDROGEN PEROXIDE Instead of chlorine bleach, use undiluted hydrogen peroxide to help whiten surfaces or remove stains from white linens and clothing.

BORAX With its grease-cutting ability, a solution of one tablespoon Borax to $1^1/_4$ cups of water can be used in place of ammonia-based kitchen and bath cleaners.

SALT If you have a burned saucepan that you don't think will ever come clean, try scrubbing it down with salt. Fill the pan with saltwater and let soak overnight. The next morning, bring the contents of the pan to a boil and rinse away the worst of the burned-on residue.

VINEGAR In addition to being an amazing all-purpose cleaner, vinegar can be used to clean teapots and coffeepots for better-tasting hot drinks. Just make sure to use white vinegar on light-colored material, as apple-cider vinegar will stain. A cup of vinegar in your laundry rinse cycle can work as a fabric softener. You can also easily clean mirrors with old newspaper and a solution of half water, half vinegar, and a splash of ammonia. This mixture works well on floors too.

LEMON The acidic properties of lemon help to dissolve some stains while leaving a pleasing scent behind. You can even use a little lemon juice to remove mild tarnishing on silver.

Friendly Cleaning Hints

■ Cold tea can clean woodwork.

■ To wash hairbrushes and combs, soak them for a few minutes in a sink of water with a tablespoon of baking soda and a drop of bleach.

■ Think that you've got tar or motor-oil stains that will never come out? Try applying eucalyptus oil to help dissolve those stubborn spots.

■ An easy way to clean a vase is to fill it half full with a cleaning solution (like a teaspoon of ammonia in water) and some uncooked rice or beans. Then shake.

■ Talcum powder can be used to dry out liquid spills on carpets. You can get rid of carpet odors by sprinkling with cornstarch and vacuuming.

■ Apply ice in a plastic bag directly to stuck-on chewing gum. Once the gum has hardened, use a knife to scrape the residue away.

■ For candle wax, first pry off as much wax as possible with a blunt knife. Next, cover the area with paper towels and apply an iron on low. As the wax heats up, it will melt into the paper towel. Keep applying fresh paper towels until all the wax has been absorbed.

■ Chalk absorbs moisture. Pieces can be placed in jewelry boxes to prevent tarnishing, or a bunch can be hung in the closet to protect clothes.

■ Remove spots on leather and suede by rubbing with stale bread.

■ Scratches on wood finishes can sometimes be disguised by rubbing the meat from pecans or walnuts into them.

Natural Polish

Some of the harshest chemicals used in a household are those used to cleanse metals. Here are some natural alternatives:

■ For cleaning brass, use a mixture of salt and vinegar as an abrasive cleaner.

■ To keep bronze shiny, rub olive oil into the surface.

■ Apple-cider vinegar is useful for cleaning copper.

■ Don't let your pewter tarnish. Polish it with leaves from a head of cabbage.

■ Remove rust from utensils by sticking them in an onion for a day or two.

■ To clean silverware, put an aluminum pan in the sink and place the silver in it. Cover with boiling water and three tablespoons of baking soda. Soak for 10 minutes, then wash with a mild soap, rinse well, and dry. The aluminum pan can be cleaned with some vinegar and water. To cut down on polishing, minimize silver's exposure to air.

An All-Purpose Cleaner

$1/2$ cup clear ammonia
1 cup baking soda
1 gallon warm water

Dissolve baking soda in warm water. Add ammonia and stir. (For extra cleaning power, add a tablespoon of grated soap.)

A recent study by the Centers for Disease Control and Prevention found over 116 chemicals in 2,000 Americans tested, and not all of them were from exposure to cleaning products. Several chemicals, such as phthalates and PBDEs found in plastics and flame retardants, are now being investigated for their danger to human health. The conclusions of some scientific studies argue that the doses we are exposed to are so small that they have no serious effect, but other experts recommend consumers keep an eye out for them. If you're concerned, try researching them at *www.fda.gov* and *www.cdc.gov*.

Cleaning Surfaces

*S*ure, sure we all know it's what's inside that really counts. But when it comes to maintaining appearances, follow these guidelines to make sure all of your household surfaces look their best and last a long time.

ACRYLIC Because acrylic is so delicate, it's best to follow the manufacturer's directions or use a specialized cleaner.

BRICK Brick is difficult to clean because it's very porous. Try vacuuming up any loose dust and dirt, and dusting off surface grit. Using a stiff, thick paintbrush, apply a heavy-duty degreaser and allow it to soak into the brick for 15 minutes, reapplying if it gets absorbed. Scrub the area and then rinse well with water. Painting on a sealer will make it easier to dust and wipe down.

CERAMIC TILES Avoid using powdered cleaners, since they scratch; instead wash with water and a bit of dishwashing liquid (too much will leave a residue) and cut mild soap scum with a vinegar and water solution. Rinse and dry thoroughly. To attack dirty grout, use a mild solution of 2 tablespoons bleach to a quart of water and scrub with a cotton swab or toothbrush. Glass: Use a nonabrasive baking-soda-and-water paste. Rinse and dry.

CONCRETE For outdoor areas, wet concrete and sprinkle with powdered detergent. Scrub with a push broom and rinse off. For indoor areas, regularly mop and sweep sealed concrete. Wet unsealed concrete thoroughly and use a heavy-duty cleaner. Get rid of dirty water with a mop or squeegee and dustpan. Soak up fresh oil stains with kitty litter and sweep away.

CORK Wipe up spills immediately, as the surface is very porous. Vacuum and dust regularly. Use a sealer to protect from moisture.

FIBERGLASS Use a nonabrasive baking-soda solution. An acidic cleaner might be useful in removing hard-water marks.

GLASS Try a solution of vinegar and water. Use newspapers or a squeegee to avoid streaking when drying.

LACQUER Clean with $1/2$ teaspoon Murphy's Oil Soap to 1 cup water. Test the cleaner on a small, inconspicuous area. Using a soft cloth, clean a small area at a time, drying as you go.

LAMINATED PLASTIC Don't use an abrasive cleaner. Wash with a mild dishwashing liquid and water. If a stain pops up, try

It's usually not advisable to wash ceilings; instead dust with a broom wrapped in an old T-shirt, or vacuum with the brush attachment. If your ceiling is very dirty, consider repainting it. For moldy bathroom ceilings, try a solution of diluted chlorine bleach, or follow instructions for ceramic cleaning if tiled.

Because metal is used in many countertops and appliances and comes in many forms, methods of cleaning vary widely. For stainless steel, try an all-purpose cleaner for general cleaning, or a paste of baking soda and water to remove stains. Boil away deposits in pots by bringing $1/2$ cup vinegar and a pot of water to boil and then simmering for an hour. To get more information on the individual care of specific metals, as well as other surfaces, try The Soap and Detergent Association's website at *www.cleaning 101.com* and consult the Fact Sheet Notebook.

squeezing fresh lemon juice on it and letting it soak for half an hour. Then follow with baking soda and wipe away. The lemon juice will also provide a nice shine.

LINOLEUM Make sure it has a wax finish. Sweep and mop regularly, and remove marks with some baking soda sprinkled on a damp cloth. Don't wash linoleum too often, or it may crack.

MARBLE Dust using a soft cloth, like an old cotton shirt. Wash occasionally with a cloth dampened with mild cleaner and water. Rinse with a clean cloth and dry. When dealing with stains, try a specialized marble cleaner or poultice found at the hardware store. Wipe up spills immediately to prevent staining. Don't use an acidic cleaner or it will scar the surface.

PAINTED SURFACES Test if the surface is washable on an inconspicuous area. Use a non-abrasive or wood cleaner, and make sure to work your way up when cleaning. This will make streaks easier to wipe away. For floors, use floor wax to make cleaning easier, and damp mop to get rid of any dirt.

PLASTIC Avoid using abrasive or harsh cleaners. Use soap and water, or a solution of 2 tablespoons baking soda to 1 quart water. Rinse and dry.

PORCELAIN Use a non-abrasive liquid cleaner with a damp sponge. Rinse well. For appliances, consider using a small amount of creamy kitchen wax. Don't wipe a hot surface with a wet cloth, or the temperature change may cause chipping.

VINYL For waxable vinyl, apply several coats of floor finish, reapplying in high-traffic areas. Mop with a cleaning solution and sweep regularly. For no-wax floors, follow the same procedure without waxing. For walls: Use a sponge dipped in a mild cleaning solution.

WALLPAPER Test washability on a small, inconspicuous area. For washable paper, use a non-abrasive cleaner or a mild solution of water and dishwashing liquid and wipe walls. Start from the bottom and work up to make marks easier to see. For non-washable paper, use a specialized wallpaper cleaning agent, or gently rub marks with a bit of white bread or a gum eraser. A thick baking soda paste can be applied to grease or crayon marks. Allow to dry and then brush off. Vacuum fabric coverings.

WOOD Because wood can be easily stained, it's important to wipe up spills immediately. Mop a small area with a damp (not wet) cloth, and wipe dry before continuing. You can use a vinegar-and-water solution for cleaning. Add 2 tablespoons furniture polish to a gallon of this mixture to revive the shine. Dark wood floors may be washed with cold tea. Don't allow water to sit on wood or it will be absorbed, and water stains are very difficult to get out. Gently rub stain with a clean cloth slightly dampened with hot water and a few drops of ammonia. Be careful not to damage the finish.

Tough Surface Cleaner

1 tablespoon ammonia
1 tablespoon laundry detergent
1 pint water

Cleaning Appliances

How crazy is your gadget? Modern appliances save us a ton of work, but taking care of them can be quite tedious. While it's sometimes tempting to simply throw the entire food processor in the dishwasher, there is a better way to maintain appliances. Here are the best ways to keep your household items clean and functioning.

BLENDER Fill halfway with water and add some dishwashing liquid. Put the lid on and turn the blender on low for about half a minute. Rinse well and dry. To clean the base, wipe down with a household cleaner. You can get around buttons with a cotton swab dipped in a cleaning solution.

COFFEEMAKER Clean pot, filter, and lid separately with soapy water. To get rid of mineral buildup within the machine, pour in a solution of 1 part vinegar to $2^1/_2$ parts water and turn on. Halfway through the cycle, turn the coffeemaker off and let sit for half an hour. Pour the mixture back in and restart. Run plain water through several cycles to thoroughly rinse out the machine.

DISHWASHER Wipe exterior down with a mild cleaning solution. Dishwashers should clean themselves, but if you notice any brown or discolored spots inside, it's because of mineral buildup. Use a solution of baking soda and water to scrub spots, then run a cup of vinegar through the dishwasher cycle.

ELECTRIC CAN OPENER Disassemble cutting mechanism, if possible, and soak. Otherwise, use a soft toothbrush to clean away debris trapped on the blade.

FOOD PROCESSOR Carefully disassemble and either put in the dishwasher or hand wash, according to manufacturer's directions. Clean the pieces immediately after processing food. Do not use abrasive cleaners; they will scratch the blades. If you coat blades with a nonstick cooking spray, food will wash away more easily next time.

GARBAGE DISPOSAL Using an adequate amount of cold water will keep blades clear and cut back on odor. You can also throw in some citrus peels to get rid of a bad smell.

GRATER Rub with a cut potato or lemon to remove stuck-on food, then rinse thoroughly.

MICROWAVE OVEN Wash the inside with a baking soda and water solution, or microwave a glass bowl containing $1/_4$ cup vinegar and 1 cup water on high for 5 minutes. Wipe down the walls. You shouldn't use commercial oven cleaners: They will damage the interior coating.

MIXER Wash beaters by hand. Wipe down base with a damp cloth, and unclog vent with a toothpick. Vacuum out debris.

General Guidelines

■ **ALWAYS** unplug appliances before cleaning. If you need to turn one on to clean it, as with the blender or coffeemaker, make sure you shut it off again.

■ **ALWAYS** consult manufacturer's instructions when disassembling and cleaning (especially for the larger appliances). Although most of the cleaning solutions described are less harsh than many commercial cleaners, it's always good to check the prescribed instructions and use your judgment.

■ **REGULARLY** wipe appliances with a damp cloth or sponge; you'll be amazed at how much cleaning time this will eventually save you.

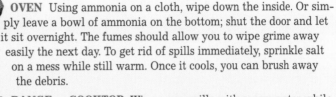

OVEN Using ammonia on a cloth, wipe down the inside. Or simply leave a bowl of ammonia on the bottom; shut the door and let it sit overnight. The fumes should allow you to wipe grime away easily the next day. To get rid of spills immediately, sprinkle salt on a mess while still warm. Once it cools, you can brush away the debris.

RANGE or COOKTOP Wipe away spills with soapy water while the surface is warm. Coils will usually burn off debris and don't need to be cleaned.

REFRIGERATOR Dust coils in the back or at the bottom regularly with a vacuum or brush to insure the fridge runs properly. Soak racks and removable compartments in warm, soapy water. Wipe down inside walls. Get rid of the gunk on top of the fridge with a solution of 1 part ammonia to 10 parts hot water.

REFRIGERATOR ICE MAKER Turn off ice maker if possible. Clean the ice bin with baking soda and water, then rinse, dry, and replace. Turn back on.

SPICE GRINDER Try running a piece of white bread through it; it will pick up stray spices and odors.

TOASTER Unplug toaster. Empty crumb tray. Turn toaster upside down over garbage can and shake out crumbs, dislodging any stuck pieces with a toothbrush. Wipe the outside down with a wet cloth.

TOASTER OVEN Unplug toaster. Empty crumb tray or sweep out with paintbrush. Knock crumbs out by turning the unit on its side. Soak and scrub removable tray. Try not to let spills sit, as they will become difficult to remove.

Cleaning Electronics

■ Unplug electronics before cleaning.

■ Don't spray directly with cleaner; spray on a soft cloth first. Or use a sponge dampened with soap and water to wipe down surfaces.

■ For computers, be sure to routinely vacuum dust away from the back of the CPU (allowing dust to accumulate here can short out your computer and cost you a very expensive trip to the repair shop, or worse). You can wipe down some monitor screens with a tissue or very slightly damp cloth. For flat-panel monitors, however, you must not touch or apply pressure to the screen; this can leave a permanent dark smudge: Follow manufacturer's directions for cleaning with special cloth. Use a cotton swab with a bit of rubbing alcohol or a spray cleaner to get between keyboard keys, but don't saturate keypad. A pressurized can of air is useful for blowing away accumulated dust, hair, and crumbs. Just be extremely careful.

■ For any metal trim or chrome, polish with a little bit of white vinegar or window cleaner on a cloth.

■ Wipe down the ear- and mouthpieces of telephones with rubbing alcohol. Periodically clean your VCR, DVD, and CD players with specialty kits found in most electronics departments.

■ One of the most common germ-spreaders is sitting in your hand. Remote controls need to be periodically cleaned, especially during cold and flu seasons. Turn off the electronics, then spray remote with a mild cleaner. Wipe dry with a soft brush, or remove grime with a thin dry bristle paintbrush.

Cleaning Upholstery

When it comes to deep cleaning of upholstery, the main consensus among cleaning experts seems to be "Don't try this at home!". Uneven cleaning and harmful agents can cause spotting and discoloration, and can even ruin furniture coverings. Whenever possible, have furniture deep cleaned professionally.

Here are some guidelines to keep your upholstery in good condition:

■ Maintain upholstery by dusting and vacuuming furniture regularly, every two weeks or so. Use the vacuum brush or wand feature to get into all crevices. This is especially important if there are allergy sufferers in the house, since cushioning can contain a large amount of dust particles.

■ Protect high-contact items like arm- and headrests from wear and tear with matching fabric covers.

■ Always follow manufacturers' cleaning instructions carefully. Most furniture pieces have a tag containing Fabric Care Codes. These codes, listed here, tell you what is the best cleaner to use for spots and mild cleaning:

S Use a mild, water-free dry-cleaning solvent to spot-clean stains and grime. Be careful: Solvents are flammable, and you should keep the area well ventilated. Water-based cleaning agents can cause water stains. A "solvent" is not water-based, and is generally used to treat grease stains, like lipstick.

W Use a water-based cleaner. This is usually a mild, foamy detergent or an upholstery shampoo. Work quickly, one small area at a time, and blot the surface dry with a clean cloth. Do not soak upholstery, as this can cause spotting and mildew. Nongreasy stains, like grass, are treated with a mild detergent.

S-W Use either a water-based cleaner or a solvent. Stains that cannot be classified as either greasy or nongreasy (like certain beverages and foods) can be worked on with a detergent, then a solvent.

X Vacuum only. Any kind of cleaner will cause material to fade or spot.

In order to check whether you can use a particular cleaner on an item, test for colorfastness and shrinkage. If the cleaner provokes either one of these reactions, it's a good idea to get the item cleaned professionally.

Leather is a good upholstery choice since it very rarely stains. To keep it in good shape, dust regularly and check the manufacturer's instructions to see if it can be cleaned with saddle soap. Never wax.

■ Press a white or light-colored cloth with some cleaning solution to an inconspicuous or hidden part of the furniture. If the color bleeds, then you can probably only use a dry-cleaning solvent for spot treatment. For full cleaning, take it to a professional.

Window Treatments

CURTAINS Vacuum them regularly with the upholstery attachment. Curtain fabric tends to shrink. Avoid over-washing them, or get them dry-cleaned (mark the places where hooks need to be reinserted with a dab of nail polish or permanent marker at the top). Otherwise, launder them in the washing machine or hand wash in your bathtub if they are especially long or heavy.

BLINDS Most can be vacuumed and wiped down with a sponge dampened with water and some dishwashing liquid. Dust venetian blinds by running your hands in cotton gloves over the slats; deep clean in the bathtub in mild solution.

SHADES Follow cleaning instructions per the fabric label and vacuum regularly. For vinyl shades, take down and lie flat. Wash each side separately with a dishwashing solution.

Carpet & Rug Care

Maintaining a carpet or rug can be as easy as regularly vacuuming and zeroing in on stains and spots immediately. To make sure your carpet doesn't wear out before its time, clean it on a monthly basis (in addition to vacuuming), and give it a deep cleaning once a year.

■ Monthly cleaning can be done by machine or hand. A powder or foam carpet cleaner is spread over the area and then either scrubbed into a lather and removed, or simply vacuumed up.

■ Deep yearly cleaning involves a machine that either shampoos or steam cleans the carpet. Sometimes the cleaning agent needs to set for several hours. It's important to try it out on an inconspicuous portion before you attempt to use it on your entire carpet (especially if you are dealing with older rugs, whose colors might bleed.) For particularly delicate materials, or if you don't have the time or patience to clean it yourself, call in a professional.

■ Some rugs, like bath mats, can be tossed in the washing machine. Others, like tapestries, simply need to be beaten out. Consult the maintenance tags before attempting to clean.

■ Natural fibers, like cotton and wool, can be cleaned using general cleaning methods, but be sure not to over-work them. Wool can be damaged by bleaches, and cotton may discolor if treated with an alkaline solution, so make sure to use neutral detergents.

Carpet & Rug Stains

Most stains require the same treatment as upholstery care (*page 56*). Remember to blot—not rub—the stain, and use a clean white cloth each time. Always pretest a cleaner on an inconspicuous part of the material first. Detergents can be applied directly to the stain, but most solutions and solvents should be added to the cleaning cloth first, and then applied. For more help, try *carpetone.com/stainremoval.cfm*.

Some helpful cleaning solutions:

■ water mixed with a non-bleaching household detergent

■ equal parts water and vinegar

■ club soda

■ cornstarch, baking soda, talcum powder (all absorb liquids and neutralize smells)

■ denatured alcohol

Common Carpet Stains

BLOOD Blot with cold water immediately. Don't let it set or it will never come out.

COFFEE/TEA Blot and apply a detergent and vinegar solution. Continue to rinse and then blot again until it is gone. You may need to apply a carpet shampoo.

COLA DRINKS Try blotting with a mild nonbleach detergent-and-water solution. Follow by blotting with a vinegar-and-water solution.

DIRT/MUD Let dry and vacuum up loose dirt. Add a teaspoon each of vinegar and dish detergent to a quart of warm water, and rub onto the stain.

FOOD Scrape up excess and use a stain remover.

FRUIT/JUICE Dampen with water, and then rub in table salt. Let it sit for a few minutes. Brush out particles and vacuum.

GRASS Rub in dishwashing liquid and let stand a few hours. Scrub with a brush, then wipe away with a dampened cloth.

GREASE/OIL Place a piece of colored paper on the stain. Using the warm setting, place the tip of an iron on the paper over the stain until grease is absorbed into it. Clean the spot with dishwashing liquid and water. Wipe off foam and repeat if necessary.

GUM Harden it with a bag of ice placed on top. Pick off carefully.

MILK Sponge with warm water, and then apply a spray rug cleaner or a vinegar and water solution with a clean cloth and dry thoroughly. If the smell remains, you may need to get it professionally cleaned.

NAIL POLISH Apply a non-oily nail polish remover with a cotton ball, first placing a thick towel under the rug, if possible, to make sure that it doesn't soak through to the floor. Apply denatured alcohol with a white cloth, and then clean with carpet shampoo.

SHOE POLISH Scrape off excess. Apply a stain remover. Rinse with water and use denatured alcohol to remove any discoloration. Then clean with detergent or carpet shampoo.

URINE Sponge with cold water and rinse with a diluted antiseptic, like hydrogen peroxide. Use a weak vinegar solution to get rid of the smell. A solution of a tablespoon of household ammonia to a $1/2$ cup water, followed by cleaning with detergent, will also work, but be warned that since urine contains ammonia, this may encourage a pet to re-mark this spot.

VOMIT Remove excess. Sponge on a mixture of one part ammonia to six parts warm water. Continue to rinse until smell disappears. You may need to use a carpet shampoo.

WINE Sprinkle on baking soda and then vacuum. Or try rinsing with club soda and blotting. For red wine, try pouring on some white wine and then blotting. Sponge with warm water and let dry.

Carpet Burns

Try rubbing small cigarette burns with fine sandpaper and then blotting with a mild detergent solution. Rinse with warm water and dry. For serious damage place a slightly larger piece of matching carpet and underlay over the burn mark, and using a razor, cut the new piece and underlying damaged carpet together. Remove the damaged piece and stick the new piece in place with industrial glue or heavy double-sided tape.

Vacuuming & Dusting

Vacuum All Your Cares Away

Every home needs a good, strong, efficient vacuum cleaner, for floors of course, and for cleaning cobwebs from corners, and dust from draperies, ceiling fixtures, and upholstered furniture. The basic choices are the canister style and the upright; each has advantages and disadvantages. Also available are handheld models, electric brooms, central vacuuming systems, and the new robot cleaners (see box opposite). If you live on two floors or in a sprawling house, invest in two vacuums and save yourself from lugging a bulky machine from one area of the house to the other. The two machines will pay for themselves over time, because each will do only half the work. Handheld wet/dry vacs work well for spills and spots and upholstered furniture, making them a good option for busy households.

Vacuuming a Carpet

The first choice for carpets has always been uprights, but there are canister vacs that do a great job. Consider what you want to clean: if you need to get under items such as a sofa or an armoire, a canister is the better choice. But if you only need to cover a large area quickly, an upright is best for you.

Before turning on the machine, search the floor for areas that need special attention as well as for items that should not be vacuumed up, such as paper clips, rubber bands, and loose earrings. Pretreat spots and stains (see page 58). Check that the bag is not full and that the intake brush and hoses are clear.

Choose the correct setting for your carpet pile. Pass the wand systematically and slowly over the carpet. Work from different directions to ensure you are covering the rug thoroughly. You may find it more efficient to vacuum the outer area first. If your rug has fringe, stand off the rug and, facing it, lift your upright vacuum over the fringe and place it on the rug; pull the vacuum toward you in the direction of the fringe. With a canister, use the furniture brush attachment in the same manner.

Next, vacuum the high-traffic areas of the room. Move furniture pieces just enough so that you can vacuum under them thoroughly. The depressions left by furniture can be finger-brushed to loosen the fibers, but they will return so long as the furniture remains there. When you cannot resist the urge to rearrange the furniture, attack the carpet depressions with a damp cloth and a steam iron.

Vacuum the rest of the room. If your room has an abundance of pet hair, you will have to vacuum several times to really clean the carpet.

An Eternal Question: Vacuum or Dust First? Although vacuuming releases dust into the air and therefore was taken care of first, with efficient appliances this is no longer a problem. Dusting and polishing first is the more efficient way to clean.

What's Available

■ **BAGLESS VACUUM CLEANERS**
The filters these models require tend to be expensive, something to consider when purchasing. Emptying their container, which can cause dust to spread, should be done outside.

■ **THE ROBOT** These little round vacs are still in their early stages of design. The ones that are on the market have a way to go before they are as effective as uprights and canisters.

■ **ELECTRIC BROOMS AND STICK MODELS** Great for their convenience, these vacuums are perfect for the kitchen. They are not as efficient as their large counterparts, but for quick cleanups, they will save you time and energy.

■ **HANDHELD MODELS** Best for keeping on countertops and in the family room, these easy-to-use vacuum cleaners pick up small messes quickly with no fuss.

■ **CENTRAL VACUUM SYSTEMS** The ultimate in convenience, these systems, which feature a receptacle in every room, have greater suction power than store-bought varieties. Good on all types of surfaces, a central-system installation is wonderful if your house can accommodate it.

That's Progress for You

Feather dusters used to define dusting, but no longer. You can now buy endless types of pre-packaged dusters, from micro-fiber cloth to duster "mittens." Each product boasts superior cleaning ability, but cotton cloth is preferable for its versatility and ability to be thrown into the washer.

Dusting! Dusting! 1, 2, 3!

All surfaces must be dusted, whether they are wood, glass, plastic, metal, or fabric, on a weekly basis. Dry dusting is sufficient for most of the dry rooms of your home—those without running water and hygiene imperatives. Damp dusting, with a moist cotton rag, every two or three weeks will usually keep surfaces clean.

With a clean cotton cloth, wipe the surface in one direction, pushing excess soil and lint into a paper towel; repeat if necessary. For framed objects and collectibles, wipe the entire surface with a clean cotton cloth, starting at the top and working your way down.

Damp dusting is for a deeper clean than dry dusting but less than an all-out scrubbing. Soft, worn cotton makes inexpensive cleaning cloths; men's shirts, for instance, have the lint-free quality that makes for efficient damp dusting. Simply moisten the cloth with water, wring it out, and begin. Dust as you would for dry dusting, turning the cloth frequently.

GREEN CLEAN FOR GLASS AND MIRRORS Paper towels are not environment-friendly. Keep on hand a bucket of clean cotton, lint-free, fabrics that have been designated rags for cleaning glass. Or use up those newspapers collecting dust in the living room. Spray the surface with cleaner and wipe, working from one side to the opposite, until the glass is dry. Check the glass for streaks and repeat the cleaning if necessary.

BUTTONS AND DIALS AND KEYPADS AND ALL THOSE REMOTES!
Dusting electronics is always a challenge; their electric field is a natural magnet for dust particles thus setting the stage for static cling. Don't despair, a quick hit with a feather duster is all that is needed during your regular cleaning routine.

Household Odors

Even the cleanest house can seem dirty if too many household odors are present. The first step is making sure your rooms are well ventilated. Then follow these solutions, and you'll never walk down the air-freshener aisle again.

LEMON Heat water and a few spoonfuls of lemon juice in a small microwave-safe bowl for two minutes on high to freshen microwaves ▪ Rub a cutting board with a cut lemon to get rid of garlic and onion smells ▪ Rub hands with lemon juice, and then wash to remove pungent fish smells ▪ Grind citrus rinds in your garbage disposal and flush with hot water ▪ Bake an unpeeled lemon at 300° F for about fifteen minutes, leaving the oven door open to let the aroma waft through your house.

WHITE VINEGAR Neutralize cigarette smells by waving a dish towel dampened with water and a little vinegar ▪ Small bowls of vinegar can freshen any room ▪ Get rid of onion odors on hands by rubbing with vinegar or celery stalks ▪ To remove an odorous spot, sponge area with white vinegar, rinse with water, and let dry.

BAKING SODA Soak plastic containers overnight in a baking-soda-and-water solution to get rid of tough odors ▪ Add 1 cup baking soda to the cat box to diminish smells ▪ Get rid of carpet odors by sprinkling on a little baking soda, letting it sit for about an hour, then vacuuming. (Be careful, as constant use of baking soda could rust gears in vacuum).

ACTIVATED CHARCOAL, KITTY LITTER Refrigerator smells can vanish if you leave a small bowl of activated charcoal or cat litter in it for a few days ▪ Sachets of kitty litter can absorb moisture and odors ▪ To remove mustiness from basement, use open containers of activated charcoal.

Instead of investing in expensive air fresheners that only mask—not get rid of—smells, use natural options, like placing open cans of coffee in refrigerators to absorb odors; simmering lemon, apple, and/or orange peelings with cinnamon or cloves in water to make the house smell sweet; and simply burning a match to get rid of offensive bathroom odors.

Make a Sachet

Sachets are wonderful additions to clothes drawers and closets. These little easy-to-make bags fill enclosed spaces with warm and comforting smells.

1. Pick a good breathable fabric, like linen, cotton, or muslin. Old lace handkerchiefs found at thrift shops are also great. Make sure fabric is clean and dry.
2. Choose a ribbon with a width of $1/4$ inch or less.
3. Measure and cut a strip of fabric 11 inches by 4 inches.
4. Make a $1/4$-inch hem on the raw edges.
5. Fold the fabric in half, right sides are together. Sew three sides of the bag closed, leaving one short side open.
6. Turn the bag right side out and fill with potpourri (*see below*). Be careful not to overfill.
7. Tie the opening closed with the ribbon. Tie a loop into it if you want to hang the sachet in your closet. Refill your sachet when you want a new scent.

A few drops of vanilla extract on the top of a light bulb will bring a homey scent to any household. Or soak a cotton ball in vanilla and leave it in an open baby food jar.

Potpourri Ingredients

■ balsam needles ■ bay leaves ■ chamomile ■ dried flower petals: roses, carnations, sunflowers ■ dried peels of citrus fruits ■ eucalyptus leaves ■ essential oils: vanilla, wintergreen, rose ■ ground/stick cinnamon ■ lavender ■ rose hips ■ rosemary ■ sage ■ small pinecones ■ thyme ■ whole cloves

Mix and match ingredients for the best possible scent combination, but always make sure you are not allergic to any before using them. Kill bugs in your mixture by placing items in a plastic Ziploc and freezing for about two weeks. This should kill insects and eggs.

63

Laundry Basics

Although nowhere near as time-consuming as the laundry days of old, washing clothes is still a process that requires a bit of attention. Here are some guidelines for washing, getting rid of stains, and knowing when to call in the professionals. Follow these steps to get clothes clean and prolong the life of your garments year after year.

Before You Wash

■ Sort clothes by color, then by degree of dirtiness. Obviously, whites and bright/dark clothes should be washed separately. If you have heavily soiled clothes, separate them from only slightly dirty clothes. In addition, think about sorting by fabric type or by clothes that easily produce lint.

■ Zippers, buttons, and ties should all be fastened to keep clothes from getting tangled, and pockets should be emptied. Repair clothes before washing them.

■ Launder dark clothes inside out to minimize fading.

■ Mix large and small items, like sheets and light clothes, together to allow them to move more freely in the washing machine.

■ Check the care label on your clothes. It's amazing the amount of information that's provided on that little tag at the back of your shirt. Use the table for fabric care symbols to decide how to best wash your clothes.

■ Decide what detergent to use. Liquids are good for most loads, and are especially great for pretreating. Powders also work well on an everyday basis, and lift out soil and most children's stains. Ultra detergents are more concentrated than normal detergents, although they offer the same cleaning power. Just make sure to follow the instructions. Also check for fragrance- and dye-free compositions, or if fabric softener has been added.

■ Other laundry aids to consider are bleaches, pretreats, fabric softeners, and starches. Bleaches are divided between oxygen (color safe) and those with sodium hypochlorite (chlorinated). Pretreaters are wonderful for use on heavily soiled and stained garments. Fabric softeners decrease static and make fabrics fluffier. Starches are used on cottons and cotton blends to provide more body to a garment and make ironing easier.

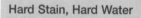

Hard Stain, Hard Water

Your water might be to blame. Hard water contains minerals that react with soap to form a white residue that might make fabrics feel stiff or scratchy. To tell if you've got hard water, look for rings around your bathtub and faucets and drains. Also, bath soap and shampoos won't lather as easily. To combat hard water, simply add a little more detergent to your normal load, or consider adding a fabric softener to your final rinse.

One of our contributors swears by Formula 409® cleaner for stains. If it's a relatively minor stain, spray the spot with 409®, let it sit for two minutes, then put it in the washer. For more challenging stains like red wine on white napkins, spray 409® on the offending spots, put the napkins into the washing machine with detergent and bleach, agitate for one minute, then turn the machine off and let everything soak overnight. In the morning, put the load through a normal cycle.

When Washing

Don't overload the washer or dryer. It wastes energy and doesn't clean or dry your clothes as well, since items can't move freely. Although washers vary, the three basic cycles are Normal, Permanent Press, and Delicates. Normal wash spins at a high speed and should be used for sturdy material and heavily soiled clothes. Permanent Press is the best bet for most loads, as it is not as vigorous and prevents creases in wrinkle-resistant garments. The Delicates cycle should be used for clothes you'd normally hand wash.

Removing Lint and Wrinkles

Remove lint with a damp sponge, clothes brush, lint roller, or masking tape wound around your hand sticky side out. Make sure to clean your dryer's lint trap regularly.

Hang clothes up immediately after laundering to avoid wrinkles. For a quick fix, hang wrinkled clothes in a steamy bathroom. A good practice is to roll your clothes when packing for a trip; this works for drawers, too. It saves space and cuts back on wrinkling.

Stain Removal

You could live in a bubble and still manage to get a stain somehow. But you don't have to spend a fortune on stain removers. Actually, most can be found around the house, including white vinegar, rubbing alcohol, detergent, and common spot remover. Here are some general steps to battling spots:

■ Identify the offender immediately. Knowing what's in that purple blob on your blouse can go a long way toward treating it.

■ Test a stain remover on an inconspicuous part of the garment (like the hem) before treating.

■ Don't use bleach on just one section of the garment; it causes uneven color.

■ Don't sponge a stain; always blot with a white cloth. Sponging will just spread it further.

■ Try to treat a spot from the wrong side out. Turn the garment inside out and treat the spot that way to ensure you don't force the stain in deeper.

DON'T WAIT The sooner you get to it, the greater the chance you have of getting rid of it. Check laundry after it comes out of the wash and look for any darker stains that didn't get washed away. Use spot removers or pretreats right away, and save yourself money at the dry cleaners.

■ Don't put a stained garment in the dryer. Heat will set it.

■ Don't mix stain removal products together.

■ When in doubt, a very general stain removal procedure is to blot with a teaspoon of mild detergent to a cup of warm water. Follow with a small amount of vinegar and water, then sponge with clean water and blot dry. You might even try using a cotton swab and dabbing at the spot with hydrogen peroxide (test this on an inconspicuous area first!).

Choosing Your Washer and Dryer

WASHING MACHINES fall into two categories: front loader and top loader. A front loader is more energy-efficient, uses less water, and is generally quieter. It also handles clothes more gently and can usually accommodate a larger load. A top loader is cheaper, but can be noisier and has a smaller load capacity. Look for models with bleach dispensers and settings for temperature, duration, and wash/spin control.

CLOTHES DRYER choices are divided between gas-powered (which costs more initially, but uses less energy and is cheaper to operate in the long run) and electric-powered. Bear in mind, gas-powered models are often more expensive to repair. A moisture sensor or thermostat will signal when clothes are dry, with the sensor being slightly better in that it will not waste energy overdrying clothes. Models with top-mounted lint filters are preferred, and side-opening doors offer easier access than down-opening doors.

White vinegar is excellent for removing detergent buildup on towels. Add a cup to the rinse cycle on a monthly basis to keep your towels extra absorbent.

Treating Common Stains

BLOOD Flush area with cold water immediately. Sprinkle with meat tenderizer and cool water. Let stand for 20 minutes, then wash. Vinegar and hydrogen peroxide can also help, but be warned: these will lighten or remove color.

COFFEE/TEA Use stain remover or lemon juice. Wash fabric in cold water and air-dry.

GRASS Use a stain remover, then launder in hot water, adding bleach if material is sturdy.

GREASE Wash in a generous amount of regular detergent and hot water. For delicate fabrics, try club soda. For heavier material, apply cornstarch and let it sit overnight.

LIPSTICK Petroleum jelly, club soda, hairspray or toothpaste can be used to pretreat the garment if it can't be washed immediately.

MUD Dry, then brush off excess dirt. Pretreat the fabric with stain remover and wash.

PERSPIRATION This is usually caused by antiperspirant. Soak in detergent, and then launder in hot water with detergent and bleach (make sure garment can handle this first). Try to use antiperspirants sparingly, and switch to one that doesn't contain aluminum chloride, which causes stains.

RED WINE Dab with club soda and sprinkle with salt. Let sit for 15 minutes. Wash in cold water.

Websites for Whiter Whites

Paint/Art Stains
www.crayola.com/canwehelp/staintips/stain.cfm

Tide Stain Care Center
www.tide.com/staindetective/selectStain.jhtml

Textile Industry Affairs
www.textileaffairs.com/stains.htm

The International Guild of Professional Butlers
www.butlersguild.com/guests/general/stain_removal.html

Know When to Throw in the Towel

When in doubt about a stain or how to care for a particular garment, it's best to take it to a dry cleaner. Take spotted garments in immediately, and make sure you tell them about each stain and what caused it.

Special Care

Caring for fabrics is not a simple job. Items of different material, different size, and different shape all have different needs. The first step towards meeting those needs is to refer to the manufacturer's instructions or care symbols on the tag. Here are some general guidelines for dealing with items that require special care.

BLANKETS Make sure blankets can fit into the washer/dryer and have room to move. If blankets are too large, send them to a professional cleaner or use an oversized machine at the laundromat. Soak them for fifteen minutes first to avoid pilling. If the blanket is wool, use cool water (too hot and it will shrink). Dry the blanket flat or drape it across two clotheslines. You may have to pull it back into shape.

CURTAINS/DRAPES If they are machine washable, use the gentlest cycle and tumble or line-dry. Fiberglass drapes need to be dry-cleaned or carefully hand washed (wear gloves or you'll get fibers in your hands). Press water out, and make sure all fiberglass fibers are washed out of the tub or washing receptacle.

DELICATES To machine wash, use mesh bags or place in a thin pillowcase and tie a knot. Turn underwear and panties inside out before washing. Use the gentle cycle, and don't overheat—it can wear out the elasticity of some clothes. Drying delicates in the dryer will age the items, so it's best to line-dry or use a drying rack if possible.

DOWN- AND FEATHER-FILLED ITEMS Try to keep these as clean as possible with covers and cases to avoid the annoyance and expense of cleaning them. If it is absolutely necessary, they can be hand washed or machine washed on the delicate cycle, but each washing extracts oils that make the pillow buoyant. Hang them to dry.

FOAM RUBBER Wash regularly with detergent, but do not machine dry them as they pose a fire hazard.

KNITS Knit articles that have not been preshrunk will shrink if heat is applied to them. Try to use cold or warm water when washing, and dry on low or no heat.

LACE Place in a mesh bag or thin pillowcase and knot before putting in washing machine. Use the gentlest cycle. If the lace is synthetic, you can dry it in the dryer. Otherwise, hang to dry and iron if necessary. You might want to hand wash very old or delicate lace.

PLASTIC SHOWER CURTAINS Wash in washing machine on warm setting, or scrub by hand. Do not put in the dryer or apply heat.

QUILTS Don't attempt if the quilt is very old or made from delicate materials; the weight of the quilt when wet will break stitches. Never wet-launder a

If you are worried about the health effects of chemicals used in dry cleaning, you may want to try wet or "green" cleaning. Cleaners use special equipment and solutions to clean clothes without resorting to harsh chemicals or solvents. Keep in mind that not all clothes can be wet cleaned, and procedures are just as expensive as regular dry cleaning.

68

handmade quilt; take it to an expert who specializes in dry-cleaning and restoring them. The main danger is fading or bleeding color, so make sure the color of a machine-made quilt is laundry-safe by testing a small patch to see if it runs. Make sure all stitches are firmly sewn; otherwise, it will fall apart in the machine. For antique quilts, get rid of surface dirt by gently vacuuming through a screen.

Accessory Care

Sure your clothes can look great, but often it's the little things that really make an outfit sparkle.

GLOVES Rub away scuffs with a pencil eraser. Wash with special cleanser and dry on your hands to retain their shape.

LEATHER Try cleaning with saddle soap or a little soap and cold water.

HATS ■ **Straw** Soak in saltwater and reshape while drying. ■ **Felt** Get rid of water spots by blotting and then rubbing with tissue paper.

TIES Steam-clean ties by hanging them in a foggy bathroom. When ironing, get rid of back crease by slipping a slim piece of cardboard in the tie.

JEWELRY ■ **Gold** Clean with $1/4$ cup ammonia in 1 cup warm water. Soak, then scrub with toothbrush and air-dry. ■ **Diamonds** Clean with a solution of $1/4$ cup ammonia, 1 cup water, and 1 tablespoon detergent. Soak for half an hour and then scrub with a toothbrush. Rinse, apply rubbing alcohol, and air-dry. ■ **Silver** Polish with toothpaste or a baking-soda solution, rinse, and towel dry. Consult our tips on page 21 to get rid of tarnish. ■ **Pearls** Polish with a little bit of olive oil on a cloth, then wipe dry. ■ **Other** Opals, ivory, jade, and turquoise should not be soaked. Just wipe with a damp cloth.

How to Hand Wash

Fill sink or bucket with cool water and add a mild detergent. Dishwashing liquid can be used to wash delicate or high-maintenance fabrics, but don't use this regularly. Pretreat stains. Place garment in water and let soak for a few minute. Swish it around for three to five minutes. Then drain the bucket or sink and rinse the item thoroughly. Dry by laying flat or on the clothesline.

SHOES ■ **Canvas** Throw in washing machine or clean with a toothbrush dipped in detergent. Stuff canvas shoes with newspaper to dry. ■ **Suede** Follow same guidelines as for gloves. Try steam-cleaning by holding over a kettle and then gently brushing them. ■ **Patent Leather** Apply some petroleum jelly, then buff. If soles are slippery, sand bottoms with sandpaper.

Ironing

The art of ironing is waning, thanks to pretreated fabrics, sophisticated washers and dryers, and a preponderance of dry-cleaning establishments. Those of us who do iron, though, find this old ritual relaxing and rewarding. The process is time-consuming and cannot be hurried, but the fragrance of steam and clean cloth is soothing. A stack or two of clean, pressed clothing and linens produces an enhanced sense of well-being for ironing enthusiasts. Slipping into a favorite shirt you've ironed for yourself is a true, if simple, pleasure.

A single shirt or blouse takes about ten minutes to iron. Delicate fabrics, detailing like pleats or ruffles, and heavy pure linen or cotton will involve a little more work. You'll need sharp, clear lighting, water for the iron, and a comfortable floor surface. Bring out the hangers (avoid wire hangers, which leave marks), fill your iron with water, and choose a book on tape or some good music or pop in a DVD. Test the heat of the iron with a cotton towel to make sure it is not too hot.

1. Iron the collar first. Lay the shirt right side out, which means the collar is wrong side up on the board. Press from the collar ends to the center. Reverse the shirt and gently iron the other side of the collar.

2. Iron the yoke (the panel under the collar that holds the back of the shirt to the sleeves).

3. Iron each sleeve. Fold the sleeve along the seam and press the seam flat. Iron the button placket at the cuff, then the rest of the sleeve. Pay careful attention to topstitched seams. Flip the sleeve and iron the other side.

4. Iron the hem of the shirt, all the way around.

5. Iron the front of the shirt that has buttons, adjusting the garment on the board to meet the seams of the yoke and sleeves. Continue to the back, and finally to the second half of the front. Pay special attention to the buttonhole placket.

6. Hang the shirt on a wood or padded hanger and button at the collar.

THE RULE OF BLACK When clothing is black, navy, or another dark color, turn it inside out before ironing. This way you avoid iron marks on the outer side and the shine from an iron that's too hot.

IRONING BORED? Though there have been many generations of design improvement in irons, the common ironing board is fundamentally unchanged. Freestanding boards that adjust in height are covered with heat-resistant pads that prevent scorching. One end is tapered and curved to allow the iron the reach intricate areas like sleeve seams and yokes.

Ironing Silk Garments...

Lay a clean wet cloth over the board. Press it quickly, remove the cloth, put the silk over the steaming board, and iron on the wrong side. Result: no streaks, no spots, no bulges. You can use this method to restore stretched material to its proper shape.

Slightly Damp

Clothes are pressed smoother if slightly dampened before ironing. Although you can use the steam function, you can also lightly spritz dry clothes, or take them out of the dryer before they have completely dried. Keep the clothes damp by placing them in a plastic bag until you are ready to iron.

For hanging curtains and clothes, steamers may be more efficient than an iron. A steamer allows you to get rid of wrinkles without setting up an ironing station, and though it takes more storage space than an iron, it can work very well on damasks and woolens, and other fabrics that are notoriously challenging to iron.

Iron Safety

After the kitchen and the bathroom, a high percentage of accidents involve an iron. Stand the iron on its heel when you are not actually pressing fabric; even though the ironing board has a scorch-resistant covering, a hot iron left face-down will eventually cause damage to the insulation. Keep the iron clean; dust can become dirt marks on pressed fabric. Empty the reservoir of water each time you've finished ironing; though the temptation is there to stow the iron with the water, mineral deposits will accumulate and stain fabric. Always turn off and unplug an iron not in use.

Let Me Down Gently

Lowering the hem of a garment (or a drape for that matter) usually leaves a strong crease where the original hem was. To remove the crease, spritz it will a mild vinegar and water solution. Cover the fabric with a pressing cloth and press with the hot iron. Good pressing cloths are all cotton with smooth weaves. A kitchen towel is a reliable, handy choice.

. . . and Pleats

Pleats, thread-marked for width before washing, are first ironed flat, and anchored with pins into folds for pressing. Tiny pleats have a better chance if the iron is pushed over them slightly sideways.

How to Store Clothes

Storing your clothes for the season is a great way to make them last longer, save money, and free up closet space (which you can then fill with more clothes!). However, it takes more than a shoebox to stow family favorites: The right temperature and atmosphere are crucial to keeping your clothes as fresh and bright as the day you bought them. Follow these hints to keep your wardrobe looking good on you, or the next generation.

■ Clean and dry clothes thoroughly before storing for the season. Do not use starch, bleach, or fabric softener, and make sure to wash all detergent out well. The chemical residue could attract insects.

■ Storage areas should have a moderate temperature (not too hot or cold), and be away from light. Bugs are attracted to dirt, hair, dust, and mold, so make sure the storage space has been properly cleaned and disinfected. Try not to store clothes in hot attics, damp basements, or unheated garages.

■ Use white tissue paper to wrap clothes, or cover them with clean cloth. Replace paper on a yearly basis for long-term storage (as for wedding and christening gowns).

■ Natural fibers (wool, cotton, etc.) need ventilation, so store in containers with holes. Don't crowd hanging clothes together; allow some space between.

■ Mothballs or cedar chests can deter bugs. Unfortunately, the strong odors that keep away bugs also keep away humans! Be sure to air garments out well for several days before wearing them. You can fight the smell of mothballs (and deter some insects) naturally with a sachet of bay leaves, or you can forsake smelly repellents altogether and use natural deterrents like cedar chips, lavender, cloves and citrus peels instead. Mothballs may discolor clothes, so keep them from coming into direct contact with garments by putting them in old pantyhose or socks. Don't expose mothballs to plastic.

Before storing (or laundering, for that matter), all clothes should be repaired. After all, who wants to pull that cute summer dress out of storage and encounter the rip down the side from last year's no-holds-barred badminton match? See pages 182–183 for basic sewing tips.

Folding

DRESS SHIRTS AND T-SHIRTS Lay shirt facedown. Fold one arm in. Fold other arm in. Fold bottom up, then once more.

SLACKS Hold pants up by cuffs and place creases together, smoothing out pant legs. Fold in thirds.

SKIRTS Lay skirt facedown. Fold in one third vertically. Fold in other. Fold up in thirds.

SOCKS Place socks together. Roll from toes to foot opening. Open the cuff of the sock that is on the outside of the roll and pull the cuff down over the roll.

UNDERPANTS Fold in half so crotch meets waistband. Then fold in thirds.

Self Storage Tips

Some materials need special consideration when storing:

■ Velvet should be padded with paper and hung on a padded hanger.

■ Most fabrics that are soft and flexible can be stored flat if padded well with white tissue paper. These include crib quilts, wool, and silk.

■ Large items like quilts should be folded over cardboard tubing to prevent creasing. Linen, as well, can be rolled over tubing. Even soft leather and suede can be stored in this way to cut back on hanging space. If you fold these, refold them in a different way every so often to avoid cracking.

■ Don't store clothes in plastic bags, since this hinders ventilation. Look for muslin bags or special acid-free cartons instead of plastic.

■ Chalk and charcoal both absorb excess moisture in the air. Try placing a container filled with charcoal in your storage space, or hang a bag of chalk in the corner.

Storing Big-Ticket Items

Storage can be expensive, but it may be the only option if you have very little space, live in a humid or hot climate, have a large amount of delicate items (such as furs), or have a recurring bug problem. Coats and furs should be placed in a cold-storage garment warehouse at a dry-cleaning plant—the cost of this includes insect deterrent and special cleaning when it's time to retrieve garments from the "icebox." Shop for best prices, and deal with an outfit you trust.

Organizing Basics

Organization and clutter control are the machines that drive good housekeeping and pleasant homemaking. A cluttered space is usually a dirty space. In a cluttered space, you don't even know where to begin cleaning; controlling clutter, therefore, in your home is one of the fundamentals of housekeeping.

Ten Tips to Help Household Organization

1 *Before you organize your home, pay attention to your current daily schedule.* Where do you usually drop the mail? What's the first thing you reach for when stepping out of the shower? Asking questions like these can help you figure out a system that is the most efficient and comfortable for you. You can then organize the house accordingly.

2 *Have a place for everything and put everything in its place.* Not only will having set places for items mean that you always know where to find things, but having a place for everything means that you have fewer places for clutter to accumulate.

3 *Schedule organizing times.* If you schedule appointments with your doctor and dentist, why not schedule appointments for removing clutter from your house? Schedule an hour weekly or monthly for set tasks, or block out an entire day a few times a year for extensive organizing projects.

4 *Never underestimate the power of plastic bins.* Whether you use them on bookcase shelves, in cabinets, or under beds, plastic bins are great for organization. Available in a variety of shapes and sizes to help group like items together, they can accommodate everything from winter clothes to household papers, divided by subject. Keep them on hand for frequently needed items such as extension cords or hand tools.

De-cluttering Hints

■ Allow yourself enough time to make decisions about what to keep. If your concentration is constantly broken, you'll disrupt that little voice that lets you know when it's time to get rid of things.

■ Evaluate the real worth of your possessions. Those home videos and photo albums are irreplaceable, and thus deserve to be archived so you can find them at any time. Sell or donate outgrown clothing that is not worn out, especially when it has no sentimental value. Board games and decks of cards with missing pieces are about as appealing to someone else as a collection of unmatched socks.

■ Check the sell-by date. Tired, faded, dusty decorations like dried flower arrangements can be honored for time served and sent on their way. Petrified foam-rubber products will never become fresh and springy again. Wood cutting boards that are split, stained, or burned, badly chipped pottery, torn curtains—all get whisked away.

Picking up, putting away, and filing are the types of activity that tend to get pushed aside and saved for another day. But once you've begun the war on clutter, you will gain momentum and develop an instinctive sense of what to keep, where to keep it, and what to send packing.

5 *Keep only what you need.* Holding on to unneeded items is the recipe for clutter disaster. If you have things you don't use, don't keep them. Chances are that the little items you keep "just in case you need them" will be difficult to find when you need them anyway.

6 *Make "de-cluttering" a habit.* Set up daily routines, such as sorting mail, washing and putting away dishes, and even making sure that clothing gets put in the hamper. Don't go around empty-handed: When you walk through a room, gather up the litter as you go.

7 *Prioritize with to-do lists.* Write up a list of all the chores that make your house neat and organized. Figure out how often these tasks need to be done. Divide your list into daily, weekly, and monthly tasks. If the month is coming to a close and there are still items on the to-do list, set aside time for a day of organizing.

8 *Make sure your furniture fits your needs.* End tables and desks are natural places for clutter to accumulate. Don't give clutter room to gain a foothold! If you find that you have lots of books lying around, invest in another bookcase. If your coffee table is only used for gathering junk mail, maybe it is time to get rid of it.

9 *Set attainable goals so you don't get discouraged.* Organizing a room is a daunting task; set smaller goals, like going through a cabinet, that you can achieve in the available time. Eventually, those small achievements will add up to big changes.

10 *Reward yourself.* Treat yourself and your helpers after an organizing job well done. Take everyone out for dinner. Not only will it be a neat reward, but it also means that you won't have to put away dishes or clean the kitchen when you are through!

Sell Your Clutter

Garage, yard, and apartment sales are a great way to get rid of your old stuff and make some money too. You might even consider holding a joint sale with a few neighbors. Here are a few tips to make your sale a success:

■ Post signs at least a week in advance at busy street corners, supermarkets, and bus stops near your home. Clearly state the date, address, and time. If you don't want people to show up early, write NO EARLY-COMERS or NO EARLY BIRDS on the sign in big letters.

■ Use tags and stickers to price merchandise. Although you will be haggling, this gives customers a starting point. Some folks won't bother with an item if they don't see a price.

■ Group similar items together. Present your wares attractively on a clean table, or hang clothes up on a dress rack or clothesline.

■ Make sure you have enough change and have a secure way of keeping it, like in a fanny pack, apron, or strongbox.

■ Discount prices during the last hour of the sale and donate all leftover items to a charity or shelter.

Organizing
Room by Room

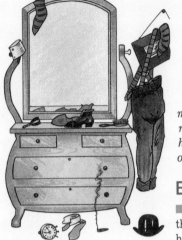

Organizing an entire house may seem like a job best handled by highly trained professionals, or at the very least, magic elves. However, by using the right tools and taking it one room at a time, you too can enjoy a neat, clutter-free household. From the musty corners of your bathroom to the overstuffed confines of your family room, you'll be amazed at how much cleaner and more comfortable your house will feel if you simply use your space creatively, stick with an organizing system, and follow Home Almanac's tips and tricks.

Bathroom

■ Hooks can accommodate towels and robes (especially on the back of the door), and towel racks keep towels organized. You can also hang up hair appliances like dryers and curling irons as well.

■ Store cotton swabs and cotton balls in clear plastic containers to cut down on bulky boxes. A metal or waterproof basket can hold extra rolled towels or spare rolls of toilet paper.

■ Make a point of going through each drawer in your storage unit and getting rid of old or unnecessary products or items. Assigning a drawer to each of your family members may be the best way to keep things organized. Or assign each drawer a subject: hair products, shower supplies, etc., and use drawer dividers.

■ Showers can stay organized if sponges, soap, and shampoos are left in caddies, like one hung from a showerhead.

■ A hamper is necessary to keep towels and clothes off the floor. If you don't have room for a large one, consider a smaller waterproof basket, or a linen bag hung on the back of the door or on the wall.

■ Go through your medicine cabinet monthly and clean out any expired medicines. Don't keep ointments or gels that have discolored or separated. Medicines that smell vinegary or have evaporated should also be thrown out. Makeup usually goes bad after about six months.

■ If your bathroom is unusually hot and humid, you might not want to store your medicines in the bathroom at all, since it could speed up the expiration of some products. Consider moving medications and liquids to a cool, dry place that is out of reach of children.

Family Room

■ Knickknacks and collectibles should be displayed only if you seriously enjoy looking at them on a daily basis. Otherwise, you're in for a whole lot of cleaning and not too much enjoyment.

Shelves can be added almost anywhere: above the toilet, on the wall facing the sink, in the bathtub area. You might even be able to get extra storage by installing a shelf above the bathroom door.

■ At least once a day, clear off the coffee and end tables and put things back where they belong. If you have several remote controls, collect them in a basket and put them in an accessible place.

■ If you enjoy keeping magazines on the table, make sure they don't get too outdated. Keep a paper collector or bin nearby to store magazines until they are ready to be recycled. A wastebasket can also cut down on litter.

■ Use a bookshelf, cabinet, or even a large, clear storage bin or chest to store miscellaneous games, books, photo albums, or other items.

■ To sort DVDs, videocassettes, and compact discs, follow the guidelines for books *(see box on right)*. When choosing a storage unit, keep in mind how large your collection is and how fast you'd like it to grow. You'll end up wasting more space if you buy something that's too big and leave most of it empty, and buying something too small renders it useless almost immediately and only adds to the clutter.

Bedrooms

■ Take it piece by piece: closet, bureau/dresser, accessory space, under the bed.

■ For each area, first take out all items so you can see the full amount when sorting; don't dump everything in the room on your bed all at once (you're trying to clean up a mess, not make one, remember?)

■ Go through your things and set aside those that are beyond repair or that

The key to storing and organizing books is to go through them about once a year, and get rid of or donate any little-used titles. This will make dusting easier and free up space. Take a hint from the library and organize into subjects, authors, or genres.

you don't want, those you wear occasionally, and those you wear regularly. Discard or donate the first pile and consider storing the second. This will leave you with the things you use regularly.

■ Organize similar things together. Categories are up to you. For clothes, you might want to divide by style (casual, dressy, etc.), color, or even type (pants, shirts, etc.). (*See Organizing Closets, page 82.*) The important thing is to find the system that comes most naturally to you; that way you won't have to think when putting things away. Hanging items of the same length together avoids wasted space. Use the space under the short garments for storage or more hanging space.

■ Use helpful storage tools like pegs, hooks, over-the-door and freestanding shoe racks, dividers, under-bed containers, and clear plastic bins to keep your things organized.

Storage Space, Where Art Thou?

Attic

PRO Usually dry and can accommodate large objects.

CON Can become extremely hot depending on your location, and is not very accessible.

WHAT TO STORE occasional-use items; sturdy things like boxes, cookware, and seasonal decorations; furniture that is covered with tarps or sheets. Bring the heat down and ventilate occasionally by opening attic windows and using roof exhaust fans.

WHAT NOT TO STORE photographs, important papers, videocassettes, film, and clothing unless it has been sealed in a garment bag (even then the dry air might damage cloth).

Basement

PRO Cool temperature and good accessibility.

CON Dampness fosters molds and can damage fabric and upholstered furniture. Flooding in basements can destroy a large amount of stuff.

WHAT TO STORE rarely used equipment or appliances, kitchenware, hard luggage. Make sure to keep things in plastic boxes and off the floor in case of flooding. You might want to install a dehumidifier to cut back on moisture.

WHAT NOT TO STORE paperwork, books, delicate clothes, tools susceptible to rust.

Garage/Shed

PRO Very accessible, especially in the case of an attached garage, which can have generally fair environmental conditions.

CON Limited space. Fluctuating temperatures in detached outbuildings can be a problem for paper and cloth.

WHAT TO STORE sports equipment, bikes, tools, folding chairs, and garden supplies. Overhead space can provide a lot of hanging storage possibilities.

Organizing The Kitchen

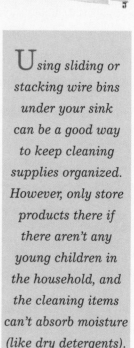

The modern kitchen, with all its gadgets and utensils, can be a place of great convenience and comfort. Unfortunately, it can also be a place of chaos. The first step to managing your kitchen is to go through everything and get rid of all expired or unnecessary items. If the whole task is too daunting, break it up into the following manageable steps:

CLEAN OFF YOUR COUNTERS Put every appliance that you don't use more than twice a week to the side. You might want to store these items in a lesser-used kitchen area, or store in another room. For small appliances you use often, consider buying stands or installing shelves to place them on. This will allow you access to them, but free up countertop space underneath.

GO THROUGH YOUR DRAWERS Empty them and divide them up by use: basic cutlery, silverware, and specialty cooking items. Where tools are placed in the kitchen will always be dictated by the importance they have in your household: Generally, silverware drawers should go by the sink or dishwasher, and other cooking items like spatulas and tongs should go by the stove for easy access. Remove seasonal items or "company" utensils from the general kitchen tools and store them in another location. If your countertop is not too cluttered, place oft-used large utensils in a stainless steel or ceramic canister.

PARE DOWN THE INVENTORY OF YOUR KITCHEN Get rid of any duplicate appliances or cookware, unless you need an extra or will need to replace that item soon. The same goes for mug and glassware selections. Sure, you love that complete set of action-figure glasses you got from a gas station, but unless you're willing to store it or use it, get rid of it.

Storage Tools and Devices

■ Invest in invaluable tools like clear plastic containers, bins and space-saving devices like lazy Susans, drawer dividers, over–the–door racks, and racks that can fold out from under counters and cabinets. These items are inexpensive and can be found at most home stores.

■ If you have very little cabinet space but quite a lot of wall space, consider installing a metal rack or rod, and then hanging utensils or even pots and pans

Using sliding or stacking wire bins under your sink can be a good way to keep cleaning supplies organized. However, only store products there if there aren't any young children in the household, and the cleaning items can't absorb moisture (like dry detergents).

A table with chairs is a welcome addition to any food-preparation area (especially if you don't have a dining room). Look for a table with a drawer to hold various household items or cutlery, and drop leaves or pull-out panels to provide more surface area without taking up too much space.

from it with S-hooks. Just make sure to wash items thoroughly before using, since they are exposed to air and dust.

■ Bookshelves are great ways to organize your recipes and cookbooks, and also to hold canisters and miscellaneous items. Keep them away from greasy stove fumes.

■ Every kitchen should have a junk drawer to serve as a catchall for necessary items that just don't fit anywhere else. Keep things together by utilizing plastic sandwich bags, twist ties, and small boxes (like those used for jewelry or cigars). Go through the drawer on a regular basis.

Refrigerator/Freezer

■ Follow the refrigerator cleaning tips on page 55.

■ Big Surprise! Using fridge compartments for what they are made for—freezer for long term storage, crisper for vegetables, etc.—can make your fridge contents more compact and keep food lasting longer.

■ Magnet department: De-clutter the door of your fridge by regularly sifting through notices and scraps. Cut back on the number of magnets by judging them based on their holding power, not their cuteness. Pictures can look nice, but they will be protected better and last longer if displayed in a photo album or frames. Consider putting a mark-up board on the fridge to write grocery lists.

Cabinets

■ When storing in cabinets, keep in mind a few things: Similar things (canned foods, dry goods, etc.) should be stored together in an area near where they are usually used; heavier items (like cans, pots, and pans) should be stored lower down, while lighter things should be placed higher up. Although it is difficult, food should be kept away from excessive heat or cold (like your oven or fridge).

■ Locate your items wisely. Plates and glassware can go near the sink for convenience after washing, but large serving dishes and oversized mixing bowls can be in their own special cabinet farther off. Pots and pans can withstand heat, so you can place them in lower-level cabinets by the stove.

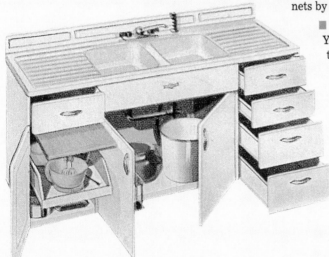

■ Don't store all china and glassware together. You don't really need to have constant access to 12 place settings if you're a household of two. Put them away for special occasions. Store baking pans, trays, cutting boards, and other slim service items vertically.

■ If you don't have enough space for a linen drawer/cabinet containing dish towels, potholders, tablecloths, and cloth napkins, try making some space in your regular towel or linen closet, even if it isn't in the kitchen.

Organizing Closets

Monsters aren't the only horrible things lurking in closets; clutter and disorganization also run rampant here. Take the bite out of the beast and have yourself an efficient and organized place to keep all of your items.

Linen Closet

■ Divide linens by theme—bedding, cleaning and table (washcloths, napkins, tablecloths), towels—and then by room. Arrange sheets by size, and fold whole sets, pillowcases and all, together.

■ Go through linens and donate ones you don't use anymore or never will. It's handy to have a few raggedy, torn-up old towels for chores, but don't go overboard and keep every single scrap of material: About four rags should be enough.

■ Make sure items used on a daily basis, like bath towels, are easy to see and reach. More seasonal articles, like holiday tablecloths, can go further in—although you don't really want to lose sight of your inventory (you may never find it again!).

■ Don't pack linen too tightly; the material needs to breathe.

■ Quilts and heavy blankets may benefit from breathable bedding bags.

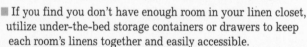

■ If you find you don't have enough room in your linen closet, utilize under-the-bed storage containers or drawers to keep each room's linens together and easily accessible.

■ Tablecloths can be hung on plastic and wooden hangers.

■ A good rule is to place the most recently used linen at the bottom of the pile. That way your linen will be constantly rotated, and you won't overuse a certain piece.

■ Labels on the shelves and drawers of your linen closet are an excellent way to quickly find what you're looking for.

■ Roll vintage textiles around cardboard tubes (gift wrap, wallpaper, or mailing tubes) for long-term storage; this will prevent tears and permanent crease marks, which can occur over time.

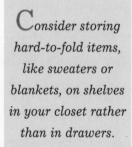

Consider storing hard-to-fold items, like sweaters or blankets, on shelves in your closet rather than in drawers.

Utility Closet

■ A utility closet is a good place to keep laundry supplies, cleaning supplies and tools, and home maintenance equipment if you do not have a workshop or garage. Although you may be tempted to use the space as a catchall for any misplaced items, realize that the more cluttered your utility closet is, the less likely you'll be to actually use it.

■ Go through your utility closet regularly and get rid of any trash, expired supplies, and broken items.

■ Plastic bins work well for keeping similar items together and accessible. They also cut down on spills and messes.

■ Hang broom and tool holders on the inside of the door, or simply install two screws spaced a bit apart to hang dustbins, brooms, and mops.

■ Don't save every cleaning product you try. Just keep the ones you use on a regular basis.

■ If the existing shelves in your utility closet are particularly deep, install shallower shelves. This will allow you to have better access to your items without having some things buried or hidden in the bottom.

Bedroom Closet

■ If your closet is too crammed, install a second rod at least 34 inches below the first, if you have room. This will accommodate shorter-length garments. Just make sure that items on the top rod can hang well. Double-tiered hangers also work great for hanging skirts and slacks. Check out your nearest container store, and you'll be amazed at the inventive contraptions available for hanging pants, ties, belts, and blouses together. If they are easy to use and save space, they are worth their cost.

■ Professional closet organizers always say, "Don't put your shoes on the floor of the closet!" This cardinal closet sin is the start of many a jumbled mess. Try to place shoes closer to eye level, on a shelf, or in a rack. This allows you to easily choose the pair that goes with your new navy suit. Plastic see-through shoe bins are helpful, too.

■ In a closet that is deeper than 24 inches, belts, scarves, and ties can all be hung on pegs on the inside of your door (without crushing clothes when door is closed).

■ Divide your closet into sections with some empty hangers, and keep everything facing in the same direction to give the appearance of neatness.

The Wonders and Shortcomings of Cedar

Cedar chips and cedar closets have long been trumpeted as the best and safest moth repellent—though they actually have barely any effect on moth larvae! Mothballs and insect repellents work well for all types of moths, but they contain chemicals and are effective only when they completely saturate or envelope the garment. The best ways to keep your clothes moth free are to make sure your closets are clean and that you wash and brush garments well before putting them away (moths are attracted to body oils, grease, and food stains).

The Life of Paperwork

Although you might want to hang on to those old check stubs just in case the IRS comes up with a nifty new tax deduction, here's some general guidance for when to put your records to rest:

■ Credit card and ATM receipts: Discard after they have been recorded and noted on your monthly statement.

■ Small-purchase receipts: Discard on a weekly basis.

■ Major home and appliance purchase receipts and warranties: Keep these together in a special file for the life of the purchases.

■ Pay stubs: Discard monthly (unless self-employed).

■ Utility bills: Discard monthly after verifying and recording information.

■ Bank statements, credit card statements and canceled checks: Discard after three years.

■ Tax returns, documentation, and medical bills: Discard after seven years.

■ Property papers: leases, deeds, and mortgages: Keep permanently in a strongbox or safety deposit box. Save property papers for at least seven years after property has been disposed of before discarding.

■ Financial papers: stocks, bonds, loan papers, broker's statements, and list of bank account information: Keep these in a strongbox; stock and bond certificates can be filed with your broker, if you have one, or in a safety deposit. Financial papers can be discarded seven years after the information has expired or closed.

■ Miscellaneous: immigration papers, wills, insurance policies, legal documents (marriage certificates, birth certificates, etc.), passports, social security cards, contracts, listing of family medical providers, etc.: Keep permanently in a strongbox or safety deposit box. Make copies of important papers and keep them in a separate, safe location.

Securing Your Paperwork

When throwing out documents or mail with personal information, make sure that you tear them up and divide the pieces among several garbage bags. This will deter identity theft.

Organizing Paperwork

Who says you have to work nine to five in order to deal with the horrors of paperwork? Before you succumb to a landslide of overdue bills and underused documents, follow our easy steps to whipping your home office into shape and keeping it that way. Whether you're ready to start a filing system or just wondering when to get rid of that old tax form, read on to find answers to your most pressing paper organizing questions.

Maintain Your Office Space

- Sort mail; get rid of junk mail and file important papers.
- Clear and clean desk surface and drawers.
- Empty wastebaskets.
- Dust surfaces.
- Sort paper and magazines for recycling.
- Check supplies.

Paperwork Tips

1 **PRESORTING** Open and sort all mail and incoming paperwork as soon as it comes in. Start with general categories, like junk mail, bills, and personal correspondence, and work from there.

2 **SORTING** Divide paperwork between that which you are keeping for reference, and that which you must take immediate action on. Reference papers can be placed to the side for filing or storage purposes. Immediate attention paperwork can be collected in a bin or visible "ACTION" folder. At the very least, divide your papers into short-term and long-term storage. In the office industry, this type of desktop organizing system is called a tickler file, to jog your memory and spur you to take care of urgent matters.

3 **FILING, STORING, AND DISCARDING** Filing should be done by categories that are neither too general nor too specific. Tickler files are often divided into the days of the month, whereas filing cabinets are usually alphabetical. The important thing, though, is for you to find a system you're most comfortable with and stick with it. Once you have come up with several general categories, divide them up further. For example, a personal file section might be divided into subcategories like "recipes," "coupons," and "magazine/newspaper clippings," while your financial file might contain folders labeled "bills and receipts," "tax documents," and "information on money-related topics." Color-code your files for easier access.

Don't label files "Miscellaneous" or "Other." It's too easy to dump everything into these types of files. Take the time to consider paperwork and organize appropriately.

Computer Hygiene

Modern computers are great helpers when getting rid of paperwork, and a number of programs are now available to organize and record insurance, financial, and tax information for you. You can even store photographs on most databases. But just like any other information system, your computer needs to be maintained and organized.

■ Make backup discs of your files, or back up your "hard drive" onto a storage device. Trust us, you'll be thankful if your hard drive ever wipes out. It's just good to have a copy of your important information in a safe place.

■ Regularly empty the desktop trash can.

■ Invest in an anti-virus, clean-up program, and run it regularly.

■ Go through programs and uninstall any unused ones. It's amazing the number of programs that are installed by computer manufacturers—a lot of these just take up space on your hard drive.

■ Don't just accept the system that came with your computer; organize applications and files you open so it's easiest for you to find them. Create folders to handle your data, and shortcuts to direct you to your most-used programs. Rename personal files so you can easily recognize them. Do not rename or rearrange files that your computer system needs in order to operate.

Tools of an Organized Office

LABELS Premade stickers, a label maker, index cards, and even self-stick notes (like Post-it™ tags) can label folders and boxes, making sure you never lose track of anything. Self-stick notes are a good temporary solution until you decide on final categories; keep in mind that while they are great for papers, they will eventually fall off folders and boxes.

FILES Hanging files are made for deep drawers. These are more effective than stacking papers or folders, since it is easier to see the work.

BINS There's a reason no desk is complete without in/out bins. Use bins to collect paperwork as it arrives and keep it from scattering. If desktop space is scarce or you find trays obtrusive, invest in clear, attractive plastic file bins that attach to a wall or door, like those you see in a doctor's office.

DRAWER DIVIDERS Keep office items neat by dividing them according to purpose. You might even be able to use a plain plastic silverware tray.

STACKING TRAYS These work for separating paperwork or just holding different types of office supplies.

PEGBOARDS Attached to a wall, these free up a lot of desk space by allowing you to hang tools and in/out bins.

Start a tax folder containing all your tax-related documents beginning January 1. This will make it much easier to pull your information when the time comes to file.

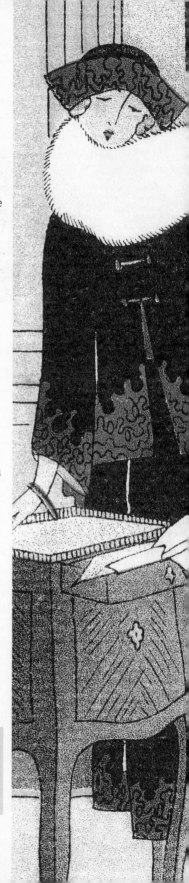

Remember to keep copies of all important documents and store them in separate safe locations.

Strongbox Inventory

■ Adoption, marriage, divorce, military papers ■ Backup computer discs of family and financial records ■ Bank account information ■ Birth certificates ■ Contracts ■ Copyrights/patents ■ Family letters or irreplaceable correspondence ■ Financial certificates (bonds, stocks, loans, etc.) ■ Immigration papers/visas ■ Important film negatives ■ Insurance policies ■ Passports ■ Photographs/household inventory—videotaped and written—for insurance purposes ■ Property papers: deeds, mortgages, etc. ■ School records and diplomas ■ Social Security cards ■ Valuable jewelry ■ Vehicle titles ■ Wills

Family Keepsakes

Nothing is more wonderful than looking back at old letters or keepsakes and enjoying the fond memories they evoke. However, it's a different story entirely when you're drowning in oceans of children's art projects you're never going to appreciate again—or you can't remember who did.

■ Although you might be tempted to save every scrap of paper your child scribbles on, pare down the collection by gathering all schoolwork together throughout the year in a file. At the end of the school year, decide on a few pieces to keep. Label accordingly and store away.

■ When storing family keepsakes and records, don't laminate documents. The chemicals will damage the paper structure over time.

■ Keep papers in a cool, dry place in acid-free cardboard boxes, or in metal and plastic containers with lids.

■ Papers should be kept out of direct light to make sure they do not fade.

■ Folding will cause creases that may crack over time. For best results, store flat, in one layer.

■ Photocopy faxes that are not printed on plain paper.

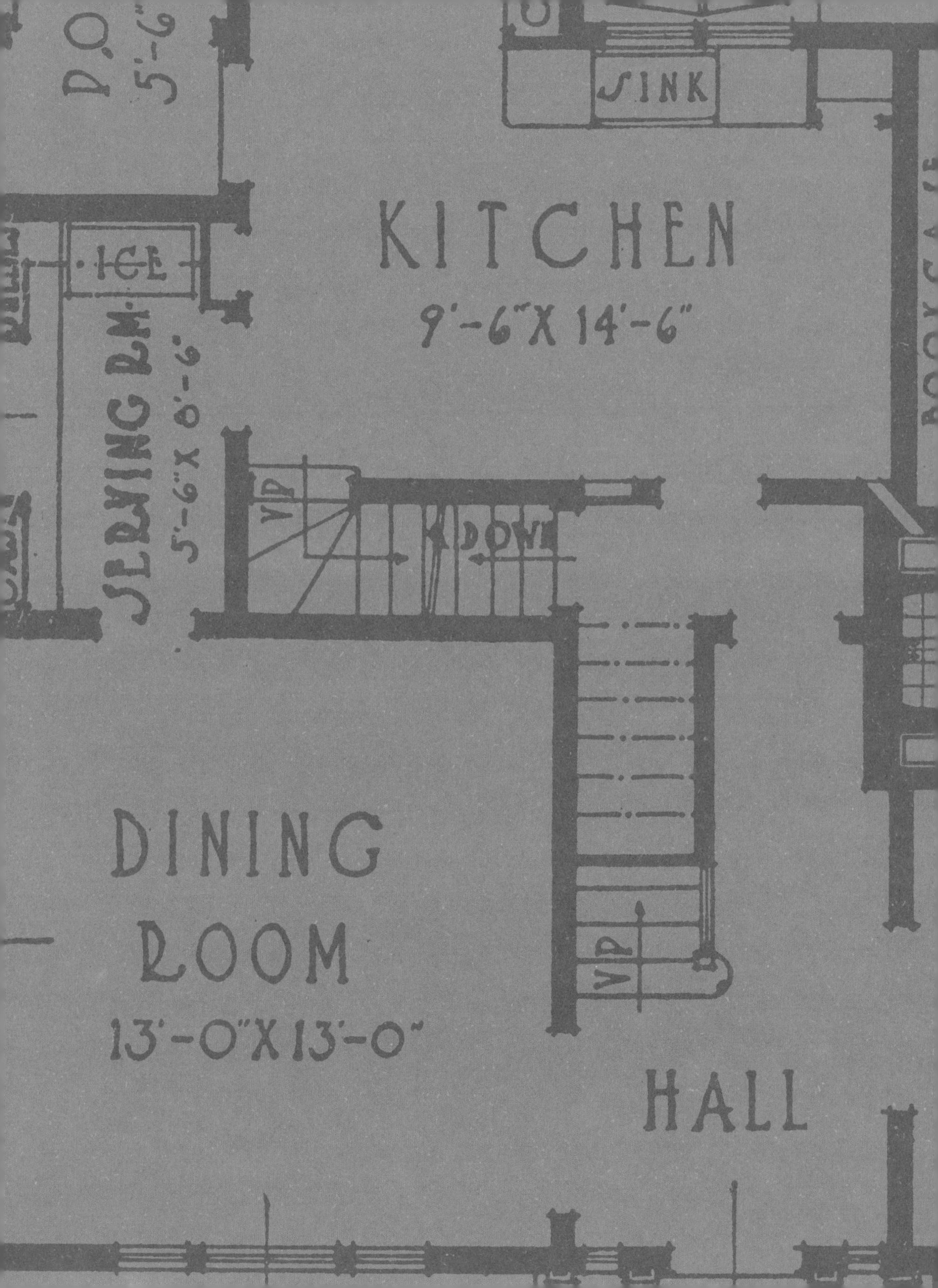

D.O.
5-6"

·ICE·

SERVING RM.
5'-6" X 6'-6"

KITCHEN
9'-6" X 14'-6"

UP

DOWN

DINING

ROOM
13'-0" X 13'-0"

UP

HALL

Chapter 3 Design &
Improvements

Design

Good design relies on harmony and balance. That sounds pretty direct, but it is a challenge that has reduced many professionals to defeat. Artfully furnishing a home is an ongoing series of decisions, from tiny ones (the doorknobs) to great leaps (adding a new kitchen). "Feathering a nest"—that is, taking an active role in design affairs—can be a deeply satisfying part of homemaking. The professional design world has provided plenty of inspiration through books and magazines, and the possibilities in every home have never been greater. The prospect of jumping into home design can be intimidating, so it is reassuring to remember that there's very little that cannot be undone—and that the results of your efforts need to please only you and your family.

Your Home-Design Checklist

Before anticipation of any project, answer the questions a professional would ask:

1 What is possible here? Take a good look at anything that you wish would go away but won't (the dropped ceiling), and anything you can alter (paneling that should be painted).

2 What are the advantages? Will your furniture look good in the room? Do you have collections that will shine on those built-in shelves?

3 Is this the right choice for me? Everyone's reality is different: Do you own or rent, plan to stay more than five years, want to start a family, or have two big dogs that shed?

4 Now I know what I want, but how does it get done? Establish your priorities and create a sensible schedule. Whether you do the work yourself, have contractors in, or plan for a combination of the two, allow reasonable overruns for time and money.

The Art of Furniture Arranging

Some rooms radiate; some just don't feel pulled together. The difference? Often, it is just a matter of furniture placement:

LIVING AREAS These gathering rooms aren't task oriented (like the kitchen) but meant for communication among household members and friends, for relaxation, for pleasing the senses. At the heart is a sofa or two, or perhaps a loveseat, upholstered chairs, ottomans, coffee tables, side tables, side chairs.

The design process in your home has already begun, whether you were actively involved or not. Before you begin transforming a bland room into a Taj Mahal, have in place a plan that's realistic in terms of time, money, and reliability.

Our favorite way to tackle this challenge is to "anchor the room" with major pieces—the sofa and chairs—to find pleasing placement. Then we gradually bring in lesser elements—experimenting with a lamp here, a pottery collection there—until the design feels comfortable. The greater elements, then, are left in place for the most part, but the accessories, like sofa throws, slipcovers, and area rugs, can be rethought for new looks. The final touches, like lampshades and candy dishes, almost seem to tell you where they will look best.

BEDROOMS Most prominent in the bedroom is, naturally, the bed itself, so where you place it will affect the atmosphere in the room. It is best to poise the bed where it has an overall view of the room. Where possible, don't position a bed with its head against the same wall as the entry door; entering the room directly alongside a bed is awkward and unharmonious. You want to enter facing the bed or so that you can walk past the foot. It is okay if one side of the bed rests against a wall in a small space; a freestanding bed will take up more space. Single beds and daybeds work well in nooks that envelope them on two or three sides. Once the bed is positioned, the bureau, dresser, and accessories can be shifted to find the most attractive arrangement.

Injecting Architectural Accents

The term "vanilla box" refers to a room with minimal built-in ornamentation: recessed doors and windows without frames, skimpy baseboards, walls that meet the ceiling without moldings. This kind of sleek design, originally inspired by the German Bauhaus movement of the early twentieth century, is not to everyone's taste. Some of us crave the crown molding, ceiling medallions, and lush millwork forsaken by modernists and foresworn by the escalating budget costs of new construction.

Recent years have seen a return to the ornamentation of interior architecture. Skylights are the most frequently installed architectural additions to a house, bringing sun to otherwise dreary center rooms, brightening kitchens, dens, and even bathrooms, bringing a supply of fresh air to a room where windows might compromise privacy.

Many other architectural embellishments are in vogue. Fortunately, affordable materials such as fiberglass and a variety of sturdy plastics make classic columns, coffered ceilings, and richly detailed mantels more affordable. Homeowners can pick and choose from a wide range of features, many of them available at the local home store. Installation is generally easy with the right tools. Once the finishes are applied and the furnishings assembled, most architectural flourishes will gracefully make themselves at home.

Create a Swatch Book of Your House

From the entrance to the storage room, a house
presents more colors than we realize. It's daunting
to stand before the thousands of paint chips at the store
and choose one or two that will hopefully look right at
home. If only you could take your sofa and drapes to the store
when you need to choose colors!

Home decorators have a secret: they rely on a swatch book to bring the
colors of the home with them when they shop. You can create your own swatch
book in a three-ring binder small enough to carry easily. Label a divider for every
room. Be sure to include ancillary spaces like hallways and staircases. In each section,
sketch a floorplan of the room (graph paper is helpful for this) and indicate the location and
dimensions of windows, doorways, closets, radiators, and anything that is built-in. Note the
room measurements and the orientation to the sun. Enter the dimensions of the room's furnishings to help keep the scale in perspective. Then add samples of the decorative elements:
paint chips, a piece of wallpaper, and swatches of the curtains, upholstery, and carpet. Do you
want to highlight a collection of pottery or painting? Take a photo and bring along a spool of
thread that matches the color.

Color

I'll Have White, White and White, Please

There are so many variations of white, who can choose? A deeply intriguing look can be created with a palette of creams, ivories, linens and other whites. Such an endeavor calls for the most precise lighting plan, right down to the colorcast of the bulbs and the lampshades.

Sometime after the invention of the wheel, an artistic Neanderthal devised the color wheel. The primary colors are red, yellow and blue; all other colors are variations and combinations of these three colors, plus white and black. Colors appearing opposite each other on the wheel are **complementary**; that means they offer the greatest possible contrast and will intensify both colors. **Adjacent** colors on the wheel will harmonize and blend, achieving soothing effects. Colors can be divided into "cool" and "warm"—the red violets to yellow greens, including yellows, oranges, and reds, are warm. The greens, blues, and violets look cool. In choosing color for a room, many professionals work on a theory of three: a main, base color; a secondary trim color; and a third accent color. Referring to the color wheel alone will not give you a divine palette. Every color is filtered through the adjacent light, whether it's natural or artificial or a combination. A designer's showroom or home furnishings store is a dreadful environment for assessing color. When you have narrowed your choice to three or four colors, bring substantial swatches of them into the room they are destined for and observe them over a few days and evenings.

Do You Dream in Color?

Behavioral scientists are enthusiastic exponents of the power color brings to virtually every aspect of life, from rich salad greens to a pair of ruby red slippers. In fact, the Inter-Society Color Council at *www.iscc.org* meets every year to study and predict trends in color—in home, fashion, commercial, and even automobile design. Manufacturers subscribe to such studies, and that accounts for the popularity of a super-saturated lime green one spring and a soft mossy green the next.

Color affects the way we feel; shades of blue give a sense of calm, reds and oranges entice your appetite, and yellows make you feel upbeat. Don't be scared off by dark colors; they can give your home a warm, cozy feeling. Tradition dictated keeping dark colors out of small spaces, but this way of thinking no longer applies: We are not always striving to make our homes look larger, and can enjoy smaller spaces for the intimacy they offer.

Think Outside the Box

Why should every wall in a room be the same color? Painting just one wall a color has an enormous effect: you do not overpower the entire room and cause overload, but you introduce the element into your décor, using it more as a decoration than a design element.

Primary Colors. These cannot be produced by mixing other colors.

Secondary Colors. These are produced by mixing two primary colors as follows:

Tertiary Colors. These are produced by mixing two secondary colors as follows:

Harmony of Colors.

Blue, Red, Violet, Yellow, Blue, Green, Yellow, Red, Orange

Orange, Violet, Russet, Green, Citrine, Green, Orange, Olive

Working with Pros

So you've decided that you need help, but what type of help do you need: a designer, architect, or contractor? A designer will tell you how to decorate your home. For major renovations, an architect is the person who draws up exact building plans, including all the measurements and sizes of what exists and what needs to be built or reconfigured. A contractor is responsible for actually making the changes to your home: building the bookshelf, refinishing the floors, or renovating the bathroom.

Major jobs obviously require professional handling, but how can you know when a smaller job needs a professional touch? Call for help when a job is one that you have not tackled before or requires breaking through a wall, floor, or ceiling. These things can be costly to repair and you want to minimize disruption. A professional will be familiar with local zoning and building codes, too.

Working with a Designer, an Architect, or a Contractor

■ Ask for references and solicit recommendations from friends and shops whose design appeals to you. Check with people who have had the type of work done that you are looking for and check at local suppliers: for instance, the town garden shop will have experience with landscape architects. Comb through magazines and books for ideas or check out home improvement programs on television.

■ Check with trade organizations (*see opposite*).

■ Go beyond the business card. See the professional's office. If it's appropriate, visit some of their earlier sites to view their work.

■ Interview prospects in your home, so they can get a sense of how your family lives. Ask them to bring along examples of the work they've done and explain the assignments. Check their references to see what others' experiences have been. When you've chosen someone, arrange for them to spend time in your home so that they can observe your family's preferences. They will submit a written proposal that will include fabric swatches, paint chips, carpet samples, and photos of furniture and fixtures.

■ Get it in writing! For contractors and architects, the building standards for your town and any permits required will have to be met and you will want a warranty; for designers you will want your agreement detailed.

■ After a design is approved, order the major components and schedule work in your home. Allow time and money for overruns, especially with large-scale improvements.

■ Negotiate a balloon payment plan, which rewards the professional when the job is complete and accepted.

■ Keep a paper trail. If a job goes sour, you'll want to have good records.

■ When the job is complete, arrange for a "walk-through" with the designer before approving the job.

■ Report your experience. Let the town, trade association, and vendor know what your experience is—positive or not. Others will benefit.

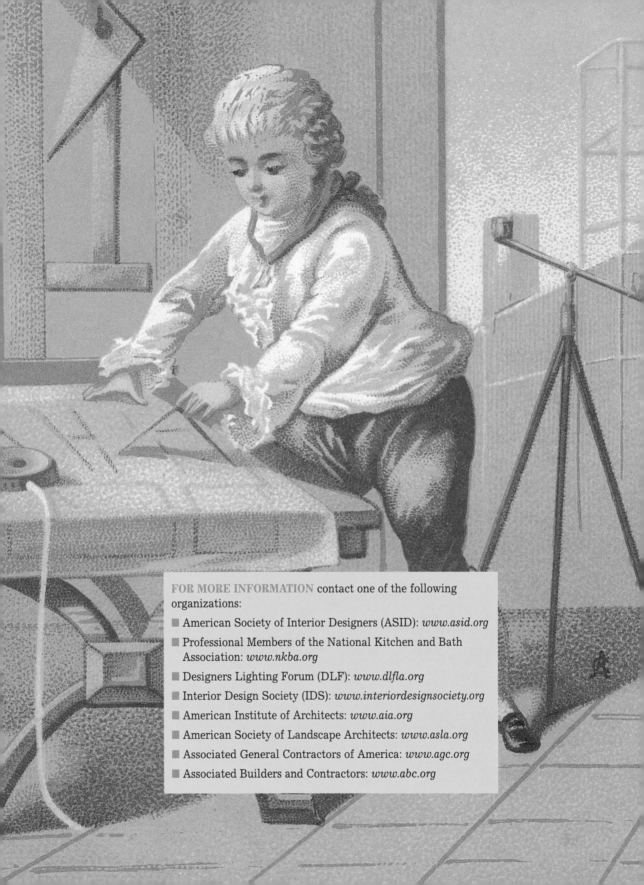

FOR MORE INFORMATION contact one of the following organizations:

- American Society of Interior Designers (ASID): *www.asid.org*
- Professional Members of the National Kitchen and Bath Association: *www.nkba.org*
- Designers Lighting Forum (DLF): *www.dlfla.org*
- Interior Design Society (IDS): *www.interiordesignsociety.org*
- American Institute of Architects: *www.aia.org*
- American Society of Landscape Architects: *www.asla.org*
- Associated General Contractors of America: *www.agc.org*
- Associated Builders and Contractors: *www.abc.org*

Schedule & Budget

"*Double the time and the cost of any quote you get!*" *This is what every prospective home renovator hears, but is it true? No. This applies to complicated jobs, and only then if you have not finalized your plans. Get everything in writing from your suppliers, and you should not have extensive exaggerations of cost and time. There are almost always some delays and cost overages, and these should be anticipated by your supplier and accounted for when they give you a quote. Some items have longer lead times than others.*

Planning a budget is a difficult process that needs to be mulled over. The amount of money you have available to spend will dictate what you will be able to do, but you should have a complete list of what you want to have done, along with a desired timetable. Work with an architect or a contractor. Tell them your goals and budget and they will guide you toward getting the most out of your money. How long will it take to paint a room? To modernize a bathroom? Everything depends on your schedule, the schedule of your contractor, and the weather (!) —if it is humid, paint will take longer to dry.

How Long Will It Take?

PAINTING A ROOM one color (including taping and priming) will take approximately two days depending upon its size. Also take into consideration the existing condition of the surface to be painted—darker colors will be harder to cover, most likely requiring at least two coats. If you are using an additional color, say for the ceiling, crown moldings, and other trim, it will take you anywhere from a half day to whole day longer. Removing and replacing wallpaper can take anywhere from four days to a week, depending on the age of the paper. You may have to repair the walls after you remove wallpaper—this can take about a day.

MODERNIZING A BATHROOM first requires one to two days for demolition and removal of old plumbing fixtures. Allow a day for any plumbing replacement and the installation of a tub. Five to seven days is needed for installation of waterproof wallboard and prepping of the bathtub area; installation of new wiring for outlets, built-in light fixtures, and fans; and for framing rough openings for installations like medicine cabinets and hampers. If you have a separate shower in a non-standard size and need a custom-size unit, allow several days for fabricating the lead pan and concrete receptor. Setting tiles on walls and floor will take at least two to three days, depending upon how complicated your pattern is and how many tiles have to be cut. After grouting, it's best not to walk on the floor for about seventy-two hours. Actual installation of the toilet and sink is quick—a few hours. Finally, painting and finishing and installation of hardware and accessories should take about two days. This is all provided you have planned ahead, had the new design drawn up and spec'd., and have ordered and received all new materials, fixtures, faucets, medicine cabinets, countertop, racks, and accessories! Remember that lead times for items can extend for weeks.

KITCHENS can be more detailed. Allow about three days for installation of appliances and plumbing fixtures. After all framing and wallboard have been installed (one to three days, depending upon how complicated your design is), the wiring and lighting, often recessed into soffits, can become more involved than in a bathroom; allow a day for your lighting contractor to install fixtures before you put in countertops (so that the electrician doesn't end up standing on them). Installation of cabinetry and countertops takes about three to five days, depending on whether you have drop-in appliances, which will be installed at the same time. Flooring takes anywhere from a half to three days.

CARPETING A HOUSE takes one to two days, depending on the square footage being covered and whether there is old carpeting and padding to take up.

HAVING YOUR DRIVEWAY AND SIDEWALKS REFURBISHED can take up to a week. Demolishing can take up to two days, and if you are pouring concrete, you need a day to build the forms. Pouring the concrete is quick, but you need five days for it to cure. Laying asphalt will take a day, plus five days to set. Driveway resurfacing takes about a day to pour and five days to dry.

> Specify the materials you wish to be used: Lumber, paint, and finishing hardware affect the cost of your renovations. Make sure that your choices in materials are specified accurately in your contract so that inferior substitutions cannot be made.

Financial Returns on Home Improvements

Homeowners always want to know what is going to add value to a home when it's time to sell.

■ Kitchen and bathroom improvements will generally earn more than their investment back when you sell your house. Most times, you can multiply your cost of renovation by a factor of two to three and add it to your basis. Choose quality fixtures, tiles, countertops and cabinetry in neutral shades that will adapt to any decorating scheme. Luxury items like Jacuzzis and professional kitchen appliances do not have universal appeal and will not always earn back their cost.

■ Other improvements that will add value to your house are carpeting, electrical upgrades, new roofing, boiler, and siding, simple paint jobs, quality windows and seals, and architectural accents like crown molding, baseboards, chair rails, and picture rails.

■ Decorative items such as window treatments and wallpapers do not add to the value of your house.

■ Outdoors, good professional landscaping will show the siting of your house to its best advantage and add to the selling price.

Furniture

When you are selecting furnishings for your home, you may choose from a variety of sources including new from department stores or used from second-hand stores, garage sales, or even family and friends. This leaves most people with a mish-mash of pieces and confusion about how to arrange them and what new pieces are needed.

Traditionally a living room has a couch, sitting chairs, a coffee table, and an entertainment center. Many times these were purchased together and kept together. Today we see people with mismatched couches, a variety of patterns for their chairs, and coffee tables that don't match their side tables. Here are tips for making it all work:

■ Make sure you like it; if it is only so-so to you, lose it.

■ Push it around! Try arranging your furniture in different ways.

■ Maintain a color scheme—either similar or completely opposite.

How to Spot Quality Furniture

Anyone who believes that the price tag is any indication of quality is in for a surprise.

IT'S IN THE DETAILS Study furniture universally regarded as superior. Whatever the nature of the piece, you will see attention to details paid to everything from pattern-making to the glue used to join a dowel.

IT'S IN THE CONSTRUCTION The balance and substance of the piece should be solid and have heft. A bookcase or bureau will be finished on all sides in the kiln-dried hardwood.

IT'S IN THE SKELETON Any number of cosmetic treatments can rescue a piece whose style has faded. Some of the best value can be found in office furniture and garden furniture from the last hundred years.

Judging the Quality of Wooden Furniture

■ The furniture finish should have no drips or air bubbles and the wood grain should be smooth, mark-free, and uniform in color. Unfinished wood should be well sanded.

■ Chair legs should stand secure, not be uneven or wobbly. Tall pieces should be stable, and not susceptible to falling over.

■ Check the joints for excess glue or adhesive. Joints should fit together cleanly.

Online auctions are a priceless resource for research. Millions of items are listed for sale every day, and knowledgeable sellers can provide just about everything you want to know about any item for the home. Check their listings for provenance and learn the going price—it's a good deal.

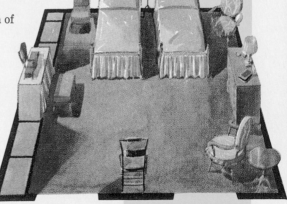

Tipping the Scales

Scale is very important in any room, but that doesn't mean that all the pieces have to be around the same size. A large, soft, cushiony sofa works wonderfully when juxtaposed with a slim wood straight-back chair.

■ Test drawers. They should glide out smoothly and fit back in snugly. Glides should be secure, and there should be stops to prevent the drawer from falling out. Handles should be secure, with nuts firmly tightened. Two side knobs are usually better than a center knob on drawers, since this cuts down on stress.

■ Doors should open easily, meet evenly, and stay closed.

■ Dressers and cabinets (anything that does more than just have stuff sit on top of it) will probably wear out first, so make sure to look for a quality piece.

■ Backs of cases or storage units should be firmly attached.

Wooden Furniture

Types of wooden furniture usually fall within three categories: hardwood, which is more durable and therefore more expensive; softwood, usually used for outdoor furniture; and composite, less expensive man-made wood products. Solid wood furniture is usually very expensive, heavy, and susceptible to warping. Generally frames are the only parts of furniture made from solid wood. Instead, thin "veneers" of wood sandwich plywood or particleboard, giving the appearance of wood without the weight or expense. You can detect a veneer by checking the inside or underside of a wooden piece: if the grain doesn't match, it's a veneer.

Popular Hardwoods

■ Cherry is a reddish-brown colored wood that is good for carving and has a strong resistance to shrinking and warping. ■ Mahogany is usually expensive, but has a good resistance to warping. It can absorb stains well and be carved, since it is a softer wood. ■ Light-colored Maple has a good resistance to warping and is very hard. ■ Oak is a light reddish-brown, all-purpose wood that carves and stains well, and is resistant to shrinking. ■ Walnut is a dark brown or brownish-gray wood with a good warping resistance that can be stained easily. ■ Other hardwoods include ash, gum, birch, beech, pecan, and rosewood.

Popular Softwoods

■ Light-brown Cedar is typically used for outdoor furniture. Its strong scent is popular in drawer linings and closets to deter pests. ■ Pine is a very soft wood so it is easy to work with, but it shows wear quickly. Painting can cover these marks.

Composites

■ Plywood is made from sheets of wood pressed together and is usually used as a support. ■ Particleboard is made from pressure-treated sawdust, wood pieces, and glue, and is inexpensive. However, since it is susceptible to shrinking and warping, the veneer may come loose.

Judging the Quality of Upholstered Furniture

■ Check the frame and the cushion. Frames should be sturdy and well made (follow the rules for inspecting wooden furniture). You shouldn't be able to feel the frame through the cushion.

■ Sofas and couches shouldn't sag in the middle. There should be even support throughout.

■ Chair cushions should have coils that are supportive, but conform to the body. Look for spring-shaped coils that are hand-tied eight times for the securest seat. Cushions should fit together snugly.

■ Make sure all decorative tassels and buttons are well secured and the seams are straight.

■ Most cushions are made from polyurethane foam. This provides cushioning, while being long lasting. Although good quality cushions can also be made from down, they need constant fluffing and are usually more expensive. Cushions filled with foam pellets are inexpensive, but could cause a real mess if the cushion breaks.

■ See Fabrics on page 110 for guidelines for choosing the best covering.

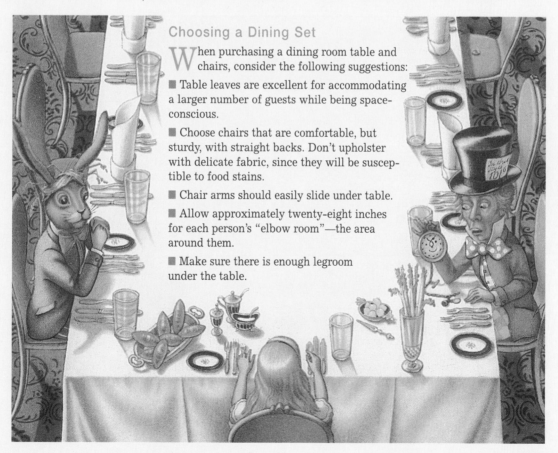

Choosing a Dining Set

When purchasing a dining room table and chairs, consider the following suggestions:

■ Table leaves are excellent for accommodating a larger number of guests while being space-conscious.

■ Choose chairs that are comfortable, but sturdy, with straight backs. Don't upholster with delicate fabric, since they will be susceptible to food stains.

■ Chair arms should easily slide under table.

■ Allow approximately twenty-eight inches for each person's "elbow room"—the area around them.

■ Make sure there is enough legroom under the table.

Floors

Choosing the right type of flooring can be surprisingly difficult. You must take the way you live into consideration, along with your personal likes. Many people love wall-to-wall carpeting, while others think there is nothing better than a shining, warm hardwood floor.

Wood Floors

For some, the feel of a hardwood floor underfoot cannot be beat. Extremely durable and long lasting, these were the floors of choice in the late part of the nineteenth century. Traditional wood floors are sealed with a gloss or matte finish and are relatively easy to clean. They are fun to decorate; painting, staining, and bleaching are all options.

You can also get wood floors that have been impregnated with acrylic, which makes the floors very durable and hard. Or consider engineered wood floors, made by gluing and pressing the wood together. In this case the grain runs in different directions, which makes the floors very strong.

Laminate Floors

These include linoleum sheet, cut linoleum squares, and vinyl tiles. Available in a wide selection of colors and patters, these are the floors most commonly installed in kitchens in the 1970s. Made from pressing components together under extreme pressure, they are easy to install, cost-efficient, easy to clean and maintain, and very durable. While the patterns of yesterday are no longer in vogue, these floor materials were appreciated enough that new patterns have been designed for today's homes.

Stone

While beautiful, these floors can be troublesome. They include concrete, marble, brick, and tile; they are costly, not only for the materials themselves (except concrete), but also difficult to install. You should probably keep the use of these floors confined to the entryway, due to the difficulty in cleaning and maintaining them. They are quite hard on your feet, making them impractical for the kitchen. They can also be very slippery and cold, thus unrealistic for the bathroom (ceramic tiles are preferable there).

There are three basic styles for wood floors: strip, plank, and parquet. Strip and plank floors run all the wood in one direction, which makes the room look longer and larger. Parquet floors create a geometric pattern when the wood is laid down, which adds visual interest to a room.

Carpeting & Rugs

Man vs. Machine:

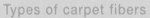

Carpets and rugs that are woven by hand are more durable and have a better overall quality. However, wovens are also substantially more expensive. Recent technology advances have turned out machine-made carpeting and rugs that are almost of the same caliber of quality, but cost much less.

TUFTED carpet is created when pieces of yarn are pushed through a carpet-backing fabric. There are options to the finish:

■ **Cut** the surface is composed of the cut ends of pile. ■ **Cut-and-loop** some yarns come to the surface in a loop, some are cut. ■ **Level-loop** all pieces form loops at the surface, creating a pebbly, smooth feel. ■ **Multilevel-loop** yarns end in loops at the surface, but are of different heights. ■ **Plush** cut-pile yarn that is luxurious and smooth since individual tufts are close together and only slightly visible. ■ **Saxony** twisted plied yarns that produce a level surface of dense tufts. ■ **Sculptured** yarns are cut at different heights to produce a pattern. ■ **Shag** extra-long pile yarns that give the impression of being densely woven. ■ **Velvet tufted** twisted ends meet closely for smooth feel.

WOVEN carpet created on a weaving loom, in which horizontal and vertical yarns are interlaced, has no separate backing. Types of wovens: ■ **Axminster** cut-pile woven carpet that looks hand-knotted. ■ **Brussels** hard-twisted loop pile that is durable. ■ **Chenille** soft and durable, high, dense pile. ■ **Velvet** very durable, but limited in color. Woven on a loom, loops are cut to create tufts. ■ **Wilton** considered the best machine-made woven rug. Limited amount of colors, thick cushion of tightly woven yarns, very durable.

NATURAL FIBER RUGS interesting texture; prone to mildew. Grass, sisal, rush, and coir.

BRAIDED RUGS also called "rag rugs," because individual fabric strips, or rags, are woven together and usually braided into a circular or oval shape.

HOOKED/RAG RUGS handmade throw rugs, made in the style of tufted rugs or braided and sewn together. They are inexpensive and usually made from wool, cotton, or synthetic fibers. Available in a variety of styles and sizes.

ORIENTAL RUGS (ALSO PERSIAN) hand-woven rugs; the very short, dense, knotted weave creates an extremely durable wear and bright design. Pieces are usually made of wool, and quality is determined by the number of knots. Hand-made rugs can be very expensive, but machine-made pieces cost much less. Authentic rugs show the pattern on the reverse side when you turn it over. Otherwise, get a professional opinion. The finest hand-knotted rugs will last centuries, so research any purchases to protect your investment.

FLAT WEAVE RUGS are khilim, dhurry, sumakh.

RYA RUGS Scandinavian wool rugs that can be hand-knotted or machine-made.

Types of carpet fibers

Natural ■ **WOOL** durable, static-resistant, comfortable, resists soil, expensive; harder to clean than synthetics. ■ **COTTON** soft, good performance, versatile appearance.

Synthetic ■ **ACRYLIC** soft, resists soil, moderate price, glossy color, has appearance of wool. ■ **NYLON** good color range, resists mildew, can be static-resistant. ■ **OLEFIN or POLYPROPYLENE** durable, limited patterns, glossy fibers, good water-resistance, colorfast, and is good for outdoor carpeting. ■ **POLYESTER** resembles wooly texture and has a wide range of colors.

Paints & Wallpaper

Paint

*P*aint is a wonderful thing. Computers can now program the color pigments to create an exact match for that fabric's pink rosebud or bandbox blue stripe. Paint is relatively inexpensive and, best of all, there is no paint choice that cannot be painted away!

Pick the Right Paint

■ Take samples of the colors in the room with you to the store to select a new color.

■ Ask for larger chips. A slender strip with half a dozen colors on it will not give you a real sense of the effect in your room. If small chips are all you can get, take several. Cut out the color choice on each strip and tape it to the wall.

■ Once you decide on a color, buy a pint of the lightest, darkest, and mid-range shades.

■ Paint a sample of each on the same wall in your room. Make each large enough to give a sense of how it would look on the entire wall or room. It is important to use the same wall for comparison, as color will always change from wall to wall.

■ Observe the colors for at least a day and night, under both natural and artificial light.

If your new paint color isn't what you had envisioned, consider applying a glaze or a color wash before starting all over. If you have gallons of unopened custom-color paint left over, bring it back to the store to be mixed with white to smooth out the color. A warm white or a cool white will temper the color accordingly.

Wallpaper

Choose wallpaper and upholstery fabric that match or compliment each other. Interior design companies offer borders and edgings that can accentuate the architectural features of a room. The quality of these matching papers and fabrics is usually quite high, for good durability. The wallpapers currently on the market are scrubbable, washable, and prepasted, eliminating the messiest and most frustrating part of installation. Some styles may also be peelable, enabling you to remove a stained pieced and replace it neatly.

Wallpaper does need good, straight walls in plumb—that is, lining up in elevation. If your walls are straight but need a better surface before being papered, try versatile wall liner. This heavy paper will conceal cracks and imperfections, unify problem ceilings, and act as a solid base for paint or wallpaper. It can be applied over paneling, stucco, and cement block walls.

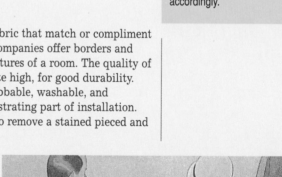

Know your paperhanger! Installing wallpaper is an art, as well as a mechanical challenge. Ask for references before hiring a contractor. When possible, try to see rooms that have been papered by the person. You'll want to look for:

■ A clean, smooth fit, with no lumps inside. ■ Tamped-down edges and neat seams. ■ A centered design. ■ Tight corners, with no gaps ■ Clean cuts at the ceiling, around the door and window frames, and at the baseboards.

A wallpaper pattern is continuous or it repeats. The repeat of a design will be indicated on back of the paper. When you are considering wallpaper that repeats, there will be wastage in order to get the repeat pattern to align properly next to each other. Take that into consideration in your estimate of yardage. Mass-produced wallpaper is between 21 and 26 inches wide. American-made paper comes in a standard roll that will cover 36 feet. Papers manufactured in Europe are measured with the metric system to a length of about 33 feet and width of 21 inches. Hand-blocked papers, which are printed manually with blocks dipped in paint, can be made to measure. Because it is applied by hand, the design is not expected to be precise and perfect; its irregularities are charming.

Wallpaper Be Gone!

If you want to remove wallpaper, investigate its history. Prepasted peelable wallpaper is easily stripped off. Older paper that was hung with wallpaper paste may be too brittle to pull off in sheets. In this case, you will have to steam the paper to release the glue bond between the paper and the wall. If you have inherited a papered room that is not to your taste but is intact, consider updating its look with a glaze or wash. Before you buy vintage wallpaper, consult a professional paperhanger to that confirm the paper is not too brittle to survive the installation. When you shop for coordinated paint and fabrics, bring along a good-size sample of the paper or fabrics.

Traditional Wallpaper Motifs

Dining Room Fruit, birds
Living Room Light plaid or floral
Library Somber stripe
Bedroom Pastel tea roses and
    band-box stripes
Every Room Toile

COPYRIGHTED BY CHAS.W FROST 1881.

How to Paint

Painting your home can actually be a relaxing task, if you approach it properly. When you go into the process without the proper supplies or plan of action, chaos is bound to reign.

Before you Paint

You will want to remove as much of the furnishings, including hanging fixtures, from the room before you begin painting. Cover the floor completely with a drop cloth and tape it down, if necessary. Thoroughly clean the surface to be painted. If it is not grimy, a wall simply needs to be thoroughly dusted with clean cotton rags. If it is a surface that gets touched frequently or is in a kitchen or bathroom, you will have to wash it down and rinse well. Let the area dry completely before painting. If the surface to be painted is glossy, lightly sand it. Be sure to remove all the dust.

Cracks and Flaking

Firmly press spackling compound into the crevices using a putty knife. Smooth the putty until flush with the surface. Fill trim joinings and door and window trim that have split by pressing the compound into the crevices and smoothing it with your finger. Allow the compound to dry, and then sand lightly. Since patching compound shrinks as it dries, large holes and cracks usually require a second application after the first has dried. Remove flaking paint with a putty knife or scraper, and sand paint edges with a fine-grade sandpaper for a smooth surface.

Paint Types

PRIMER This layer of paint is applied to absorbent walls. Priming is always necessary, even if painting white on white or painting a wall that has many coats of paint already on it. Priming seals the surface, which will ensure uniformity of color. You can have primer tinted so it becomes close to the color of the topcoat. This will reduce the amount of coats of topcoat paint you ultimately need to apply.

UNDERCOAT This paint goes over the primer, but is applied before the topcoat. It will allow paint

to go on smoothly, and is usually necessary for wood surfaces.

OIL-BASED or ALKYD PAINTS Can be more difficult to apply then water-based paints, but last a long time and are usually easily washable, making them ideal for kitchens, bathrooms, and basements.

WATER-BASED or LATEX PAINTS Dry quickly and are easy to apply. Clean up with soap and water. The only drawbacks are that it sometimes doesn't age as well as oil-based paint and it has a tendency to soil easily. Water-based paints are ideal for bedrooms, hallways, and other places not susceptible to dirt or moisture.

TEXTURED PAINT Often used on ceilings, it is a rough paint that hides cracks and irregularities in surfaces.

Gather Your Supplies

- Bucket ■ Flat-head screwdriver ■ Drop cloths ■ Stepladder ■ Extension pole, such as a broom handle ■ Painter's tape ■ Rags ■ 3'' Paintbrush ■ Roller and handle ■ Roller tray ■ Stirring sticks

How Much Paint Do You Need?

Add the length and width of the room and double it. Then multiple the total by the height of the room. This will give you the square footage of all four walls. To calculate the ceiling, multiply the width by the length, and add to the previous room total. For each window or door, multiply the length by the width for each, and then subtract those totals from the total square footage of the room. Use these figures when shopping for paint, since most paint labels state how many square feet one can will cover. If in doubt, always buy a little extra.

Now You're Ready...

Begin painting where the ceiling meets the walls. Brush a 3-inch-wide strip of the coating along the ceiling and wall beginning at the corner. Dip your roller in the paint tray and slowly roll it back and forth over the ridges to remove the excess paint. Start near the corner, and paint across the width rather than the length of the ceiling.

Once the ceiling has dried, begin painting along the baseboard and around the door and window trim with the 3-inch-wide brush. Using the same technique as for the ceiling, paint one wall at a time. Repeat if necessary. To prevent paint marks on windows, apply masking tape along glass edges before painting. When you remove the tape, you will have clean edges and corners with no drips.

Conquer drips with these tips:

- Wipe excess paint off brushes by dragging them across a wide elastic band stretched across the open paint can.

- Poke the handle of a paintbrush through a small paper plate to collect drips when painting the ceiling.

- Line buckets and trays with aluminum foil or plastic liners before pouring paint. This will help immensely with clean up.

Fabrics

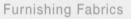

There are three basic applications for home furnishing fabrics: curtains, upholstery, and slipcovers. A few fabrics—cotton twill for instance, can conceivably be used for all three. More often, particular fabric traits eliminate one or two of the applications. For instance, delicate silks, organdies and taffetas, all wonderful for curtains, are simply not practical for slipcover and upholstery projects. (One exception could be the side chair that is rarely called on to serve as more than an accent piece; its precious fabric can be admired yet not become worn.) Crafting curtains and slipcovers, or upholstering even a simple piece is time-consuming and labor-intensive (and expensive, if you hire someone to do it for you!). Since you are investing a lot of time, it makes sense to invest in the right fabric.

Furnishing Fabrics

PLAIN WEAVES like chintz, duck, and linen are most versatile, generally easy to sew, and long lasting. Though it is available in many weights, from delicate handkerchief to canvaslike weave, pure linen wrinkles easily and is quite costly. Cotton/linen blends are convincing alternatives, and they won't play havoc with the budget.

TWILLS such as mattress ticking, denim, and tartans are longwearing, long-suffering choices for households with children, pets, and lots of visitors. Stains are more easily removed than with less-durable fabrics.

JACQUARD WEAVES—the brocades, tapestries and damasks—are rich, formal, and generally expensive. Save these for your bedroom or, if you really, really want them on the sofa, when your children have left for college.

FABRICS WITH A NAP, like velour, velvet, and corduroy, have a luxurious texture. Velour and velvet are available in embossed and even printed versions. You will need extra fabric so that the nap, or pile, runs in a consistent direction. Cottons are the most affordable.

LEATHERS AND VINYL-BASED FABRICS are appropriate for upholstery but do not make the grade for curtains and slipcovers. That said, curtaining fabric could be edged with leather to match upholstered furniture.

Buying Fabric

■ Be sure. Take your time and get what you really want. Linen will wrinkle; fabrics with a nap will flatten; leathers will crack and become distressed-looking. If you are determined to have a pristine home, these will not make you happy.

Choose a fabric for slipcovers, bedcovers, or curtains, then purchase a yard or two to test in your home. Cover a pillow with the fabric and observe, over a few days, how it looks in your room, if it wrinkles, and how it stands up to spills.

■ Read the label or the contents listed along the selvage, or plain edge, of the fabric.

■ Look for fabric that is colorfast, preshrunk, and wrinkle-resistant.

■ Check to see if the fabric has been treated with a stain-resistor.

■ If you are considering a distinctive pattern or color, make sure the manufacturer is established and that your choice will be available in the future should you need more.

■ Measure twice. Know how much you need. Then order some extra to insure against damages and to have on hand for new projects. If you're hiring someone to provide curtains, slipcovers, or upholstery, ask for several yards of the fabric and any coordinating trim or fringe.

Reupholster or Slipcover? How to Decide

Is your sofa in need of a change? Is that spot just not coming out? If you're thinking about slipcovering your upholstered furniture, it's worth a look. Slipcovers for sofas, chairs, ottomans, and dining-room chairs are now very much in style, readily available, and affordable. Log on to the Internet or visit your local home-décor shop to find a wide variety of practical and handsome covers. If your budget allows or you have children and pets, consider getting two covers to switch off when one gets dirty and needs laundering. Custom slipcovers are more expensive, but they look polished and elegant. If you know a reliable source for slipcovers, this is a very good option.

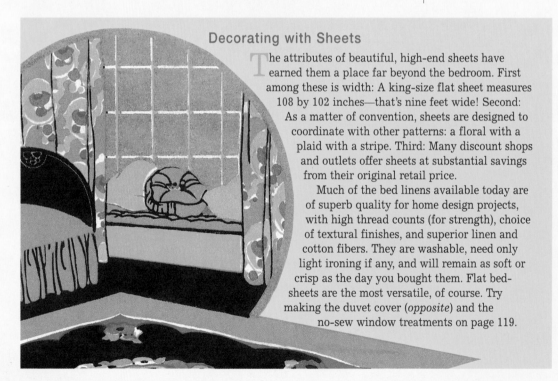

Decorating with Sheets

The attributes of beautiful, high-end sheets have earned them a place far beyond the bedroom. First among these is width: A king-size flat sheet measures 108 by 102 inches—that's nine feet wide! Second: As a matter of convention, sheets are designed to coordinate with other patterns: a floral with a plaid with a stripe. Third: Many discount shops and outlets offer sheets at substantial savings from their original retail price.

Much of the bed linens available today are of superb quality for home design projects, with high thread counts (for strength), choice of textural finishes, and superior linen and cotton fibers. They are washable, need only light ironing if any, and will remain as soft or crisp as the day you bought them. Flat bed-sheets are the most versatile, of course. Try making the duvet cover (*opposite*) and the no-sew window treatments on page 119.

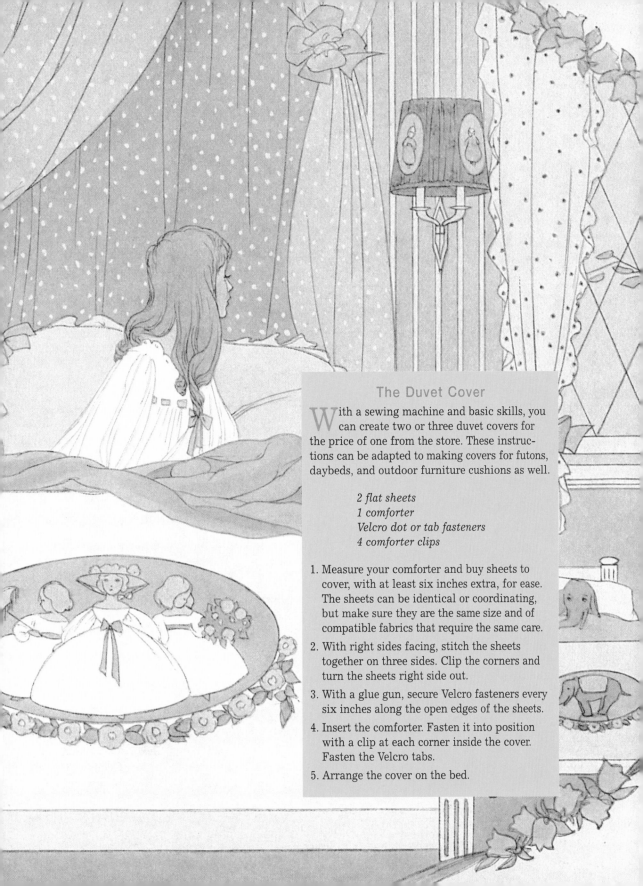

The Duvet Cover

With a sewing machine and basic skills, you can create two or three duvet covers for the price of one from the store. These instructions can be adapted to making covers for futons, daybeds, and outdoor furniture cushions as well.

2 flat sheets
1 comforter
Velcro dot or tab fasteners
4 comforter clips

1. Measure your comforter and buy sheets to cover, with at least six inches extra, for ease. The sheets can be identical or coordinating, but make sure they are the same size and of compatible fabrics that require the same care.

2. With right sides facing, stitch the sheets together on three sides. Clip the corners and turn the sheets right side out.

3. With a glue gun, secure Velcro fasteners every six inches along the open edges of the sheets.

4. Insert the comforter. Fasten it into position with a clip at each corner inside the cover. Fasten the Velcro tabs.

5. Arrange the cover on the bed.

Cushions & Pillows

Throw pillows, floor cushions, sofa pillows, chair cushions—all these soft, comforting, fabric-covered additions have a place in the home. You will often see them in pricey boutiques and specialty stores, where they can cost hundreds of dollars. They are endlessly useful as well as decorative, and making covers for them can be downright addictive (as well as a budget saver!). Any piece of fabric can be a cover for a cushion—which can be anything ranging from the fattest, most sprawling one that is a seat in itself to a delicate little pincushion. Covers themselves are quickly put together with a sewing machine; some do not even need to be sewn.

The Hardest-Working Decorative Accents

For durability, buy pillows with good cotton case covers. Make new covers and dress them up on a whim for a fast, easy, fresh look in any room. Preshrink any fabric and test it for color fastness. Pillow covers are easygoing, easily removed and replaced, so have fun making them. Mix weights and textures (organdy and a charcoal-stripe wool, for instance), fancy and plain fabrics (embroidered handkerchief linen with canvas), color and pattern (a pastel floral chintz with a gingham check).

Like the proverbial little black dress, cushions take well to all kinds of ornamentation: appliqué, cord trim, fringe, welting, ribbon, ruffles, tassels, buttons, silk flowers, sequins and beads, pearls and crystals. Embroidered monograms and homilies, from *Home Sweet Home* to Alice Roosevelt's famous *If You Have Nothing Good to Say, Sit Next to Me*, turn projects into instant heirlooms.

Some of our favorite pillow covers have been made from silk scarves, Oriental carpet, tapestry, remnants, clothing, quilts, tablecloths, curtains, leather, felt, and sweaters. Even fur (or faux fur) from an old coat that's no longer worn works; curly Persian lamb, for instance, can be sewn on most machines, as can pony skin and other hides.

IF I HAD A HAMMOCK Bliss: a slow swinging hammock in dappled shade on a sunny summer day. A chubby pillow at the top of the hammock cossets your head comfortably for reading or snoozing.

SANTA, HAVE A PILLOW Christmas-print fabric has a pretty short moment in the spotlight. If you have some old holiday

For a party, make quick pillow covers of white fabric on which the guest of honor's photo has been scanned and printed (this can be done at most major photocopying centers).

Throw Pillow Shapes
- Oblongs, Rounds, and Squares, starting at 12"
- European Squares, up to 34"
- Bolsters, up to 60"

Bed Pillows Sizes
- Standard, 20" x 27"
- Queen, 20" x 30"
- King, 20" x 37"

tablecloths, Santa-print fabric, or a Christmas sweater, you can have the perfect cushions to toss around the living room for the season.

A SILK PILLOW WITHOUT A STITCH Many women have beautiful, even exquiste silk scarves that languish in drawers waiting for the one or two times a year they'll be worn. Align two same-size scarves with right sides facing out. Center a pillow form on one scarf. Tie a square knot at each corner, fluff the pillow, smooth the top, and you have a luxurious silk pillow.

A Basic Pillow Cover

Whether it's luxurious silk damask or a sturdy length of homespun, this cover is the easiest one to sew, and can be put on an existing covered pillow:

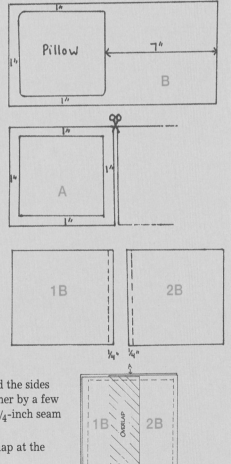

1. Measure the pillow from seam to seam and mark on a piece of paper. Add one inch to three sides and seven inches to one side and mark on the paper. Cut out the pattern.

2. Lay the pattern on the fabric, pin to secure and then cut. This will be the back of the sham, with extra fabric for the overlap. (Piece B)

3. For the front of the sham, cut six inches from the long side of the pattern (pattern should be roughly the size of the pillow now with a one inch border on all 4 sides). Pin pattern to a new piece of fabric, cut fabric and set aside. (Piece A)

4. Fold the longer piece fabric in half (Piece B), so the crease is vertical and the sides match. Steam press the crease. Open the fabric back up and cut along the crease to make two equal sized back pieces. (Pieces 1B and 2B)

5. Lay the two back pieces (Pieces 1B and 2B) wrong side up. On one side of each piece, measure $1/4$ inch in and fold the material. Sew material to make a hem. These will be the edges where the flap is open at the back of the sham.

6. Iron the edges to make them flat.

7. Lay the back pieces (Pieces 1B and 2B) on the front fabric piece (Piece A) so the top sides face together and the sides match up. The two back pieces should overlap each other by a few inches in the middle. Pin the edges all around. Sew a $1/4$-inch seam all the way around the edge.

8. Turn the sham right side out. Steam press. Using the flap at the back, tuck the pillow into the cover.

Windows

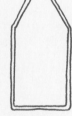

Centuries ago, window glass was expensive to produce, generally site-specific, and highly valued in a home. In the new millennium, these factors can still apply. Good windows enjoy a high rate of return on their investment. The best-quality ones are expensive, but they are expected to last indefinitely (and they do; in New York City, for example, the original windows still sparkle in landmark buildings from the 1700s!). Windows occupy a powerful design position in our residences: They are seen from the exterior as well as the interior.

Basic window styles:

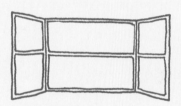

■ Bay window

■ Double-hung

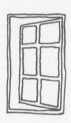

■ Casement

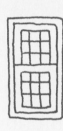

■ Nine-over-nine

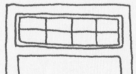

■ Transom

■ Fanlight

■ Picture windows

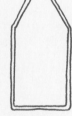

■ Gothic

■ French doors

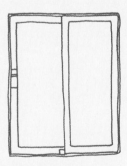

■ Sliding glass door

A Parade of Skylights

Natural light is the ally of kind weather. Tropical houses boast expansive openings for light (and breezes), and as one travels farther north the windows become fewer and smaller in order to keep rooms warm. Glass was a luxury when many American homes were built.

Glass still is a luxury, though a much more affordable and even democratic one. Bring a skylight to that dark room and a stream of natural light will fill out every corner and help conserve energy. Because they do not take up wall space, skylights are superb remedies for tight areas.

POPULAR SKYLIGHT FEATURES AND OPTIONS

■ Acrylic dome or flat glass ■ Tinted glass that filters the sun's rays ■ Screens to keep out insects ■ Shades to block sun ■ Remote operation for opening and closing

Consider Before Purchase

■ STYLE: whether it is operable

■ GLAZING: the glass itself, and whether a window is single, double, or triple glazed for insulation

■ TINT: the coating that goes on the glass or acrylic to filter the sun's rays

■ SIZE: based on how much light and air you need

STAINED-GLASS and LEADED-GLASS windows were popular in homes built before World War II. Today they are highly sought after, as are new designs handcrafted by artisans. If you have even one such window, try to have it installed in your home where the sunlight is strongest, perhaps in a sunny bathroom, where stained glass can also afford some privacy.

Window Treatments

Dressing windows is one of the most popular decorating activities, and for good reason: It provides an opportunity to express creativity, to freshen the look of a room, and to instill a strong sense of the seasons, all for as much or as little as you would want spend. Window shades and drapes filter light, play up a good view, minimize a homely one, supply privacy, and lend architectural definition.

If you are dressing a window, your primary choices are blinds, shades, curtains, and, the most formal, customized curtains with valances.

BLINDS AND SHADES are made of paper or cloth that is rolled around a ballister and installed in the window frame. These are best underneath another window treatment to keep out the sunlight, perhaps in a baby's room.

PURCHASED CURTAINS work well in any room, even if money is not a concern. Today you can find many styles to match your furnishings. Prefabricated curtains also allow you to easily change them whenever you desire. This choice is wonderful for family rooms and, if your style is casual, bedrooms.

CUSTOM CURTAINS AND DRAPES are one of the major purchases for your home, often involving coordinating fabrics to complete a look. Custom treatments are often reserved for dining and living rooms.

Curtain Terminology

VALANCE is a shallow band that spans the width of the window at the top of the curtains or decorative shade. Valances are often covered with fabric that matches the curtains, or are made of plastic or metal that matches shades, or of wood.

SWAG is a drape of fabric that hangs in a curve from a curtain rod or decorative hooks at the top corners of a window.

TIEBACK holds a pulled-back curtain at the side of the window.

TASSEL is an ornament made from twirled or twisted cords gathered at the top and cut to a uniform length.

BALLOON SHADE is raised by cords inserted in two or three fabric runners to give fullness.

PUDDLING is the term for a curtain or drape that falls two or three inches over the floor.

Windows, like lots of women, are dressed in layers. Directly over the window can be a pull-down shade, wood shutters, screen panels, or delicate and gauzy sheers. Curtains are next: from purest white to exuberant florals or bold plaids. Draperies are heaviest of all, of rich damasks or velvets, and in addition are lined with muslin or a coordinating pattern.

No-Sew Window Treatments

Bare, undressed windows can shatter the design harmony of any room. But you might be surprised what wonders can be wrought at a window with practically nothing. The secret? Lots and lots of fabric, way more than a tailored treatment would require.

Draping fabric over a rod creates a classic, lush line that flatters any window. If you're looking for a simple and inexpensive window dressing, the drape curtain is fast and easy. It's removable, and leaves the fabric undamaged. Many decorators routinely give window fabrics a test run, before the significant investment is made in elaborate tailoring.

Types of Fabrics that Work Well

■ Scrim, an open-weave cotton or linen that is semi-transparent ■ Sailcloth, a heavy cotton canvas ■ Lace panels ■ Canvas tarps ■ Sheets

If you do not have formal brackets, rods, and finials in place, get a tension rod. The tension rod is spring-loaded, with rubber feet at each end. Sizes range from several inches to rods that will fill a doorway. To install a tension rod, simply twist it open enough to wedge in the window frame. A heavy-duty tension rod is strong enough to support a quilt, a tapestry, or a panel of needlework.

Lighting

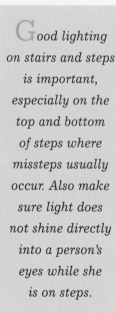

Once you realize how important lighting is to a room, you will be amazed it is so often ignored. People invest in architectural elements, furnishings, and other details, right down to a bowl of tulips, and still somehow leave lighting to chance. But when you step into a room that is well lit, you will know it and feel it. Like the subject itself, mastering light is elusive. Natural, task, general or ambient, and mood lighting are all contributors to the light design in your home.

NATURAL LIGHT is your starting point, whether you want to temper it or play it up. Artists and photographers know that the light of early morning is as different as that of high noon and late afternoon.

GENERAL OR AMBIENT LIGHTING lights up a room as a whole.

TASK LIGHTING is evenly directed, sharp, non-shaded light that is at least twice as strong as ambient lighting. The rule of thumb is that halogen bulbs will give the clearest light for task lighting.

READING LIGHT at a desk, computer station, or in bed, is the most exacting light in the home beyond the kitchen and bathrooms.

MOOD LIGHT, like that of a wall sconce, is background decoration, contributing to the atmosphere.

Guidelines

If new lighting is one of your options, keep in mind that most homes are over-lit and there is a tendency to saturate rooms with light. Other points to remember are:

■ Avoid recessed ceiling lights in period rooms. If your dining room furniture is inspired by Shaker sensibilities, ceiling lights will clash.

■ Hide wiring whenever possible. Take advantage of renovations to sink wire for chandeliers and wall fixtures.

■ Install dimmers, devices that allow you to create limitless special effects.

■ Use candles carefully. The most flattering light comes from candles, which also provide a sense of warmth and shelter.

Good lighting on stairs and steps is important, especially on the top and bottom of steps where missteps usually occur. Also make sure light does not shine directly into a person's eyes while she is on steps.

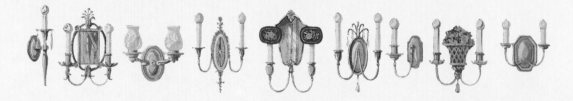

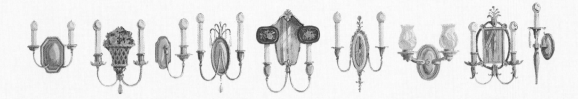

Common Bulbs

INCANDESCENT BULBS Usually referred to as "regular" bulbs, these dimmable, low-cost lights have warm, pleasing tone with color options. Some types are available in protective coatings. They work excellently with dimmers. Some incandescent lights offer long-life options, and they come in a wide variety of bulb shapes, wattages, and voltages.

- **Reflector** Economical for directional placement of light, these bulbs are generally used indoors and come in multiple diameters, wattages, and colors.

- **Globe** Spherical-shaped lamps offer a decorative element where bare lamps are acceptable. They will add interest to light fixture and are available in various finishes, wattages, and diameters.

- **Candle** Decorative lamps can recreate the warm romantic ambience of candlelight. They are best on dimmers to provide accent lighting, and come in a variety of wattages, shapes, and colors.

- **Bullet** Offers all the benefits of the incandescent candle, but with a more contemporary shape. Multiple wattages are available in a variety of bases.

- **Flame** This intriguing shape offers an architectural alternative to decorative lighting.

- **PAR** Classic outdoor flood lamp providing resistance to damp and wet locations; excellent for landscape lighting, and lighting for safety and security; available in multiple sizes and wattages

HALOGEN BULBS Crisper, whiter light closer to that of daylight, a halogen bulb produces beam control that allows light to be directed accurately. They are up to 50 percent more efficient than incandescent lights and are compact in size.

- **A-Line** This bulb has a classic lightbulb shape, good color, and a long shelf life that provides a lower operational cost.

- **Mini Candle** This very compact bulb has excellent distribution control when used in new compact fixtures.

- **PAR** A PAR bulb offers crisp, white light and excellent beam in a compact size.

- **Single-Ended Quartz (SEQ)** This bulb provides all the benefits of quartz lighting in a single-ended lamp that fits in compact light fixtures. It is available in a variety of wattages and sizes.

Dirty bulbs can reduce lighting efficiency by up to 50 percent. Clean bulbs regularly by switching off electricity, removing the cool bulb from the socket, and carefully wiping with a slightly damp cloth. Use a feather duster to clean light fixtures.

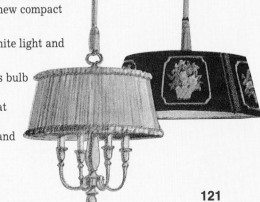

121

■ **Double-Ended Quartz (DEQ)** The linear quartz lamp provides excellent color-rendering and cooler operations, which may increase fixture life.

FLORESCENT BULBS Florescent bulbs consume up to 80 percent less energy than similar incandescent bulbs. They lasts up to eighteen times longer than their incandescent counterparts (up to 20,000 hours), come in many shades of white, from warm to cool, and provide diffused, soft light that is excellent for general lighting.

■ **Shoplite** Most commonly for residential shop light and work light fixtures, they have an average five-year life, providing bright, even light

■ **Universal Residential** These bulbs consume up to 80 percent less energy compared with incandescent bulbs of similar brightness. They last up to eighteen times longer than an incandescent, with a life of up to 20,000 hours.

■ **Kitchen and Bath** These versatile bulbs are energy efficient, provide pleasing color, and are available in a variety of lengths.

To remove a lightbulb that has broken off in the socket of a fixture that is out of reach, first make sure the power is off. Use a wooden-handled (never metal) broom, insert the handle end into the socket and twist to remove the base. To remove a broken bulb in a reachable fixture, get a raw potato, cut the potato in half and press into the filament of the bulb. Turn the potato to take out the bulb.

Lamps and Their Shades, A Timeless Love Story

Freestanding lamps provide light that can be customized to any area. Table and floor lamps also inject some architectural energy into a room, and present an opportunity to have a bit of fun with decorating. Lamps and shades regularly segue in and out of vogue, so look to please yourself in their design and feel free to change shades often. Remember to always keep old shades.

To liven up lamps, look for dark shades that are lined with a contrasting color, translucent paper shades, or textured shades. Trimmings like ball fringe, dried flowers, and beading bring another level of design. Plain shades are widely available and can be a starting point for custom tailoring in any number of ways. Remove the shade and use it for a pattern to design a shade of your choice, or slipcover a plain shade with fabric.

What Watt

The average life of an incandescent bulb is 750–1,000 hours. The average life of a halogen bulb is 2,000–4,000 hours. The average life of a florescent bulb is 6,000–24,000 hours.

100 watt = 750 hours
75 watt = 750 hours
60 watt = 1,000 hours
40 watt = 1,000–1,500 hours

Decorating Hotspots

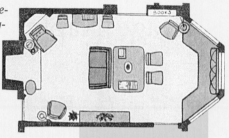

E very home has a troubled area or two—a space that is an eye-sore, an inconvenience, or a hazard. The problem can be any-thing from architectural casement windows that do not visually balance with double-hung windows on the next wall to a floor in bad shape or a corner that is more like 100 degrees than 90. In other cases, the trouble is less tangible: an impractical traffic pattern, a lack of privacy, a poorly functioning conversation area.

No matter how hard you wish it would, that ugly fireplace isn't going away. But you can usually make changes—a new mantel, a fresh coat of paint, a beam of light that highlights nice woodwork. Cosmetic tools—furniture arrangement, lighting adjustments, and clever design tricks fill the homemaker's arsenal. The worst aspect of a room can sometimes be a catalyst for a massive improvement. These challenges should be met with imagination and a little energy. Here are some classic problems and solutions.

CORNERS Easy to overlook, empty corners can suck the rhythm out of any room. Easy fixes? A tall, graceful, spectacular houseplant like a banana palm, an artful folding screen, an elegant and versatile round table with a floor-length cloth. Always provide illumination in corners to prevent them from becoming dark holes.

MISMATCHED WINDOWS Bring in the harmony with matching window treatments that conceal the shape of each window. Opaque ceiling-to-floor cur-tains are the most reliable, and they can move with you from home to home. If you want to control the natural light, install translucent sheers behind draperies.

BAD FLOORS Your new apartment is fitted with nasty wall-to-wall carpeting! The first step is to get it steam-cleaned, then cover as much as possible with area rugs.

INTERRUPTED WALLS Ground-floor rooms especially are vulnerable to in-and-out traffic patterns. If your kitchen, dining room, or living room is the path to another area, arrange the major furnishings to direct travelers around work areas and out of the middle of conversation areas.

RADIATORS AND HEAT RISERS If custom radiator cabinets are impossible, improvise a seat with uprights and shelving. Attach a gathered curtain to the front to allow the heat to travel out. Risers are nearly impossible to camou-flage. Instead, apply the same paint treatment as the wall behind it and look the other way. Or, in a contemporary treatment, paint pipes an accent color.

ELECTRIC OUTLETS AND CORDS The price of living in our electronic age is a spaghetti bowl of electric cords in each room. Overloaded electric outlets remain one of the most dangerous conditions in the home, the cause of thousands

Walking Room

S pace planners know that for easy access and an uncluttered look, they need to have a cer-tain amount of room:

■ A minimum of three feet of open space for walking around furniture.

■ A minimum of three feet of clearance for desk, dining and kitchen chairs.

■ At least eighteen inch-es between a sofa or chair and coffee table.

■ Two feet of open space around a bed.

■ Three feet in front of a cupboard, bureau, or desk.

■ A three-foot arc of space around a door.

B*e vigilant in checking outlets to assure they have not been over-loaded; regularly inspect your children's rooms and behind the scenes at the television, DVD, VCR, or stereo center.*

and thousands of fires every year. Surge protectors prevent a pile-up of plugs from computers, electric chargers, and all kinds of electronics, and may save you from blowing a fuse or throwing a circuit breaker. Exposed electrical cords, running along walls or floors, pose a trip hazard as well as a threat to young children and pets, who will often chew on them. Rigid plastic cord covers are readily available at hardware stores and can be trimmed to fit. If money is not an issue, ask a carpenter to conceal the cords behind custom baseboards that will provide coverage and allow you to adjust the cords within.

DOORS IN SMALL ROOMS You can live with the tiny space, but opening the full-size door to the room or the closet means having to nudge a chair or table out of the way each time. Replace the door with a pair of shutters, sliding doors or a bi-fold door. Another solution is to remove the door, install a tension rod, and hang a curtain.

Small spaces

These quick tips will help you design your room to make it appear larger and more comfortable

- Use mirrors to double and triple the sense of square footage.
- Choose fabrics that reflect light.
- Raise furniture from the floor with casters or feet.
- Edit your possessions; stow them in a larger room.
- Choose oversize furniture to play up the room's small proportions.

- Bring depth to the room with lighting.
- Think out of the box with unconventional furniture choices and placement. Try a sleigh bed in the living room that can serve an overnight guest.

Televisions

The question is not TV; the question is how many and where? They are everywhere! They are magnets for junk, too . . . loose DVDs, CDs, remote controls, the television listings.

- Decide on the best place for the television in each room, the kitchen countertop, a living-room cabinet, the home office.
- Create realistic storage for newspapers, magazines, and other related materials that will accumulate near the TV, and reserve space for your collections of tapes and discs to grow.
- Designate comfortable, well-lit viewing stations.
- Add coffee tables and side tables to accommodate drinks and snacks. If your family likes to watch TV while eating, allow space for that. Set aside ample room for household chores that are done mostly while watching TV, like folding the laundry and exercising.
- Fine-tune acoustics and viewing light.

Buying Kitchen Appliances

L ittle is worse than the growling of a refrigerator that is slowly giving out or the puddle underfoot that indicates that your water heater has sprung a leak. Here is your opportunity to look for an appliance that meets the needs that your old one did not.

It's the American way: Select the largest appliance your space will accommodate. There are other criteria, though, besides size:

KEEP CURRENT WITH THE MARKETPLACE. Manufacturers continually introduce major technological improvements—e.g., the frost-free refrigerator, the self-cleaning oven.

PREDICT WHEN YOU WILL NEED A NEW APPLIANCE. You get signals from your dishwasher that it is getting old, and you will save by buying when prices are low.

TAKE ACCURATE MEASUREMENTS of your door openings to make sure you don't buy an appliance that is too big to fit. Most important, check exact measurements on spec sheets for the models you are interested in. These would include overall depth including handles and depth when the door is standing open. Make sure you have the recommended clearances and that you have enough room to comfortably work around the appliance. Check to see that your wiring can safely provide the power needed.

VISIT RETAIL OUTLETS TO INSPECT MODELS PERSONALLY. Read the use and care manual before you buy; ask questions.

CHECK AROUND. Talk with friends, with your contractor, and with organizations that publish ratings, such as Good Housekeeping and Consumer Reports. Study the warranty.

INSPECT AN APPLIANCE AS SOON AS IT IS INSTALLED. Try each feature and contact the seller and the manufacturer immediately if there is a defect. Complete and return the warranty card to the manufacturer and store the appliance information where it can be easily retrieved.

Ranges and Ovens

A range is a freestanding unit with a cooking surface and an oven beneath. Cooktops no longer need to be anchored by ovens, and ovens are free to "move" about the kitchen in various configurations:

■ A wall oven is installed and vented directly in the wall.

■ Ovens can be conventional or convection (a fan circulates the heat), powered by electricity or gas.

THE ENERGY EFFICIENCY GUIDE

T he desirability for new features prodded manufacturers to lavish their designs with options. This came with a price tag: increased energy costs. Government mandates require that each appliance disclose its energy efficiency, now shown on the distinctive yellow-and-black label on the front of every appliance. Read it carefully to find out whether the extra features your household likes will cost dearly in electricity charges.

Which Cooktop Is Right?

Conventional Gas Pros: Cooks with a flame; no warm-up time. Easily controlled heat; accommodates any type of cookware. Can be used during a power outage by lighting with a match. Cons: Difficult to clean, food can spill through openings in burners; gas leaks are dangerous.

Gas Sealed Burner Pros: Spilled food can't seep inside cooktop; accommodates any type of cookware; can operate during power outage. Con: Not every burner supplies a full range of temperatures.

Electric Coiled Element Pros: Inexpensive; accommodates any type of cookware. Cons: Coils take time to heat up, although some manufacturers are now offering "almost instant" heat; for cooking, heat is not as easily controlled as with gas heat; difficult to clean as food can spill inside; not operable during power outage.

Electric Solid Disk Element (Cast iron) Pros: Even heat, durable surface. Cons: Slowest to heat up and cool; accommodates flat-bottom cookware only; not operable during power outage.

Electric Glass Ceramic Pros: Sealed; easy to clean Cons: Accommodates flat-bottom cookware only; not operable during power outage.

Radiant Element Pros: Least expensive to operate; provides the precise control of gas in an electric appliance; easy to clean. Cons: Most expensive to buy; not operable during power outage.

Halogen Elements These are radiant elements also; the only difference is they have a halogen bulb circling their radiant element that shows you that the cooktop is turned on.

Induction Pros: Unlike other electric elements, provides the precise temperature control of gas burners; magnetic waves have no effect on skin; energy efficient. Cons: Expensive; accommodates iron and steel cookware only; not operable during power outage.

Modular units (plug-in coils, grills, pots, and griddles) Pros: Offer versatility. Cons: Must be stored when not in use; can be problematical to clean.

■ Grills, broilers, pizza ovens, bread ovens, and rotisseries are available to the home cook.

■ Custom kitchens usually have more than one oven.

■ Self-cleaning ovens achieve an intense heat that burns up food particles.

Zap—Let's Nuke It!

Since electric-powered microwave ovens came into our homes in the 1970s, they have become one of the most popular of all cooking appliances: Over 95 percent of households surveyed had at least one. Units range from 750 to 1500 watts, and they provide one of the safest ways to prepare cooked food.

Large microwaves generally range from 900 to 1,350 watts, but a difference of 100 watts is not too noticeable. Less-expensive compact models don't generally heat as fast as medium- to large-size ones, since they usually have lower wattage ratings. Although most microwaves are countertop models, over-the-range ovens can preserve much-needed space in your kitchen. They are heavier and more costly to install, but if you're really pressed for space, an over-the-range microwave may be the way to go. Combination convection microwaves, which can brown food, have been in wide use by restaurants and are also available for residential use.

127

Dishwashers

Depending on your tolerance for noise, your need for special features, or your desire for better water and energy efficiency, a dishwasher can run anywhere from $300 to almost $2,000. Cheaper models get dishes clean, but can be noisy and waste a lot of water.

If you are concerned with noise, look for models with rubber insulators that act as soundproofers. While touchpads are easier to clean, manual button dishwashers are usually cheaper. If loading all your dishes seems to be a problem, consider buying a dishwasher with removable racks, glassware holders, and even fold-down shelves. Energy efficiency is important when choosing an appliance, so consult Energy Guide stickers, and choose a dishwasher that will safety accommodate your dishes without being too overwhelming. Dirt sensors are readily available in most models, but they are not foolproof in detecting how dirty your dishes really are. Inspect them yourself and decide on a wash cycle that will get them adequately clean.

Purchase appliances from reputable stores and make sure they have a return policy. Compare prices, as you are often able to convince one dealer to "price-match" another.

All About Refrigerators

How much refrigerator does your household need? Industry guidelines recommend a minimum of 12 cubic feet of storage for two people, plus 2 cubic feet for each additional household member. Hence, two parents and three children would need 18 cubic feet.

Refrigerator-freezers are available in four configurations:

- **TOP MOUNT** Two doors, with the freezer compartment at the top.
- **SIDE-BY-SIDE** A full-length door for refrigerator and another for freezer; good for smaller spaces, since full size doors often require more swing space.
- **BOTTOM MOUNT** Two doors, with the freezer at the bottom.
- **SINGLE DOOR** Small freezer compartment within the refrigerator. This is the most basic model, and least efficient for longer-term storage; good temporary storage for entertaining.

A built-in refrigerator can align with kitchen cabinetry and sport matching panels on its doors. The most adaptable model to custom-fit is the side-by-side.

Specialty Refrigerators

MINI-FRIDGE Installed in an armoire or bathroom vanity.

WINE BOX Clear glass door; precisely controlled temperature/humidity ratio.

ICEMAKER Produces clear ice automatically.

FREEZER For seasonal storage.

REFRIGERATED KITCHEN DRAWERS Useful in preparing large meals or for storing snacks.

Eggs-actly Where Does That Go?

Consider the various storage features available before you choose a refrigerator. Cooking and eating patterns change with the seasons, with technology, and with a growing family. Will you be able to adjust the shelves to allow for 2-litre bottles of soda the kids will guzzle? For the average family, those individual egg holders built into the door take up more space than the shelf storage of a carton of eggs.

The No-Frost Trade-Off

Frost-free technology pulls moisture from inside the refrigerator and freezer compartments, limiting the frost crystallization. At the same time, unprotected food will lose its moisture—fresh vegetables become limp, bread goes stale, ice cubes shrink. Wrap each food in moisture-proof material to prolong its life.

Smaller Kitchen Appliances

Toaster Look for ones with extra-wide, non-stick slots, a manual lift, and removable crumb tray for easier clean up. Many models now have settings for bagels.

Coffeemaker Automatic-drip coffeemakers are the most popular models. Look for removable filter baskets, although you may want to invest in a metal mesh filter rather than continuing to buy paper filters. Transparent fill tubes can tell you how much water is available in the tank, and a thermal carafe will hold heat longer than a glass container. Higher priced models can come equipped with a programmable timer (for setting up the coffee the night before) and small-batch settings.

Food Processor Good for chopping, slicing, and shredding foods. Get one with an interchangeable container and blades to multitask with food. Convenient models may come with a plastic food pusher, pulse settings, and even special small bowls that fit within large ones when chopping only a small amount. Lighter models are good for small jobs, but larger eleven-cup ones are more versatile. If you find you only need minor jobs done, such as chopping garlic, try a mini-chopper instead.

Blender Great for pureeing mixtures and creating drinks. Sturdy models made from stainless steel or thick glass are preferable to the more easily scarred plastic containers. A standard power setting falls at about 350 watts. Removable blades are easier to clean and maintain than those attached to the container. A convenient alternative to countertop blenders is the handheld, wand-like immersion blender. Although it doesn't have as much power, it is useful for a wide range of small jobs and frees up counter space.

Bathroom Improvements

L ike the kitchen, a bathroom is driven by utility. Its major furnishings are bolted into place, to put an emphasis on safety even above utility. Only when these two concerns are dealt with does decoration come to the front. Happily, the sterile hospital operating room style of bathroom is a thing of the past, and we now can enjoy bathrooms with softened light, plants, and even art.

Bathrooms need lighting that is efficient, yet humane. Replacing harsh lighting with ambient light and limiting task lighting to the area where it is used immediately improve the overall look of a bathroom. Mirrors can be too much of a good thing, and when they are overused, the room becomes a series of harsh reflections. Diffuse the power of large mirrors by hanging artwork in front of them. Bring in items that are not standard issue in a bathroom, like a table lamp or a side chair. Look for storage that is both functional and stylish. For example, replace plastic laundry baskets with woven or metal ones.

A garden piece looks at home in the bathroom. A birdhouse, a concrete cherub, or a decorative rock bring a feeling of fresh air along with them. A weathervane becomes sculpture, and a lush plant invokes the sense of a botanic garden.

The appearance of a bathroom gets tired easily. If it's messy, it is distressing. The first principle for good bathroom design is to make it easy to be cleaned and kept tidy. No wall covering or lighting will look good when the fixtures aren't sparkling and bright.

Bathroom Walls

Look for a bathroom wall covering that is durable, hygienic, and will provide traction. You want a material that will be easy to clean and stand up to water pressure without buckling or cracking. Here are some pros and cons to different coverings:

Ceramic Tile PROS: Durable, many design choices
CONS: Expensive

Terracotta Tile PROS: Inexpensive and warm CONS: Porous tile will stain without sealer

Mirrors and Glass PROS: Easy to clean CONS: Dangerous when broken; easy to overlight

Moisture-proof Wallpapers PROS: Wide range of designs and patterns CONS: Not especially practical

Wood Paneling PROS: Natural finish adds warmth CONS: Needs to be waterproofed; can be slippery

Faucet Styles

Their combination of utility and design makes it important to choose wisely when it comes to bathroom faucets in sinks, tubs, and showers. Look at samples for heft and attention to detail, as well as their profile. Sinks children will use should be fitted with faucets that are easily controlled, to reduce the possibility that they will be scalded with hot water. Before making a final choice, consider how responsive the faucet will be when it is adjusted by a wet, soapy hand.

Showers

Most bathtubs can accommodate a shower fitting, or a separate stall shower can be installed. Look for a good-quality showerhead that can be adjusted for angle, stream, and power.

Toilets

Low-water-use toilets assist with energy conservation every day, thanks to the advances of modern design. A 1.5-gallon flush toilet is more than three times as efficient as an older 5-gallon flush model. Siphon flushing is quiet, traps odors, and uses less water than side flushing. Side-flush toilets swish water around the side of the bowl with each flush; the reverse-trap flush provides the conservation advantages of siphon flushing at a more practical price.

Sinks

The sink is generally made of enameled steel and porcelain. The most widely chosen style for set-in bathroom designs is the round sink. Faucets and fittings are made of chrome, brass, colored coatings, and combinations of porcelain and metal. Gold-plated faucets are the most expensive, but are long lasting. Take care when making your choice and invest in a design you will love for years.

The most often used installation for bathroom sinks is the vanity, a stylized cupboard in which the sink is installed. Vanities are characterized by their Formica-like finishes and swing-style cupboard doors, which serve as access to the wastewater pipe. The trend now is toward separate sinks in the shared bathroom, often side by side, installed along a common wall, with shared counterspace and a mirror.

The pedestal sink is a self-contained unit; the plumbing lines are concealed in the pedestal and the sink is freestanding. Pedestal sinks come in designs that will fit any bathroom, from antique Victorian to the most modern look.

Wall-hung sinks take up the least space, since plumbing lines run independently underneath. For a stylish resolution, they are often dressed with fabric skirts to hide exposed pipes.

Rx for the Medicine Cabinet

The medicine cabinet is probably the most neglected element of bathroom design. In theory, it provides safe and accessible storage for medicinal supplies. In practice, its narrow shelves are just too small. Though it has pride of place, the average medicine cabinet is manufactured to a lower standard than bathroom fittings. One solution? Abandon it! Organize storage for medications and first aid in the kitchen, where you spend far more time and they are safer from children. Keep toiletries in baskets under the sink. Replace the medicine cabinet with a large, framed mirror in the style of your décor.

Bathtubs

Vitreous china and enameled case iron were the earliest materials for tubs, and both are still highly desirable. Lighter units of fiberglass and acrylic tubs are easier to install. The tub can be set into a surround, which in turn can be finished with ceramic or stone tile. Be sure that a molded tub and a wall unit will fit through your bathroom door before you purchase them!

The Home Spa

Forget the harsh, sterile, in-and-out concept of the bathroom. Open this room to pleasure and you will be rewarded many times over. While it would be grand to have a Jacuzzi or a Japanese soaking tub, most bathrooms can be made more luxurious with some simple additions:

- **LIGHT** Soften and diffuse it; burn candles.
- **SURFACES** Cover hard floors with cotton rugs.
- **BATH CADDY** Fit your tub with a wire tray to hold soaps and sponges as well as a hand mirror, bath oils, and a book.
- **FRAGRANCE** Good ventilation is the first element for a restful bathroom.
- **SOUND** A circulating fountain gurgling takes away your stress. Or try music, mighty fine music.
- **GRAB BAR** Feel safe in the bath.
- **HOOKS AND RODS** Robes and towels deserve to be hung up, not sit in a puddle on a wet bathroom floor.

Luxurious Interludes

Create ceremony for your home spa time. Lay a fresh-from-the-dryer bath mat at the floor of the tub. Bring out the plushest, thickest bath towels you have, and pile up two or three on a chair alongside the tub, folded just so. Place a flowering plant on the tub. Set a cherished framed photograph nearby as a focus object. Unwrap a new bar of soap. While your bath is filling, moisten two face cloths, roll them up and heat them in the microwave. Chill two used tea bags for refreshing your eyes. Sprinkle a handful of rose petals over the bathwater and position a neck roll at the end of the tub to support your head.

Treat the bathwater with your favorite scented oil and allow the steam to build in the room. The most relaxing beverage to accompany a delicious soak is a cup of green tea—it sends the toxins from your body and restores your spirit. (Beware the proverbial bottle of champagne in the silver ice bucket. This delicate wine does not respond well to the warm humidity you're looking to create, and its alcohol will dehydrate you.) Reading a book in the bath can be awkward and its pages will curl; the television is a bit of an intrusion in this most private setting. We recommend playing music you particularly enjoy or listening to a good book on tape. And muse, by all means, muse. Let your thoughts drift into daydreams. When you've finished bathing, slather your body with top-quality creams and lotions.

Instant Spa Treatments

Toning Face Mask

Make yourself a toning facial mask with a quick trip to the kitchen. This mixture will unblock pores and improve skin texture.

$1/2$ cup plain oatmeal, cooked and cooled
$1/4$ cup honey

Combine the oatmeal and honey and blend into a sticky paste. Apply the mixture to the face, avoiding the sensitive area around the eyes. Leave on for twenty minutes, then rinse with warm water and pat your skin dry.

Lavender-Almond Bath Oil

6 ounces almond oil
60 drops lavender essential oil
Dried lavender sprig

In a glass bottle, combine the oils. Press the lavender sprig into the bottle.

The Perfect Bed

I n this hectic modern world, who doesn't dream of simply dropping everything and heading directly for the most remote spa or retreat they can find? But few places actually offer more relaxation from a busy schedule than your own bedroom. Follow these helpful hints on making the perfect bed and creating a soothing atmosphere that will get you the good night's rest you truly deserve. Just remember to venture out once in a while!

Sheets

While high-quality sheets usually have a thread count of 600 or higher, 300 is considered standard. The quality of the sheet is actually determined more by fiber and fabric than count. Use the weight of the sheet and the way it feels to make your choice: Don't base it on thread count alone.

Regardless of thread count, experts agree that the best sheets are made from Egyptian cotton. The long fiber lengths ensure a luxurious feeling as well as durability.

Types of sheets include:
Linen: versatile, but needs to be ironed
Percale: closely woven cotton
Sateen: cotton in a satin weave; has a polished sheen
Voile: semi-sheer, gauze-like material
T-shirt knits: soft cotton jersey, recently popular
Flannel: napped cotton fabric for added warmth
Satin: closely woven silk with a lustrous face

Pillows

Keep an eye out for a high count of "down clusters," fluff balls that are mixed with the flat-feathered filler to provide airiness and volume. Most pillows have at least 75 percent down clusters, but many top-quality pillows contain from 85 to 90 percent.

Look for the highest "fill power" available, usually above 600. This measures the quality of the down and means an ounce of flattened down will fill 600 cubic inches when expanded.

Watch for high thread count on the pillowcase: It will keep the pillow edges from fraying and down from escaping.

Although the National Sleep Foundation recommends at least eight hours sleep a night, a recent study shows that only 30 percent of the population between the ages of 18 to 54 actually get the correct amount. Chronic sleep loss has been found to contribute to obesity, illness, the risk of heart attacks, and poor memory retention.

136

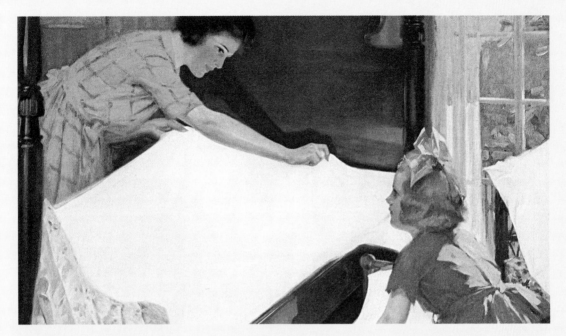

Making your Bed the Classic Way

Tuck the bottom sheet in along the edges under the mattress, starting from the head and working to the foot. At the foot, pull the sheet tight and fold into an envelope shape before tucking over the already made corners. Place the top sheet so that any decorative design is at the headboard. Lay any blankets on top, then tuck everything under the mattress. Envelope the corners, as with the bottom sheet, to keep it neat. Finish by placing the bed cover on top and turning the top sheet and blanket over it. Add some pillows and your bed is complete!

Mattresses

Although many are made with polyurethane foam, it's better to have a mattress created from natural materials like cotton, wool, cashmere, or flax. Quality mattresses made with these materials can last up to 30 years in comparison to the 9- to 10-year life span of a standard foam mattress.

Support coils are important. A queen-size mattress should have at least 375 coils, with five turns per coil. Look for tufted-inner-layer mattresses, especially hand tufted. This means each layer of the mattress has been threaded from top to bottom, locking everything in place and preventing bunching.

Make sure to put the mattress on a box spring rather than a foundation. Box springs make use of hourglass coils that not only provide support, but also adapt to the shape of the body. Futons are comfortable and convenient, but turn the mattress each week to reduce wear.

Caring for a Mattress

Ideally, mattresses should be alternately flipped from top to bottom and rotated from side to side every six weeks, but four times a year is usually adequate. Air the mattress out in the sun once or twice a year and always use a mattress pad; it will keep the mattress's fabric clean.

If a mattress is getting lumpy before its time, an egg-crate foam top may help even it out. Also, a board placed between the box spring and the mattress can perk up a sagging or too-soft mattress.

Slipping and Sliding

Mattress slippage usually caused by two synthetic materials rubbing against each other. Try replacing the bed skirt or mattress cover with one made entirely of cotton. A foot- or headboard can also stop the shifting.

137

Relax

Although your bed is the obvious focal point of your bedroom, it's important to create a relaxing atmosphere all around to ensure a restful night. The National Sleep Foundation provides these tips for creating a healthy sleep environment:

■ Use dark curtains for windows, sleep masks, earplugs, and "white noise" devices to get rid of outside distractions.

■ Your bedroom should be free of allergens. To reduce them, get a synthetic pillow rather than a down-filled one and invest in an air purifier. Waterproof mattress pads reduce dust accumulation, and dust-mite-proof mattress and pillow enclosures eliminate a major allergen. Do make sure your mattress does not rest on the floor—dust and pollen collect there. Eliminating carpets and pets from the bedroom is also recommended for allergy sufferers.

■ Keep the area around your bed clear of objects that may cause you to slip or fall if you get up during the night.

■ Associate your bedroom with only sleep and intimacy. It's easier to fall asleep if you don't connect your bed to any stressful or hectic activity.

■ The tranquility of your bedroom environment is greatly enhanced by pacifying color schemes. Try decorating in calming colors like green, purple, and blue, or shades of pink and coral, which have been shown to comfort and refresh the spirit.

■ When installing lighting, 60- to 100-watt bulbs are preferable, and use table lamps next to the bed or wall sconces instead of downlights, spots, or overheads directly above the bed.

Attic & Basement Improvements

Tired of never having enough space? Always wanted that extra bedroom, family room, or home office? You might have the additional space right under your feet or over your head. With the right improvements, your attic or basement could become whole new additions to your home without major renovations.

The Attic

While often seen as isolated and remote, attics can be quite spacious and ideal for a variety of new purposes, from simple storage to guest bedrooms.

■ Temperature will play a major part in whatever you wish to renovate up there. Since heat rises, attics can sometimes become sweltering sites. Install window fans or a ventilation system to keep the temperature manageable.

■ To increase natural light, place windows on different walls, or install a skylight. Use glazing to reduce heat from direct sunlight. To keep areas warm during the winter, install thermal windows and good insulation.

■ If your attic simply has rafters, you probably won't be able to do much more than store boxes. However, if your attic has a sturdy floor and ample room, you can utilize this part of your house for a number of things.

■ Roof leaks can also be a problem when it comes to fixing up your attic. Wait for a rainy day and check for moisture before you go ahead with any renovation.

Renovation Suggestions

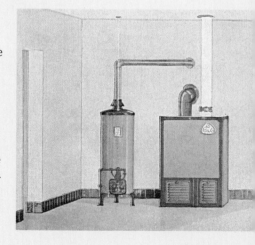

HOME OFFICE Whether you work from home or just need a quiet place to organize the household, a home office is a welcome addition. You'll need power outlets and a phone jack, as well as space for a desk, chair, and containers for files and office supplies. Good lighting is also necessary to minimize eyestrain. Soundproofing will maintain a quiet environment while you work.

GUEST BEDROOM Guests tired of that lumpy foldout couch in the living room? Create a guest bedroom with electricity, a phone jack, and at least eighty square feet for a bed, dresser, and closet. Easy access to the rest of the house will keep your guest connected, but soundproofing will provide her with privacy. Install a smoke alarm for safety.

If you're going to be remodeling, check with your local buildings department to see if there are zoning laws you need to be aware of. Even if the job doesn't seem that big, it's always a good idea to check community restrictions first.

LAUNDRY ROOM You can create a hidden place for all of your laundry needs. In addition to the basics (washer, dryer, sink, and ironing board), hanging cabinets and shelves hold laundry supplies, countertops make folding and stacking clothes easy, while the hamper hides dirty clothes. Make sure you have enough electrical outlets to accommodate your appliances. Next, you can install a laundry chute throughout the rest of your house.

TOOL WORKSHOP Safety is key in your workshop, so have an adequate amount of electrical outlets and good, general-purpose lighting. Install workbenches and counters, and add soft, rubber flooring to relieve foot stress. Lockable storage units and a pegboard wall to hang tools on make the room complete.

STORAGE SPACE Keep in mind moisture and temperature restrictions, and consult our tips on page 79 for the best place to store items.

Other possible home projects to install in an attic or basement are a family room or a personal gym.

The Basement

Dank, damp, dark—these three words seem to sum up most people's view of the lowest level of their houses. But the basement can also hide valuable storage space, even a new laundry room or office. The key to improving your basement is recognizing its limitations. If you have high levels of radon or constant flooding and humidity, your basement probably will not be good for much more than storage purposes (and only sturdy items at that.) But if you find your basement stays relatively dry and has good air quality, there's no limit to the amount of transformation that can occur.

■ One of the first things to consider when renovating your basement is the amount of radon and toxic mold present. See page 196 to learn what you can do to test for and combat these household menaces.

■ The basement is usually one of the dampest places in your house, making it less than ideal for storing delicate items or paperwork. Deal with this moisture problem before you begin remodeling. Walls and leaks can be sealed, but you might also want to install a sump pump. This will help combat flooding when it rains.

■ If you are susceptible to flooding, all items should be placed on raised platforms, at least three inches above the ground.

■ A dehumidifier can cut down on mold growth and help the air quality. Keep walls clean and free of mildew, insulate basement pipes, and make sure your wall insulation has a vapor barrier.

■ Your gutter system could cause leaks around the foundation of your house and in your basement.

■ If worse comes to worst, you may need a contractor to check and remodel your drainage system.

HVAC

The federal government set requirements for minimum efficiency for all heating, ventilating, and air-conditioning equipment in 1992; if your units were manufactured before then, they are most likely not energy efficient. You can realize a savings by replacing even a well-functioning unit that was not energy efficient. When upgrading your heating, ventilation, and air conditioning systems, known by the acronym HVACs, bear in mind that:

■ Products that have earned the Energy Star rating meet the guidelines set by the Environmental Protection Agency and the Department of Energy

■ You should choose cooling products that have high seasonal energy efficiency ratings (SEER)

■ Look for a high AFUE (Annual Fuel Utilization Efficiency) percentage and a high heating seasonal performance factor (HSPF)

The basics of HVAC may seem daunting, but they represent an opportunity to save considerably on energy bills and keep the air in your home clean and pure. Perform heating- and cooling-load calculations before adding upgrades and new systems, and make sure the equipment under consideration can handle your home's loads. Getting the right system for your space is critical; if you install oversize equipment, you will be paying higher electrical bills. What's more, a too-big air-conditioning unit will not control the humidity properly and the air in the house will feel stale.

Before You Commit

■ You can figure your home's heating and cooling loads calculations by calling your local utility or visiting their website. Be wary of having contractors or appliance salespeople do these calculations and make recommendations for you: It is far more common for consumers to be sold units that are too big for their space than too small. Consult a heating and cooling (HVAC) engineer. The charge for a site visit can be surprisingly reasonable, and it pays for itself in long-term savings.

■ A contractor or engineer should listen to your reasons for upgrading: Quite often, the problems perceived to be related to a unit that is too small are in fact caused by inadequate ductwork, improper balancing, or improper humidity control—or simply a dirty coil.

■ Cooling loads are more expensive to deal with than heating loads; it takes more energy to cool a space than to warm it. If you live in an area with high cooling loads, such as Florida, make sure you install the most efficient air-conditioning system available, and use it wisely.

Radiant heating is a system of coils installed under or embedded in your flooring, powered by air or water pressure. Radiant heat is desirable for its ability to warm rooms without circulating the allergens common to forced air vents. Also, radiant systems save energy. Though the installation involves major reconstruction for flooring already in place, consider it seriously if you are building a new home or laying new floors: Coils are cast into concrete floors or laid under plywood subfloors or wood flooring. Radiant heating means no more vents, ducts, or radiators.

143

Gardening

The keys to a beautiful and bountiful garden are as simple as understanding what kind of growing environment you have, learning what types of flowers and plants will flourish in your area, and having the right gardening tools. The wide variety of plants that can accommodate almost any environment is truly amazing, so take the time to research what each plant needs to thrive. Ask questions at your local garden supply center. You'll eventually come up with ideas for a garden that lifts your spirit and satisfies your green thumb.

What to Take Into Account Before You Break Soil

CLIMATE How hot does your area get? How long are the seasons? How much rain do you receive? What kind of sun exposure does your yard have?

ELEVATION Do you live in a hilly region or a valley? By the coast or on a plain? Each of these conditions could affect the temperature and frost factors.

SOIL TYPE Is your soil rocky? Sandy? Muddy? Rich? Research the types of plants that can thrive with your soil.

Watering Tips

Water gardens in the morning. This will allow enough time for the soil to soak up moisture before night falls, and will halt the growth of damaging fungi. If you'd like to add drip irrigation to your garden, try poking holes in the bottom of a gallon milk carton. Bury most of the carton in the dirt and fill it with water. This will slowly add moisture below ground level.

Essential Garden Tools

■ Garden spade: a shovel-like tool that is used for breaking up soil for planting, making drainage ditches, and delineating bed edges ■ Garden trowel: breaks up small patches of dirt, digs out weeds, makes holes for seeds and plantings, and transplants grown plants. A narrow trowel is good for planting, and a wider trowel can be used on flowers ■ Gloves ■ Hose ■ Kneeling pad ■ Pruners: keep trees and shrubs well maintained and trimmed with these sharp blades ■ Rake: not only can you collect and discard leaves, you can also use a strong rake to break up soft soil and make lines for planting ■ Watering can: use this to gently water individual plants and easily transport water to places inaccessible by a hose

There's no need to stop at a handful of vegetable or flower rows. Explore other garden options, such as rock and shade gardens, butterfly gardens, herb gardens, and Japanese sand gardens.

Types of Flowers and Plants

ANNUALS, as their name suggests, last only one year and must be replanted.

BIENNIALS grow for two years, but only produce leaves in the first year. They die after blossoming in the second year.

PERENNIALS come back annually and have specific growing seasons. It's a good idea to plant perennials that blossom at different times throughout the year; that way something is always in season. Asters, roses, lavender, and peonies are all timeless garden favorites.

EVERGREENS AND CONIFERS (pinecone bearing) are perennial plants. These shrubs and trees make good hedges and borders.

FRESH FRUIT is one of the benefits of growing fruit trees, but they blossom only seasonally and usually need specific growing conditions.

Helpful Gardening Websites

- *www.bhg.com* (Better Homes and Gardens)
- *www.houseandhome.msn.com*
- *www.gardenweb.com* (directory of garden web sites)
- *www.burpee.com* (Burpee)
- *www.garden.org* (National Gardening Association)
- *www.organicgardening.com*
- *www.gardening.about.com*
- *www.gardenguides.com*

Weed and Pest Control

It goes without saying that the loveliest garden in the world is still prone to various garden pests and weeds. Weeds steal valuable nutrients from the soil and can crowd out other plants and flowers. They can be removed easiest after a heavy rain. Undiluted white vinegar, boiling water with a little salt in it, or chlorine bleach can all kill weeds when poured directly on individual plants. Be careful though! Only use a little of these treatments, since they can join run-off water and kill other plants.

SLUGS Place a cup of beer in your garden. Slugs and snails will drink the alcohol, not be able to get out of the cup, and drown. Replace regularly.

RODENTS The strong scent of marigolds deters these nuisances. Marigolds also work well on tomato worms and whiteflies. Plant them around vegetables.

RABBITS Baby powder sprinkled around your plants can send rabbits running back to their holes.

MOTHS Protect against these damaging pests by planting mint, sage, or thyme around cabbages and broccoli.

APHIDS Onion, garlic, basil, coriander, and anise all safely discourage these annoyances.

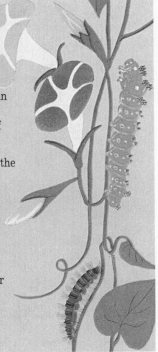

Houseplants

Houseplants are a beautiful and inexpensive way to stylize your house and provide cleaner indoor air. Choose houseplants that fit your lifestyle. Will you be around to give the care each one needs? What kind of sun exposure do you have at home? Do you prefer large, leafy plants or trailing, hanging ones? Check gardening websites, and don't be afraid to ask garden center experts. It's their job to match customers up with the right plants.

The Essential Three

Once you've decided on your perfect plants, here are some basic tips to make sure they stay healthy:

SOIL Healthy soil goes a long way toward a healthy plant, so make sure you change it at least once a year, or until the roots reach the bottom of the pot. To re-pot, hold your hand against the soil and around the stem, tip the pot upside down, and pull the plant out gently. Keep the root ball as undamaged as possible, loosening it a little with your finger if it is too compact. Move to a clean pot that has some broken crockery or marbles in the bottom. Place a little new soil in the bottom, then the plant. Fill around the plant with more soil, and tap the pot to even it out. Add more as needed and water. Don't pack the soil too tightly, or water won't reach the roots, and don't use garden soil if it is an indoor potted plant.

WATERING One of the main causes of plant death is overwatering, so it's important to pay attention and do it right. Test if your plant needs water by poking your finger, or a pencil, halfway down. If dirt clings, don't water. If not, the plant is dry. Water in the morning, if possible, with lukewarm water. Saturate the soil until water runs out the drainage hole. Wait for it to drain, and then dump the excess water. Don't let water stand in the pot more than a day, or root rot will occur. Check for yellowing leaves and a slimy stem: these are both signs of too much watering.

SUNLIGHT Depending on the type, your plant will need low, medium, or high light to grow. Flowering plants usually need more light than foliage plants, but there are exceptions to the rule. Keep your plant in bright, indirect light and look for signs that it is getting the right amount. Pale, wilted, and spindly leaves usually mean too much sunlight. Small, yellow leaves signify it isn't getting enough. Give your plant half a turn each week to make sure it is getting evenly sunned.

Greenhouse

Some areas are just particularly good for particular plants: African violets and ferns thrive on humidity, so keep them in steamy bathrooms. Cacti need sunny conditions that could be provided in a bright living room or south-facing bedroom. Most plants come equipped with tags detailing their ideal growing conditions. Read the tag to see what room in your house it will perform best in.

Like some greenery in the house that's also practical? Why not try growing herbs on your kitchen windowsill? Chives, oregano, spearmint, and basil are all excellent indoor choices. Just make sure to keep them in direct sunlight for at least five hours a day, and water them regularly.

Poisonous Plants

Plants can benefit the whole family, but it goes without saying that they should be kept out of reach of young children and pets. The following plants are just a few that have been deemed poisonous when ingested. Make sure you know what kind of plant you're purchasing!

■ Amaryllis ■ Azalea ■ Caladium ■
Dieffenbachia ("dumb cane") ■ English ivy
■ Foxglove ■ Holly Berries ■ Hyacinth ■
Hydrangea ■ Jerusalem cherry ■
Philodendron ■ Poinsettia ■ Pokeweed

For a more comprehensive list, contact your local Poison Control Center or the American Association of Poison Control Centers at www.aapcc.org.

Plants that Just Won't Die!

Do you have such a "black thumb" that it seems you can make fake plants wilt? Try one of these household favorites and everyone will wonder why your green thumb was dormant so long.

■ African violet ■ Aspidistra ■ Bamboo palm ■ Chinese evergreen ■
Jade plant ■ Kangaroo vine ■ Peace lily ■ Pothos ■ Rubber plant ■
Snake plant ■ Spider plant ■ Strawberry begonia ■ Striped dracaena

Plants that Provide a Breath of Fresh Air

Most plants promote a healthier home atmosphere, but these are especially good for keeping your indoor air clean.

■ Chinese evergreen ■ Ficus ■ Gerbera daisy ■
Golden pothos ■ Mauna Loa ■ Spider plant

Houseplant Hints

■ At the nursery or garden center, ask if you can lift the plant out of the pot to check the roots. If they are too loose, it's probably because they have just been transplanted and haven't adjusted yet. If they are packed into a tight ball, they are probably suffering from a cramped pot, and will need to be put in a larger pot immediately. Also, check for any bugs or visible diseases on the leaves.

■ Save the pieces of that plate that slipped out of your hand last week! Placing pieces of crockery in the bottom of a pot before adding soil creates an ideal drainage system that will allow your plant to flourish.

■ An excellent way to nourish your plant is to water it with the cooled liquid left from boiling or steaming vegetables or eggs. Just make sure there's no salt in the water, or it will wither the plant. Cold tea also works well as an occasional vitality shot.

Maintaining Fresh Flowers

Most flowers can be maintained with a few simple steps: remove any leaves that fall below the waterline, cut the stems often, and change the water regularly. Add two tablespoons of bleach and three ounces of 7-Up to the water to preserve flowers longer. Here are some tips for more specific blossoms:

■ **ROSES** Remove all but the topmost leaves. Submerge the whole flower in cool water in the sink and cut the stem. Place in a vase of warm water, bleach, and 7-Up solution. To revive wilted roses, try submerging the entire flower in cool water for half an hour. Then fill the sink halfway with hot water and cut the stems beneath the water surface. Leave the stems in the water and keep the rose heads supported until the stems become rigid again. ■ **BULB FLOWERS** Always cut stems with a knife, not scissors. Add $1/2$ ounce of vodka and a couple of pennies to the water to keep them looking fresh. ■ **HYDRANGEA** The leaves drink up much of the water, so remove most of them first. Soak the whole flower in cool water. Shake off the excess water and cut the stems. To revive the blooms, repeat the soaking procedure for up to three hours. To dry hydrangea, simply allow the vase water to evaporate. ■ **WOODY-STEMMED FLOWERS** (lilac and other shrub flowers): Crush the bottom inch of the stem with a hammer. Plunge the flower into cool water, then place in a vase with a solution of warm water, bleach, and 7-Up.

Flowers

Flower arranging can be considered both a science and an art. Whether you're a major horticulturist or just an admirer of pretty blooms, there's definitely something about flowers, be they silk or fresh, that make rooms come alive. Take a cue from nature: you don't need a degree in interior design to brighten and revive your house—just a few well-placed blossoms.

Creating a Fresh Flower Arrangement

1. Gather fresh flowers in the early morning or early evening. Cut stems on an angle under water to minimize air bubbles. If stems are especially thick, split them or mash them at the bottom with a hammer. This works well on roses.

2. Fill your container about halfway full with clean water. A few drops of chlorine bleach can keep water from clouding, and will keep cut flowers fresh longer by killing off some bacteria.

3. Remove any leaves that fall below the waterline.

4. A nice beginner's bouquet should have at least three items: greenery (like ferns) and two kinds of different flowers (one larger, like roses or carnations, and one smaller, like small daisies).

5. Start with a few pieces of greenery and add them to the holder. This will serve as the base of your arrangement.

6. Add the flowers to the greenery base one at a time. Start with large flowers. Then fill in spaces with smaller ones. Make sure to distribute the flowers evenly, that way the colors aren't clumped together.

7. Use a lot of blooms, but be careful not to overfill the vase. All of the stems should have access to the water.

8. Occasionally redistribute the flowers as blossoms open or wilt. Adjust the arrangement daily and pick out any dead items. Recut the stems every few days and change the water.

Drying Flowers

Beautiful flowers don't need to end up in the garbage. Tie a small group of flowers together with string and hang them upside down in a dry, dark place. Leave them for a few days until all the moisture has evaporated. Be careful when arranging them in rooms with fluctuating temperatures, such as the bathroom and the kitchen, since high levels of steam or moisture can cause the flowers to rot. Good drying flowers are roses, sea lavender, marjoram, larkspur, and hydrangea.

Flower Power

Help winter out the door by forcing forsythia and branches of flowering trees to bloom.

1. Harvest the branches when small buds show. This is usually towards the end of winter.

2. Trim the bottoms of the stems to size for your arrangement.

3. With pruners, cut an X into the bottom of each stem to help the branch to absorb more water.

4. Set branches in a container of warm water.

Cleaning Silk Flowers

Place sturdy silk flowers in a plastic bag with two tablespoons of salt and shake. This will cause dust to adhere to the salt. You can also use a hair dryer on the warm setting to blow away dust particles.

149

Hanging Pictures

A picture may speak a thousand words, but if it is hung incorrectly, it might not convey the meaning you're going for. Framed photographs and pictures are an easy way to dress up any room and give your house a warm, personal touch. Whether it's a group of family photos or a heavy oil painting, here are a few tips to ensure that your pictures are always hanging pretty, no matter where you decide to display them.

To Hang a Picture

■ To avoid having to re-hang a picture that doesn't look right, take your time to determine the best place in a room and position and height on a wall for the frame before proceeding to the steps below. Have someone assist you by holding up the frame against the desired location as you look at it from a distance and from different angles. Once you are satisfied with your choice, make a small mark on the wall that corresponds to the center point of the top edge of the frame. This will help you determine where to position the actual picture hook.

■ Assuming the frame already has a horizontal braided wire attached to it for hanging, use your finger to pull the middle of the wire toward the top edge of the frame, and then measure the remaining distance. Referencing the mark you already made on the wall, make a second mark below the first, equal to the remaining distance you just measured. This is the point on the wall to attach the hook.

■ Generally speaking, it is better to use a real picture hook, which is inexpensive and comes in many sizes for different frame weights, than a plain nail. A nail will certainly hold up a frame, but if a person brushes up against the frame, the picture might be knocked off the nail. This is less likely to happen with a hook.

■ Hammering picture hook nails into plaster walls can often cause small pieces of the wall to chip off, so it helps to apply a piece of masking tape over the marked spot and embed the nail directly through the middle of the tape. The

If you find your picture is slipping to one side, try twisting some tape around the picture hook or nail.

tape also helps prevent the wall from chipping if, for some reason, you have to extract the nail later.

■ Brick walls, in particular, are difficult to hang frames on. In the case of brick and other kinds of masonry, you will want to use a wall anchor. Create a hole with a proper drill and a special masonry bit, and insert a plastic or metal wall anchor. Then drive in a screw. Like picture hooks, these anchors and screws come in many sizes. It's important for the anchor to fit snugly in its hole, since the function of the screw is to expand the anchor, thereby pressing it out against the sides of the hole and creating a firm, secure hook (in this case, the screw head, which you don't completely tighten against the wall, so there is space for the frame's hanging wire to catch it).

■ While picture hooks and wall anchors make it easy for you to hang frames of many sizes and weights (even up to 30 to 40 pounds), for particularly heavy objects it may be best for a professional to install it. In the end, you don't want to create a potential hazard by improperly securing a heavy object, framed or otherwise, to your wall.

Picture Perfect

■ Don't apply cleaner directly to the glass on a picture frame, since it could seep around the edges to the back and possibly damage the image. Instead, apply the cleaner to a cloth first and then wipe the glass.

■ For items framed in plastic or Lucite, it's important to use only specially formulated cleaners, as regular glass cleaners will damage the plastic. These special cleaners can also help remove scratches, to which plastic can be prone.

■ Clean picture glass with denatured alcohol or vinegar on a tissue. Wipe dry.

■ Clean wooden frames with furniture polish.

■ Save money and make your own custom frame. Framing kits are sold in frame shops and art supply stores.

Comb through thrift shops, garage sales, and flea markets for old, empty frames or even framed items that may not be too expensive. Antique frames are easily spruced up and can look great—at a fraction of the cost of purchasing new custom frames.

Feng Shui

According to the American Feng Shui Institute, the words feng shui literally mean "wind and water." This ancient Chinese art, also called the art of placement, relies on observation of the environment in relation to astrological factors. Using the principles of feng shui, one can adjust the flow of chi, or vital energy, to benefit the folks in a home or business. Feng shui is a set of techniques, not a religion, and can be used by anyone, at home or office.

Are Professionals Worth Their Fees?

Today, the many feng shui practitioners out there charge a wide range of fees for their services. Your best bet is to find one that is licensed, accredited, or certified by an organization such as the Feng Shui Institute, the Feng Shui Society, or the Feng Shui Academy. Use your judgment before you hire a feng shui consultant. Ask for their qualifications, training, and references. If they are unable or unwilling to provide this information, take your business elsewhere.

Basic Feng Shui

Although feng shui is a complex art that requires years of study to master, there are some simple tricks you can use to improve the energy flow in your home.

■ **Be aware of your surroundings** Start by surveying your house or workspace. Look at your use of color, shapes, patterns, designs, and how they interact with each other. Just like different brushstrokes make one painting, every element in your house plays into "the big picture."

■ **Conquer clutter** A tidy house is the sign of a tidy life. Looking for a missing item can be a source of stress, and just living surrounded by clutter makes you think of all the things that you could be doing to make your house perfect. Make sure that every item has a place, and keep clutter under control.

■ **Strike out sharp edges** Sharp corners are the feng shui energy equivalent of knife blades. Select furniture with rounded edges, round picture frames instead of rectangular ones, and circle motifs in decorations. As bonus, reducing the number of sharp corners from your household might mean fewer bumps and bruises from running into them in the middle of the night.

■ **Remember the importance of color** Different hues can produce different moods. Warm colors can create a "homey" feeling and a sense of activity. Cool colors bring out the calming and quiet side of a location. In addition, some feng shui sources say that certain colors work best in

Do your research

Read a variety of different authors from different schools of thought to discover their similarities and differences. Experiment to see what works for you, and don't discount the benefits of working with a professional.

certain corners of your house. In the north, use bold and cool colors, like black, blue, and white. For the south, use fiery colors, like red, orange, and yellow. In the east, use colors from nature, including green, brown, and earth tones. For the west, use muted and neutral colors like white, gray, and beige.

■ **Learn about personal interaction with your environment** Some feng shui consultants will do an analysis that encompasses everything from astrological sign to numerology of your house number to discover how you as a person interact with the energy of your house. While a professional can compile a detailed profile for you, many websites provide free reports. The Center for Applied Feng Shui Research runs a site that deals with everything from finding your personal environment to the best sleeping position. Log in at *www.geomancy.net/reports/reports.htm.*

■ **Use bells and wind chimes** Cultures throughout the world have valued their soft sounds for everything from attracting fairies to driving away evil spirits. Hanging bells or coins on the inside of the door to your house is said to draw money in whenever they ring. Wind chimes are said to remove bad luck from a household, and their tones can be quite soothing to the listener.

■ **Use mirrors** Traditionally, mirrors were not a standard part of the feng shui practitioner's arsenal of treatments for ailing buildings, but modern culture has embraced their use. Although they are not a cure for bad energy flow, they can create a more pleasing environment by making a room seem brighter or larger. Be cautious about any practitioner who suggests that a mirror is a cure-all for your house's feng shui problems. A decorative placebo is still a placebo.

The Significance of Fish

In feng shui, fish represent wealth and good fortune. In addition, having an aquarium with fish has been proven to reduce stress. Keep an aquarium prominently displayed in a home office or workspace to keep your cool during stressful situations.

■ **Take note of the significance of plants** Living plants are a source of positive energy in a household. Plants are said to have specific symbolism (for example, bamboo is representative of good fortune over the long term) or the ability to create moods. Spider plants lend a soothing feeling. Fresh flowers can provide a sense of stability and calm. Placing plants in an empty corner can prevent a stagnant pool of energy from forming in the room. Some practitioners advise against using cactus, with its sharp spines, or bonsai, which represents stunted growth.

FOUNDATIONS

LIGHTING AND WIRING

INSULATION

HEATING

PLUMBING

ROOF

FLOORS

FRAMING

WINDOWS

BATHROOMS

Chapter 4 Repairs & Maintenance

Home Maintenance

No instructions needed!

■ Test the fire extinguisher

■ Test the batteries in your carbon monoxide and smoke alarms, flashlights, garage door opener, telephones and answering machine, alarm clocks, and radios

■ Make sure you have candles and matches in one place (and that they still work)

■ Check for bugs and rodents

■ Label the electrical panel circuit breakers

■ Keep the oven and microwave clean of grease and debris

Whether you live in a house or apartment, own or rent, your home will need maintenance and repairs. At some point, maintenance stretches beyond cleaning and decorating. A home is as sound as its architectural elements—walls, ceilings and floors, doors and windows—and all the paint and wallpaper in the world won't bring solidity to these surfaces. The structural integrity of a building is literally its foundation. Buildings that survive from Colonial times bear out how durable proper home construction can be.

Popular building materials vary by region: wood in the east, brick in the mid-Atlantic, adobe in the southwest. On the other hand, good craftsmanship is universal. The higher the structural quality of your home, the less you will find yourself spending on its systems. And the less you spend on repairing the basic structure of the house, the more you can spend on cosmetic and decorative projects. Still, even the finest materials need upkeep, and a home with plaster walls, hardwood floors, and a coffered ceiling deserves tender care.

Why wait for something to break and need repair? Periodic maintenance can extend the life of many of the items in your home. Don't skimp when it comes to these repairs, especially if you own. Proper repairs are an essential part of a well-maintained home. Anything less is not an efficient use of your time, energy, and money.

To properly repair your home and its contents, you must have a familiarity with all the systems in it and their age. The best way to do this is by keeping a home log. Your home log should contain the dates of repairs, major purchases (including where it was purchased and the serial and model numbers), warranty information, renovations, and contact information of people who have done work on your house. Having this information handy makes life much easier when it comes time to do additional work.

Keeping your home running smoothly is not a job that you should tackle alone; you will need help with pest control, home security, water and electrical systems, as well as the exterior of your house, including the roof, well, and septic tank. The best way to find suppliers is by word of mouth. Talk to your neighbors, work colleagues, and fellow church members. Be sure to tell people your experiences, too—good and bad. Don't shy away from delegating tasks, either. Children can help paint or your next-door neighbors' teenager might be looking for work mowing lawns in the summer. Keeping your house well maintained takes work, and you will need assistance.

Have a prospective home inspection before moving, even if you are dealing with new construction or are renting. You will want to know that the ventilation is proper, the walls and floors are plumb, and there is no likelihood of pest infestation. Try to get copies of architectural drawings. If you are buying an older house, they will be invaluable for repairs and upkeep as well as renovations. In lieu of plans, ask the home inspector to point out load-bearing walls, key joists, and other critical construction points.

Doors & Screens

The exterior and screen doors on your house are some of the most used pieces of equipment in your home, and need to be well maintained to endure all the abuse they receive. If you purchase quality equipment, you will have a much better experience. Second-rate models may be appealing at the store, but they can look shabby when installed, and their life expectancy is much shorter. The styles are vast—solid wood doors, metal doors, sliding glass doors— and each door has its own needs for maintenance and repair.

Cleaning Doors

Clean exterior doors twice a year, at least. If you have had a wet season, chances are your door is pretty dirty. Check the manufacturer's directions for suggestions. A general rule of thumb is to rinse doors down with a hose and use a clean sponge (not the scouring kind) to wipe off any additional dirt. If there are serious stains, use a little wood soap in a bowl of warm water to clean wooden doors. Using a clean sponge, gently apply the soap to the dirt spot and rub to remove the stain, then rinse with clean water. If your door is metal, a soft sponge and some mild dishwashing liquid will do the trick. Remember to rinse with clean water.

Screen Doors

Maintain and repair your screen doors in the same way as window screens (see page 162). Keep the hinges of both screen and storm doors oiled and tight, and lubricate the door closers once a year. Check that the latches work well. Replace hardware, glass, and screens, as necessary. In addition, replace the clips holding the screens and glass in place if they become bent, broken, or lost. Replacement parts are usually available at building supply centers and hardware stores. Because each manufacturer's hardware may be slightly different, be sure the replacement part will fit your particular door.

Tips for Keeping Doors in Shape

■ Treat painted wooden doors with a heavy-duty sealant, then choose exterior-grade paint or marine-grade enamel. Prime doors before painting.

■ If you have a squeaky door, try coating the hinges with silicone spray or light penetrating oil. If the squeaking persists, remove and clean the pin, barrel, and hinge leaves with steel wool. Coat them lightly with silicone spray or light penetrating oil and replace the parts.

■ Clean and vacuum sliding door tracks instead of lubricating them. The lubricant will attract more dirt and cause problems.

■ To protect exterior doors from damage, all storm and screen doors should have a door closer, either a chain-linked snubber or a pneumatic or hydraulic closer

■ You can lubricate door locks by rubbing the point of a No. 2 graphite pencil on both sides of your house key and working the key into its lock.

■ Some glass in doors can be replaced using the same methods as replacing the glass in a window (see page 161). Do not attempt to replace the glass in sliding glass doors yourself.

Scuff marks are easily removed using a new eraser. Scuff marks that have indented the door should be cleaned out using a new toothbrush.

Windows & Screens

The windows in your home are huge assets. Whether you have a few windows or floor to ceiling windows in every room, these valuable resources will need some type of maintenance from you, be it a simple cleaning or a full-blown replacement. You probably have screens of wire weave or fiberglass on your windows or doors to keep out bugs and let the sun and fresh air in.

Replacing Glass

Windows made after 1970 are usually factory sealed. You will need to consult the manufacturer before replacing the glass. Here are general guidelines for replacing glass in older windows. *Remember: Always protect your hands and eyes when working with glass.*

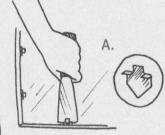

For wood frames:

1. Remove old glass.
2. Remove the triangular metal glazier points with pliers or a putty knife (see figure A).
3. Remove the putty or glazing compound from the frame using a putty knife.
4. Spread new glazing compound around the frame in a thin layer.
5. Select glass that is $1/8$ inch smaller than the groove length and width.
6. Insert the glass in the opening.
7. Insert the glazier points and gently press them halfway into the wood.

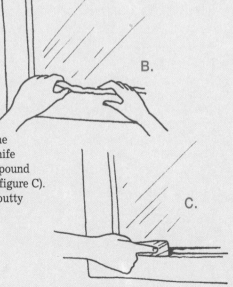

8. Carefully smooth a roll of glazing compound rope, approximately $3/8$ inch in diameter, around the glass next to the frame (see figure B). Holding a putty knife at a slight angle, smooth the compound out and clean off any excess (see figure C). If necessary, lightly moisten the putty knife for a smooth finish.

For metal frames:

1. Remove the old glass.
2. Pry out the spline (the rubber strip that holds the window and screen in place in the frame).
3. Wrap the spline around the new glass and put the window back together the way you disassembled it.

Shutters

Shutters add a decorative element to houses, one that is often not even functional. This does not mean that you do not need to care for your shutters. Check them annually to make sure there are no missing or loose pieces, they are securely attached to the house, and the hinges and screws are not rusted. Also check the shutters for wood rot, particularly around the hinges. When painting shutters you need to remove them from the house. Remove all the hardware and clean them well to remove any dirt. Dry them thoroughly. If there is damage, fix it before you put them back up. For wood rot, use a flat-head screwdriver to scrape out the damage and fill with wood putty. Let dry completely before painting. Paint on both sides—a spray painter can speed this job if there are more than two or four shutters.

Screens

SEASONAL CLEANING OF THE SCREENS To clean your screens, take the screens outside and rinse with a hose on both sides. Using a soft brush, lightly scrub the screens and rinse well. Set aside to dry completely, preferably upright.

PATCHING A SCREEN Repair a very small tear in metal or fiberglass screening with epoxy- or acetone-type glue. Clean the screen and layer the glue on until the tear is filled. For larger holes, trim the loose edges of the mesh with scissors. Cut a patch one inch larger all around than the hole. Remove several wires on each side of the patch and bend the protruding wires at a right angle to the patch. Center the patch over the hole in the screen, making sure the bent wires feed through screen. Bend the wires over on the reverse side to secure the patch to the screen.

TIGHTENING A SCREEN Remove the fasteners from three sides of the screen. Pull the screen taut and smooth it out. Refasten on the opposite side of the remaining fastener. Repeat for the remaining two sides.

REPLACING A SCREEN Cut the replacement screen to a size one inch wider than the frame all around.

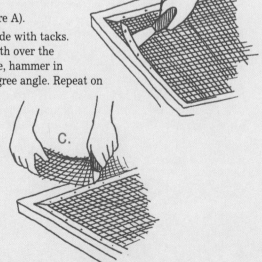

A.

For wooden frames:

1. Remove the moldings and tacks or staples (see figure A).

2. Attach the screen to the frame and secure on one side with tacks. Clamp screen in the middle and pull taut and smooth over the window opening (see figure B). On the opposite side, hammer in tacks, with the heads toward the center, at a 45-degree angle. Repeat on the remaining sides. Remove clamps.

3. Replace and refasten the moldings.

4. Trim away the excess screening falling outside the frame's edge with a utility knife (see figure C).

C.

B.

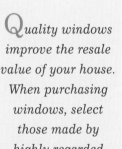

For vinyl or aluminum frames:

1. Carefully pry off the splines with a screwdriver (see figure A).

2. Trim screen corners at a 45-degree angle. Cover the opening with the replacement screen. Clamp on one side and pull taut and smooth.

3. Press in the spline on one end over the screen using a splining tool (it looks like a mini-pizza cutter) or use a slim piece of wood and hammer spline (see figure B). Remove the clamp. Pull the screen taut and smooth out. Insert the spline on the opposite side. Repeat procedure for all sides.

4. Trim away excess screen that falls over the edge (see figure C).

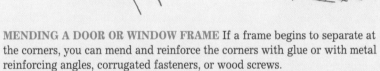

Quality windows improve the resale value of your house. When purchasing windows, select those made by highly regarded manufacturers that carry the Energy Star rating.

MENDING A DOOR OR WINDOW FRAME If a frame begins to separate at the corners, you can mend and reinforce the corners with glue or with metal reinforcing angles, corrugated fasteners, or wood screws.

1. Lay the screen or storm window on a flat surface and clean out the gap in the joint.

2. Pour waterproof glue into the joint and clamp it.

3. If the frame is still loose, attach metal reinforcing angles or corrugated fasteners at the corners, or fasten with wood screws.

Roof & Gutter

hink of your roof and gutter system as the hat of your home—the shingles are the top and the gutter system is the brim. Without one, the other could not function properly to protect your house from nature's elements. There is not only the rain to consider, but the heat and cold, leaves, snow and ice. All of these issues need to be addressed. Proper maintenance depends on your skill level. Do not attempt to do repairs on your roof if you are not sure you can do them correctly, because incorrect repairs can lead to big trouble that will affect the rest of the roof.

The Roof of Your House

Inspect and repair your roof in the fall, before the winter freeze. You should also examine the roof again in the spring, to assess any damage that may have occurred during the winter. A typical roof consists of rafters that support a roof deck (sometimes called a "subroof"). The roof deck consists of sheathing and underlayment, and provides a nailing base for the roofing. Tile, slate, metal, and plastic roofs are extremely slippery. If your house has one of these out-of-the-ordinary roofs, leave inspection and repairs to a professional.

Inspecting Your Roof from the Inside

■ Begin in the attic, using a strong flashlight, a thin screwdriver, and a piece of chalk.

■ Keep an eye out for water stains, dark-colored areas of wet wood, moisture, and soft spots that may indicate dry rot. Circle the spots with chalk.

■ On sunny days, turn off the lights and look for holes in the roof. If you find some, stick long nails through the holes so they'll be visible from the roof's exterior.

Inspecting Your Roof from the Outside

■ Don't walk on your roof more than necessary.

■ When you examine the roof from outdoors, evaluate the condition of the structure, surface material, flashings, eaves, and gutters.

■ If you see sags in the roof, call a professional. Your roof may have a structural problem.

■ Check flashings (the metal seaming around eaves and chimneys) for rust and broken seals.

■ Examine the roof surface for signs of wear, loose or broken nails, or curled, broken, or missing shingles.

■ Scrape out minor damage caused by dry rot. Treat the surface with a wood preservative, and fill the holes with wood putty. If there is extensive damage, call in a professional.

Better Downspout Drainage

Water that's allowed to flow from downspouts directly into the ground can erode the soil alongside the house, making the ground too wet and causing settling of the structure. To divert water, attach flexible plastic sleeves to the downspouts (or clay drainage pipes) to carry water to a dry well several yards from the house. You could also purchase flexible tubing with regularly spaced holes in it that attaches to the end of the downspout and distributes the water throughout your garden. This is inspired by a technique called a French drain.

Quick Help for a Leak

Roof leaks usually appear during storms when they are impossible to fix. The best step is to try to trace the course of water to find the hole (the hole is usually far from where the leak actually is). Mark the hole with chalk and stick a nail or wire up through the hole. Tie a cord from the nail and put a bucket directly under the cord. The cord will act as a wick to keep the water from dripping outside the bucket. Patch when the roof is completely dry or call in the professionals.

The Gutters

The gutter and downspout system carry water away from the house. Regular inspection and maintenance are essential for keeping your gutters and downspouts clear and in working order. Inspect them in fall and spring, and clean out the accumulated debris. Check the slope of a gutter by running water through it. If the drainage is slow, reposition the gutter for the correct slope. A gutter should slope toward the downspout at a rate of one inch for every twenty feet.

Keeping Gutters Clean

Wearing gloves, remove leaves, twigs, and other debris from gutter troughs. Loosen any dirt with a stiff brush and hose out all the debris. If a downspout is blocked with debris, spray water down it with a garden hose turned on full force. If necessary, feed a plumbers snake into the downspout and then flush all loosened debris out with the hose. Avoid debris buildup by installing some type of gutter guard such as mesh screen.

Do not jostle or remove fiberglass insulation without first checking with a professional to make sure it is safe.

Gutter Repairs

- Do not attempt to repair any damage until the rain or snow has stopped and the gutters are dry.

- Examine gutters for flaking or peeling paint, rust spots, broken hangers, and holes or leaky joints.

- Tighten loose hangers and replace broken ones. Check that the downspout straps are secured to the sides and that all elbow connections fit tightly. Thoroughly clean and patch leaky joints and holes in gutters. If a large section of your gutters is badly damaged, it will need to be replaced.

- If you have a small hole, use a putty knife to patch it with a thin coat of roofing cement. Extend the cement beyond the hole in all directions. For larger holes, half an inch and over, use a putty knife to cover the hole with roofing cement and embed a sheet metal patch in the cement. Apply another coat of cement over the patch and allow to dry completely.

- If you have a leaky joint, apply silicone sealant or caulking around the seams between sections on the inside and outside of the gutter.

Interior Walls

*T*he walls on the interior of our homes not only define the rooms, they also hold the house together. The walls can be finished with plaster, sheetrock, brick, paneling, or tile. Beneath these superficial materials, wood framing, metal studs, or cinder block provide structure, and insulation buffers temperatures, moisture, and noise. Also running behind the walls are the water and electrical systems. This makes extensive repairs to the walls tricky. Make sure you know what is behind your walls before you begin extreme changes.

Lead-based paint is a serious danger in homes with children, because exposure to lead can cause learning and behavior problems. If your home was built before 1978, it should be tested for lead contamination. You cannot remove lead-based paint yourself; you must call in a professional.

Patching & Filling

Patching Fine Cracks in Plaster and Sheetrock

1. Chisel the crack to a width of $1/8$-inch.
2. Fill the crack with spackle and smooth the edges with a putty knife.
3. When dry, sand the spackle using a block wrapped with fine-grade sandpaper.
4. Prime the patch with sealer before painting or papering.

Patching Wide Cracks

1. Undercut the crack with a chisel and a putty knife.
2. Dampen the crack with a wet sponge.
3. With a putty knife, fill up to half the area of the crack with wet plaster.
4. When the plaster has dried, rough up the surface with coarse sandpaper or steel wool.
5. Repeat the process of filling the plaster.
6. Fill with finishing plaster and scrape with a straight edge to remove excess plaster.
7. Allow to dry thoroughly.

Filling Holes

1. Sand the surface to remove loose bits of plaster, gypsum board, and wallpaper.
2. Using a scraper, fill the hole with spackle or joint compound.
3. When the spackle is thoroughly dry, sand the area.
4. Dust the surface and paint the area.

*P*lastered walls are composed of three layers: a base coat, a thick coat of plaster for strength, and a finishing coat for appearance.

Patching Paint

1. Wash down the damaged surface and allow it to dry.
2. Sand with fine-grade sandpaper until smooth.
3. Seal the area with primer.
4. Paint the area, feathering the edges to blend in the patched area.
5. If the balance of the paint is faded, you may want to paint the entire wall.

Patching Wallpaper

If the wallpaper you are patching is old, try leaving the patch in the sun for a few days to better match the surrounding paper.

1. Cut a matching patch from the wallpaper design.
2. Use thumbtacks to position the patch in line with the pattern.
3. Cut through both the patch and the wallpaper underneath using a utility knife.
4. Dampen the scored, damaged wallpaper with a wet sponge and peel it off.
5. Clean the wall and let it dry. Apply a thin layer of adhesive to the back of the wallpaper patch.
6. Position the patch carefully and smooth it down with a clean, damp cloth or a seam roller. Wipe off excess adhesive.

Replacing Ceramic Tiles

These directions apply to walls, floors, and countertops, and to tiles with a thin set mastic or mortar type adhesive, not the thick mortar bed that professionals use.

1. Match the mastic. Have on hand patching plaster to create a base for the new tile, and latex primer and grout for filling the spaces between tiles.
2. Wearing safety goggles, chip away the damaged tile and remove the surrounding grout.
3. Clean the area behind tile, removing all old adhesive and grout. Use sandpaper to smooth rough spots and dust thoroughly.
4. Fill the backing with patching plaster, if necessary, to make it level. When dry, paint with latex primer.
5. When the primer is dry apply mastic to the back of the tile with a putty knife. Keep the mastic one-half inch from the edges.
6. Center the tile and, using a hammer and wood block, gently tap it flush with the surface. Wait twenty-four hours before grouting.
7. Fill the joints with grout, using a damp sponge or cloth. Smooth the joints with a wet finger. Sponge off excess grout.

Not Again!
How Many Coats of Paint and Wallpaper Can You Layer?

PAINT Check out the walls. If you find your paint peeling and bringing up more than one layer, you need to have the wall stripped. If your paint job is bubbling in places, you may have a leak behind your wall, and won't necessarily have to have the wall stripped. As a rule of thumb, you should have the paint removed from your walls after seven to ten coatings.

WALLPAPER Old wallpaper generally needs to be removed before another application of wallpaper or paint. However, if you find that your old wallpaper has worn well and there are no bubbles or loose seams, then you can safely paper over it. But two coats is the maximum. After that, you must remove the bottom layers before applying new ones. Painting over wallpaper can be difficult. It is best to remove the paper rather than paint over it.

Floors

Floors take more abuse than any other surface in the house and require practical finishes. Permanent flooring is installed over subflooring, typically concrete or plywood. When you decide how to finish the floors throughout your rooms, be realistic about the wear and tear involved. The most common types of flooring are tile, wood, linoleum and other petro-based synthetic materials, and carpeting.

Repairing Wood Floors

Water Marks

1. Rub the marks with fine-grade steel wool and furniture paste.
2. If the marks remain, wipe away the paste with a soft cloth and rub again with steel wool and odorless mineral spirits.
3. Wipe clean and finish.

Burns

1. Burns that darken the wood's surface should be sanded.
2. Deeper burns need to be scraped out of the wood.
3. Apply wood filler or paste.
4. Finish as desired.

Warping

1. Cover the warp with a damp cloth for two days.
2. Drill pilot holes every few inches along the board.
3. Insert and tighten screws.
4. Fill the holes with wood putty and finish.

Architectural salvage is being recognized as the valuable material that it is. When older buildings are demolished, the fixtures and fittings can be removed and given new life in a fresh environment. Popular items are mantels, doors, cupboards, paneling, and even windows. Carefully removed and transported to new locations, gargoyles and frescoes bring a stylish solidity to new homes. In fact, entire shells of rooms—the flooring, the walls, and the ceilings—have been dissembled and reinstalled at other locations. (It is possible to move an entire house to a new location; based on the building itself and the distance. Prices start at $10,000.)

Patching a Carpet

1. With a utility knife, remove the damaged area in a square or rectangle. Cut through the carpet's backing, but not through the separate padding on the floor.
2. Cut a replacement that matches in pattern and pile direction.
3. Spread a thin layer of carpet adhesive under the patch and on the padding. Press the patch into place, using your fingers to fluff the pile.
4. Allow the adhesive to dry completely.

Replacing Linoleum and Vinyl Tiles

1. Warm the old floor with an iron to soften the adhesive.
2. Remove the damaged tile or linoleum with a paint scraper and hammer.
3. With a utility knife and ruler, trim sheet linoleum to a square area. Dust the surface.
4. Prepare a small amount of the grout or adhesive originally used.
5. Spread grout over the area and over the back of the patch itself.
6. Position the patch. Force a broomstick or another lever over the patch and allow it to remain until the patch is completely set.
7. Rinse off any remaining grout or adhesive.

Replacing Wood Flooring

Before starting, determine how the floors were nailed. In blind nailing, nails are driven through each board's tongue, and they don't show from the finished surface. Dots of wood putty indicate face nailing. Plugs on plank flooring often cover screws. If the plugs are just decorative, the flooring is blind nailed (some flooring secured with screws may be blind nailed as well). For any of these, you can use the following approach:

1. Lay each board in place, fitting the cut end tightly.
2. Mark the other end and saw on the waste side.
3. Slip the groove of the new board over the tongue of the board in place and blind nail.
4. Remove the tongue of the last board.
5. Tap the last board down and face nail the ends.
6. Countersink nails, fill holes with wood putty, and finish.

Fix It or Replace It?

When considering fixing an item in your home, a good rule of thumb is to rely on your instincts: if you feel a project is above your skill level, don't do it. If fixing it is within your capabilities, take the price of the item and the amount of use it receives into consideration as well. If your coffeemaker stops keeping the coffee warm, this is not a problem you want to tackle yourself. Coffeemakers are affordable, and when you use an item everyday it takes a lot of wear and tear and will most likely break again. If, however, your ice cream maker stops churning, this is a project you may enjoy looking into. If you are not mechanically inclined or know nothing about electricity, do not attempt to fix anything.

What You Can Tackle Yourself

Projects you will be able to accomplish yourself will depend not only on the problem, but also on your skills and the time you are willing to invest. Some simple maintenance and repair projects anyone can do are: wiring lamps, installing counter-top appliances, installing linoleum flooring, installing hardware for curtains and shower rods, and replacing knobs and buttons on appliances.

More advanced maintenance and repair projects are: structural repairs, installation of major appliances, tile work, and structural wiring jobs.

If I Had A Glue Gun: Quick Temporary Fixes

A glue gun can fix a wide range of problems, from a broken wooden frame to minor upholstery damage. Some of our favorite glue gun fixes are:

■ Keep felt feet on furniture ■ Keep rubber feet on tension rods ■ Put a dot on the back of a picture frame to keep it from damaging the wall and sliding around ■ Replace the leg of a chair ■ Fix broken pottery ■ Keep the gasket on the refrigerator and freezer doors secure ■ Fix faux flowers and plants ■ Fix hands of a clock ■ Replace loose ceramic tiles

When to Rent or Buy Power Tools

Power tools, such as a circular saw, an air hammer, a table saw, a power sander, and a router, are not found in most households, but they make most major jobs easier on you physically and help save time. Ask yourself: How often will I use this? How difficult is renting one? How expensive is renting one compared to buying one?

If it will be a frequently used tool and renting is expensive, you should purchase the item. If, however, this is a one-time use item, such as a concrete mixer, you will be better off renting one.

Got a big clean up or demo job? Rent a dumpster!

MOST EASILY FIXED
mechanical components

MOST DIFFICULT TO FIX
wiring element

IMPOSSIBLE TO FIX
digital components

Keep your warranties in a place where they are easily accessible, with the date of purchase, receipt, and model and serial numbers. Manufacturers realize that most people do not claim their warranties, finding it easier to replace the broken item. Do not attempt to fix anything that is still under warranty. This will negate the warranty.

The Essential Tool Kit

The art of using tools is essentially what makes us human, yet some people still get nervous over even the simplest home repair. What many don't realize is that having the proper tools is the most important step toward a better house (and a fatter wallet). We've put together the basics of a practical toobox that can give you a helping hand, even if you can't tell a screwdriver from a ratchet wrench. So before you put your local handyman on speed dial, consider investing in these.

Tools of the Trade: Basic Tools

- **ADJUSTABLE WRENCH** tightens and loosens nuts and bolts. Look for an 8-inch wrench that adjusts smoothly to about $1^1/_4$-inch for most common jobs. A locking mechanism is also good for making sure the wrench does not come free.

Adjustable Wrench

- **ASSORTED FASTENERS** box nails, finishing nails, masonry nails, wood screws, sheet-metal screws, lead or plastic scr anchors, screw-in hooks, S-hooks, eyes. ■ **ASSORTMENT OF SMALL WASHERS AND RUBBER GASKETS** small plastic bag available from the supermarket (usually with the laundry kits and vacuum-cleaner bags) for quick faucet repairs. ■ **CLAW HAMMER** removes and drives nails. A 16-ounce claw hammer is the most basic hammer to start with. However, some may prefer a different weight (like a 13-ounce) for smaller jobs or more precise work. ■ **GLUE GUN** uses hot glue as an adhesive. Glue guns are excellent for small adhesive jobs, as the glue dries fast and the gun makes maneuvering easy. ■ **HEAVY GLOVES** protect hands when working with sharp blades or cleaning tools.

- **LUBRICATING OIL** ■ **PLIERS** (slip-joint, needle-nose, tongue-and-groove) slip-joint pliers grip and turn metal pieces. Needle-nose pliers are used to turn small pieces in cramped spaces, and most come with a wire cutter for electrical repairs. Although slip-joint pliers have long been the basic pliers of choice, tongue-and-groove pliers are now considered to grip better.

Slip-joint Pliers

- **PUTTY KNIFE** spackles, scrapes, and pulls out nails. ■ **SAFETY GOGGLES** protect your eyes from any flying debris. Keep them wrapped in a cloth to prevent them being scratching in your toolbox. ■ **SANDPAPER** smoothes edges and corners. Sandpaper

Needle-nose Pliers

Purchasing Tools

With the wide array of implements and gadgets out there, it's no wonder that buying tools is almost as stressful as picking out a car. After all, a set of tools is an investment, and you want to use them as long as possible. This is why you should look for tools that fall in the mid-price range. Cheap tools will fall apart sooner, and more expensive ones are usually meant for professionals.

Sometimes the basic tools simply aren't enough. For large projects, it might be necessary to use power tools like a circular saw, sander, or power drill. If you plan on using one of these on a regular basis, go ahead and purchase it. Otherwise, research how much it is to rent these from your local home improvement or tool center. Most chains, like Home Depot, offer a tool rental program that allows you to test out tools before you purchase.

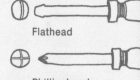
Flathead

Phillipshead

To prevent rust, clean tools with a stiff brush after every use and rub them with an oily rag. Clean rusted parts with a rust-remover on steel wool. Rub on a little oil or petroleum jelly afterward. You might want to put small tools (especially those for the garden) in a bucket of clean, dry sand, since this also will hinder rust.

comes in many different sizes and grades.
■ **SCREWDRIVERS** drive and remove screws. There are two types of screwdrivers: flathead and Phillips. A flathead has a single straight edge. Phillipsheads have a cross shape. They fit corresponding screws. A small, medium, and large size of each type of screwdriver covers all bases. Or purchase a 4-way screwdriver with an assortment of tips. ■ **TAPE MEASURE** measures dimensions. A 25-foot tape measure, with a width of 1 inch, is the most convenient. ■ **TAPE** duct, basic adhesive, electrical insulating, Teflon (for plumbing connections) ■ **UTILITY KNIFE** cuts wood, plastic, cardboard, and particleboard. Look for a retractable blade that can be replaced. ■ **WIRE CUTTERS**

Beyond the Basic

Once you've become comfortable with these basic tools, you might consider expanding your tool kit to include the following:

■ **CARPENTER'S LEVEL** accurately checks the level of horizontal or vertical surfaces. Small vials use a bubble to show whether surfaces are plumb, or "true." This has nothing to do with evenness. A surface can be perfectly smooth or even with another surface and not be truly level. Want to test a horizontal surface for slope without a level? In a pinch, you can fill a soda bottle half full of water, lay it on its side on the surface pointing lengthwise, and see if the water line is level. ■ **FILE** smoothes metal edges and surfaces. Look for a file about 10 inches long and $1^1/_8$-inch wide, with a rounded and a flat side. ■ **HACKSAW** a bow-shaped manual saw that cuts through metal and wood. An all-purpose blade with 18 teeth per inch is a good tool to start with. ■ **HANDSAW** cuts wood. A small one will fit in your toolbox and be easy to maneuver. A thick blade with 12 teeth to an inch is the best basic model. ■ **NAILSET** drives nailheads below the wood surface. ■ **PUSH DRILL** hand-drills small holes in wood and plastic. ■ **RATCHET WRENCH AND SOCKETS** removes tightly bolted nuts with a crank mechanism and socket. ■ **WOOD CHISEL** trims wood pieces. A $1/_2$-inch wood chisel is useful, but be careful of the very sharp edge.

Level

Nail Set

Hacksaw

Push Drill

Wood Chisel

Where's It All Gonna Go?

Although a toolbox is the storage container of choice for many people, if you're not keen on having a big, clunky metal box around, consider using a heavy canvas bag with a closable opening and a stiff bottom. Or a large plastic storage container. A kid's lunch box will work for a small number of tools. Distribute chalk pieces among your tools: they absorb rust-promoting moisture. Keep your nails and screws in baby food or jam jars. And don't store tools in damp places.

Bathroom Repairs

The bathroom is one of the busiest places in the house, so when something goes wrong in there you'll want to fix it, and fix it fast! Fortunately, with a little help from the plumber's best friend, the plunger, you'll be maintaining the flow of bathroom traffic in no time. Although some repairs need professional attention, here are some simple things you can do to take care of the most common problems.

Unclog a Toilet

1. Turn off the water using the shut-off valve, usually located behind the lower part of the toilet.

2. If bowl is full, bail out water until it's half full. Or fill bowl to more than half full by adding water. Place the plunger over the drain hole and pump a dozen times to get good suction going. If you're unable to get a good grip, try applying a thin layer of petroleum jelly to the plunger rim first. This should suck the obstacle through the drain hole.

3. Follow with some more water from a cup or bucket to make sure obstacle is gone. Turn water valve back on.

4. If you are still having problems, you may need to use a closet auger on the pipe. This twisted item can be found at hardware stores. Follow the instructions when using.

5. Don't use drain cleaners on toilets, since it can collect in pipe curves and damage the toilet.

6. Make sure you have a wastebasket available so people are less inclined to throw trash in the toilet.

Fix a Running Toilet

A running toilet is loud and wastes a lot of water, so it's best to take care of it when you first notice the problem.

1. Remove the lid of the toilet tank and check the water level. It should be about an inch below where the tube begins on the overflow pipe. If it is too low or too high, this is probably what's causing the problem.

2. If you have a float arm device (a metal arm has a rubber hollow ball on the end), slightly bend arm downward to bring water level down, or upward to bring it up. Plastic arms can usually be adjusted where they connect. If the hollow ball has water in it, it has a leak and needs to be replaced.

Float Device

Dripping faucet driving you crazy? Tie a piece of string around the mouth and trail it to the drain. Water will noiselessly follow the string.

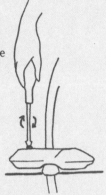

3. If you have a float cup device, you'll have to slide the metal clip to the side of the apparatus up or down to regulate the water level. Flush and check if the level comes back to normal and stops running.

4. If you have a metered fill valve, you'll need to use a screwdriver to turn the screw on the fill valve clockwise to raise water levels, counterclockwise to lower it. Don't overtighten, or you could crack the screw.

5. If your tank continues to run constantly, you might have to replace the toilet flapper (that black rubber item that covers and uncovers the drain hole) or the fill valve itself.

Unclog The Bathtub

Nothing will clog up a drain like hair and soap pieces, so make sure to use drain baskets and clean them out often.

1. Insert needle-nose pliers into two holes of the strainer and turn counterclockwise to remove. Remove accumulation and run water. Replace strainer by turning clockwise to tighten.

2. If you have a pop-up drain stopper, loosen and remove stopper by turning counterclockwise. Clear of any obstacles. Run water to see if drain clears, and then replace stopper.

3. If the tub is still clogged, remove stopper or drainer as described above. Remove the overflow cover (on that little hole just below the faucet) with a screwdriver, and stuff with a rag. Using a plunger, place over the bathtub drain and fill tub so water covers most of the plunger head. Pump a dozen times. This should unclog the drain and allow water to run out. Don't forget to replace the overflow cover and stopper/drainer.

4. You might want to follow with a cup of baking soda and some boiling water to clear away any additional debris.

Plumbing

We need it, we want it, we want it to behave. Our forefathers would be astounded at the hot and cold running water we take for granted. And they would be flabbergasted to learn that most plumbing problems are the result of carelessness. The cost of an ounce of prevention pales in comparison to a bill from a plumber, and whether you own or rent, whether your pipes are antique or new, whether you are a man or a woman, you should take care of your plumbing. Beneath every sink you will find a cold-water line, a hot-water line, shut-off valves, and a wastewater pipe. When a clog presents itself, you must deal with the wastewater pipe. The sink that's clogged may be a clue to the nature of a bigger problem. Kitchen and work-room sinks carry the heaviest load; bathroom sinks tend to clog less often, and powder room sinks rarely spit up. Assume a positive attitude, assess the situation, and take action.

If the drain has been treated with an agent such as a de-clogger, do not try to remove the trap yourself. Bring in a plumber and be direct about the techniques and materials you've used. Commercial de-cloggers are highly toxic, and must be used according to manufacturers' directions. Always wear latex gloves and be sure the bathroom is well ventilated.

1. If the cause is unknown, start with the simplest approach. Empty the sink of standing water. Bring a quart of water to a boil, add $1/4$ cup of ammonia to the water, and pour this down the drain. After 15 minutes, flush the drain to see if it's still clogged.

2. Most sink drains have strainers; remove this and pour several inches of hot water into the sink. Cover the drain completely with the rubber cup of a plunger. Force the cup up and down several times; remove the plunger and see if the clog has been cleared. If not, repeat the process several times more.

3. When you know the plunger will not do and there is no water in the sink, examine the trap (the U-shaped section of the waste pipe). At the bottom of the trap, if you're lucky, is a "plug nut." You want to unscrew this large nut to get access inside the pipe. Place a bucket or container under the trap. Fit an adjustable wrench around the plug nut and rotate counterclockwise. Remove the plug nut and see if you can reach inside to remove the clog. Run a little water through the trap into the bucket to clean it out, replace the plug nut, tighten it down securely, and congratulate yourself.

4. If your trap does not have a plug nut, you'll have to remove the pipe. With the bucket in place, use a large wrench to loosen the fittings or ring nuts at either end of the trap. Remove any rubber gaskets at the joints. Clean the clog from the trap and re-assemble the plumbing.

5. If the trap is not clogged, or the clog cannot be cleaned out, it's best to call a plumber.

Commercial drain cleaners are highly toxic and volatile. Unclogging a drain need not involve toxic plumbing formulas. Follow the simple steps on this page and demystify what's under your sink.

Save the Planet

A drip from a sink spout with a worn-out washer or tap may not seem urgent, but it is. One drop every second can, in 24 hours, add up to more than six gallons. And if that drop is coming from the hot-water line, you're overburdening the water heater and wasting energy. A trip to the hardware store for a simple replacement part is much less costly, both to you and the environment.

Troubleshooting your Refrigerator

■ If your refrigerator surface is sweating, it may be because the inner temperature is too low. Try 40° F. If temperature isn't cold enough, make sure the refrigerator coils in back are properly vacuumed and that air circulates freely around food.

■ Make sure your fridge gasket (the lining around the door) seals tightly when the door is closed.

■ A fridge may make noise because of a loose shelf or a floor surface that is not level. Check for any rattling shelves when the unit goes on. Use a level to see if the fridge is correctly balanced. Adjust the feet if necessary.

Kitchen Repairs

Appliances make up a large part of your kitchen, so it's important to keep them running. After all, if something goes wrong, you might not be eating for a while! Follow these helpful hints for dealing with some of the biggest machines that occupy your kitchen.

Clearing a Garbage Disposal

Loud grinding and other noises usually indicate a jammed disposal system, so take care of it as soon as you hear something different.

1. First turn off the disposal and look inside to see if you can locate the jammed article. Remove carefully with tongs and turn back on.

2. If your disposal has a reversal feature, run the cold water function and try this feature. It will operate the shredder in reverse, which could dislodge the item.

3. If you don't have a reversal function, turn the main power off. Stick a broomstick handle into the disposal, resting it against the blades. Turn the handle to clear obstructions. Remove all clogged items and the broom handle. Turn on the power and run the cold water function for a few minutes to make sure it's clear. You may have to press a reset button on the disposal.

Maintaining the Dishwasher

- If your dishwasher doesn't drain, try cleaning the filter screen.

- If you find your dishes are not getting clean, check the water heater temperature. It should be set at 120° F. If it is too low, it might be what's causing gunk to stay on dishes.

- Test the actual temperature of the machine by opening the dishwasher during the first cycle. Use a meat thermometer to test the water at the bottom of the dishwasher (be very, very careful!!!) Or let water collect in a glass and place the thermometer in that. If there's a major discrepancy between this temperature and the water heater, you may have to contact a repair service.

- You may need to clean the spray arm. Check to see if the arm is moving properly by opening in the middle of the cycle and checking the position. To clean the arm, remove the racks, unscrew the holding cap, and remove the arm. Unclog the holes and flush well before reinstalling.

- Make sure you are loading your dishwasher correctly. Improperly stacked dishes could be leaving your dinner items dirty. See page 47 for loading tips.

If a lot of frost is building up in your freezer, make sure the door is sealing properly. Frost can obstruct a power unit, so make sure to defrost your freezer regularly.

Sewing Kit

Sewing is not only a time-honored and comforting tradition, but also a practical way to save and maintain garments. Even if you've never seen yourself as a seamstress, it's a good idea to keep a handy sewing kit around for last-minute repairs: fixing tears, sewing on buttons, and making hem changes. And with our quick overview of basic stitches, you might surprise yourself at how well you can keep clothes with a little bit of tender sewing care.

Basic Sewing Kit Ingredients

- Assorted-size needles and pins (safety and straight) ■ Needle threader ■ Tape measure ■ Small, sharp scissors ■ Spools of black, white, and "invisible" thread ■ Thimble ■ Buttons (black and white) ■ Iron-on invisible mending tape for hems ■ Small magnet for picking up stray needles and pins ■ Pin holder/cushion

Basic Sewing Stitches

RUNNING STITCH Push a threaded needle in and out in a straight line about $1/4$ inch apart. Try to keep the stitch size and distance between even. Place a knot in the thread when you are finished.

BACK STITCH stronger than a running stitch and the closest thing to machine-stitching. First, make a running stitch. At the middle of the running stitch, bring the needle back down and make another running stitch (beginning at the middle of the previous one). This new stitch should extent halfway past the old stitch. At the middle of the new running stitch, bring the needle back down and make another equal size stitch. In this way, you'll always be starting a stitch in the middle of a previous stitch. This produces smaller, more closely linked stitches.

OVERCAST STITCH used on edges of material to prevent fraying. Pull the needle through about $1/8$ inch from the edge of the cloth. Then loop it over the edge and pull the needle through from the back again, beginning another stitch. Repeat, keeping stitches close together in a spiral pattern all along the edge of the material. Make sure not to pull stitches tight or the fabric will bunch up.

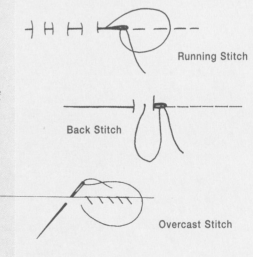

Running Stitch

Back Stitch

Overcast Stitch

How to Sew on a Button

1. Remove a broken or old button by sliding a comb between it and the fabric. Lift the button up and then cut the exposed threads.

2. Thread a needle, making sure the length isn't too long or it will become tangled. Tie a knot at the ends of the thread.

3. Hold the button in place on the fabric. Push the needle up through one hole on the button and then back through the opposite hole.

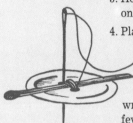

4. Place a matchstick between the button and thread. This will insure there is enough room for the button to move a little without snapping the thread. Continue to sew in and out of the holes. After about ten passes, remove the matchstick and wrap thread around the bottom of the button a few times.

5. Push the needle back to underside of garment. Make a few stitches, then knot and cut off excess.

6. Make sure buttons don't come loose by dabbing a bit of clear nail polish or superglue on the exposed threads.

How to Hand-Sew a Hem

1. Remove old hem if present. Try on the garment and make a mark where you'd like the new hem to be. Fasten it with straight pins and press the hem. Then try it on again just to be sure.

Rub a little bit of soap on thread ends to make them easier to thread.

2. Trim away excess material, leaving three inches of fabric. Turn under $1/4$ inch and press.

3. Place the garment inside out in front of you with the fold closest to you. Using a hemming stitch, insert the tip of a threaded needle facing away from you, just below the raw edge of the hem. Push the tip through the inside layer of fabric, and then hold it so it just takes a tiny bite of the outside fabric a little above the edge. Pull the needle through and repeat. This will make a slanted stitch. Don't pull the stitches too tight or the garment will bunch, and make sure your stitches are even and not too far apart. When you have gone around the entire garment, knot securely and trim excess thread.

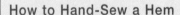

Hemming Stitch

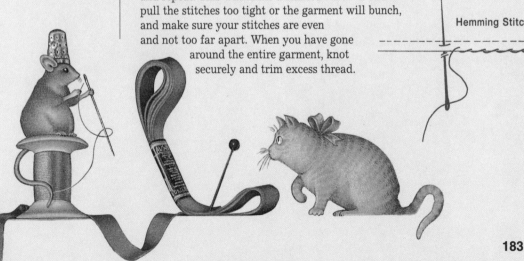

183

Home Safety

According to a report conducted by the Home Safety Council, Americans make approximately 20 million hospital visits each year due to accidents in the home. These are frightening statistics, especially since we typically think of our homes as the safest places in our lives. Fortunately, many home accidents can be prevented. By taking precautions and educating families, we can sidestep a wide variety of household disasters.

General Accident Prevention

■ Make sure you have well-maintained and sufficient lighting in hallways and staircases. Attach a strip of reflector tape to the top and bottom steps of your basement stairway to help people find the steps easily. All staircases should have sturdy railings.

■ Stop rugs from slipping by attaching non-slip backing strips to the underside of all rugs, and make sure carpet is firmly nailed down and without any tears.

■ Keep electrical cords close to the wall, not under the carpet, as the bump could cause falls.

■ Make sure you don't overload a wall socket, and that all cords are well wrapped—not damaged or frayed.

■ Use non-slip rubber mats in the bathtub, and have a non-slipping rug on the floor outside the tub. If you have an elderly person in your household, it's important to have a secure handrail in the shower to make getting in and out easier.

■ You should never have electronic appliances near running or standing water—even cordless items!

■ Have an emergency list with contact information for fire, police, poison control centers, personal relations, doctors, and the hospital emergency room posted near your home's primary telephone.

Kitchen Safety

Safety is important in every room of the house, but especially in the kitchen, where things can get dangerous very quickly. From burns to cuts to food contamination, it's important to practice awareness and organization when preparing, cooking, and serving food. Before you resign yourself to a life of ordering takeout, consider the following helpful hints to make your kitchen the cozy and safe heart of your home.

Stove/Oven

■ Prevent spills by making sure all cookware handles face inward, but not over any other burners.

■ Try to use the rear burners as much as possible, especially if you have small children in the house.

■ Make sure the range top is cool before cleaning. You can get burned from using a wet sponge on a hot range.

■ Adjust oven racks before you turn the oven on.

Appliances

■ Keep cords unplugged and away from water.

■ Never use a metal utensil to loosen bread from a toaster while it is turned on or plugged in. You can receive a very bad shock.

■ Fill a blender only halfway when mixing hot liquids, and blend at the lowest speed. This will minimize the risk of the liquid spurting out due to steam pressure.

■ Kitchen blades can cause many accidents if improperly handled. Store knives and other sharp utensils so that you can grab them by their handles. Take the blade out of the food processor before emptying its contents.

■ Smoke detectors are important in the kitchen area. Use a photoelectric model, and you won't have to worry about false alarms from steam and cooking fumes.

Most fires that occur in the kitchen are caused by grease. Don't use water to put out a grease fire, as it might spread the flames or splatter grease on you. Instead, put a lid or wet towel on the pot, or throw salt, baking soda, or flour on the flames. Investing in a small fire extinguisher is another inexpensive way to insure kitchen safety. See page 186 for fire safety in the kitchen.

Toxic Kitchens?

Recently experts have noted high levels of emissions from a chemical called PFOA in kitchens. This chemical is used in nonstick coatings and can be released into the environment when such surfaces are overheated. The fumes can cause flu-like symptoms in humans, and can sicken or kill pets. They kill pet birds almost instantly. To avoid this hazard, don't use metal tools with coatings. If you do have nonstick pans, avoid harsh scrubbing. Also, don't reheat food in fast food wrappings or boxes, since they also contain chemicals that can give off noxious fumes.

Fire Safety

I n the blink of an eye, a fire at home can wipe out belongings and heirlooms that took a lifetime to collect. You can drastically reduce your likelihood of fire damage by installing and maintaining smoke detectors and creating an emergency escape plan. The sooner a fire is detected, the greater your chances are for keeping your house and loved ones safe.

■ Install a smoke detector on each level of your house. Regularly dust or vacuum them every four weeks, and test them periodically, either by pressing a test button or holding a smoking, extinguished candle up to them. Replace batteries promptly: Most detectors emit a beeping or chirping sound when batteries become weak. Replace smoke detectors about once a decade.

S ome homeowners keep a fire blanket on hand to smother any small fires that might break out. Automatic sprinkler systems, required by code in some commercial buildings, also are becoming popular in homes where escape is not easy. The cost of one of these systems is substantial.

■ Create an emergency escape plan: The ideal home will have two exits per room (it could be a door and a window); if this is not possible, you might consider other measures discussed here, like fire blankets or keeping a phone in the less accessible room. If you live on the second floor, consider investing in an emergency fire ladder. Make sure your whole family knows what to do and where to meet outside once they leave the house, and that they must never go back into a burning building.

■ If you become trapped in a room, try to seal off all vents and duct openings with towels or blankets. Open a window, but be sure to close it if smoke builds (fire feeds on oxygen). Hang a brightly colored cloth in the window to signal to outsiders where you are. If a phone is available, call 911 and give your exact location.

Fire Safety in the Kitchen

GREASE FIRE Never pour water on a grease fire. Use a fire extinguisher, baking soda, or flour to quench the flame.

POT FIRE Throw a wet dish towel over it or put the lid on; turn off the burner.

FIRES IN OVENS, BROILERS, AND MICROWAVES Keep door closed and turn off appliance. Make sure flame goes out before attempting to remove food.

ELECTRICAL FIRES Use a fire extinguisher made for use on electrical fires; don't use water. Avoid electrical fires by making sure all appliance cords are intact, not frayed, and wall sockets have not been overloaded. Each major appliance should have its own outlet.

Fireplace Safety
■ Don't use lighter fluid to start a fire. ■ Don't burn coal, trash paper, cardboard, or scrap wood. ■ Don't leave a fire unattended. ■ Don't keep paper or stacks of firewood too close to the blaze (about five feet away is good). ■ Always keep a screen in front of the fire. ■ Keep a fire extinguisher on hand. ■ Build small manageable fires rather than large ones. They use less energy and actually create more heat.

Helpful Websites
www.redcross.org
www.nfpa.org
(National Fire Protection Association)
www.homesafety council.org

the kitchen fire.

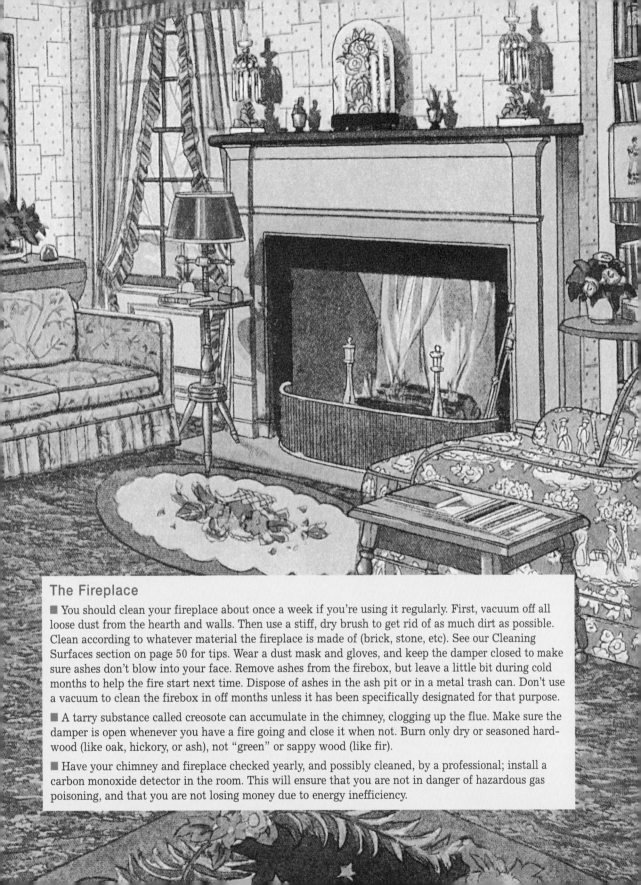

The Fireplace

■ You should clean your fireplace about once a week if you're using it regularly. First, vacuum off all loose dust from the hearth and walls. Then use a stiff, dry brush to get rid of as much dirt as possible. Clean according to whatever material the fireplace is made of (brick, stone, etc). See our Cleaning Surfaces section on page 50 for tips. Wear a dust mask and gloves, and keep the damper closed to make sure ashes don't blow into your face. Remove ashes from the firebox, but leave a little bit during cold months to help the fire start next time. Dispose of ashes in the ash pit or in a metal trash can. Don't use a vacuum to clean the firebox in off months unless it has been specifically designated for that purpose.

■ A tarry substance called creosote can accumulate in the chimney, clogging up the flue. Make sure the damper is open whenever you have a fire going and close it when not. Burn only dry or seasoned hardwood (like oak, hickory, or ash), not "green" or sappy wood (like fir).

■ Have your chimney and fireplace checked yearly, and possibly cleaned, by a professional; install a carbon monoxide detector in the room. This will ensure that you are not in danger of hazardous gas poisoning, and that you are not losing money due to energy inefficiency.

Home Protection

A burglary occurs in America about once every 15 seconds. Make sure your house doesn't fall victim by securing all known entry points and being aware of your surroundings. You don't have to go overboard when it comes to deterring robberies. By taking steps to secure your home, you'll be protecting your cherished belongings and gaining valuable peace of mind.

Key Areas of Entry

Doors

■ Obviously hollow doors are a lot easier to break down than metal or solid core doors. Replace any exterior hollow-core wood or particleboard doors with ones made of stronger materials. Hinges should be durable and well maintained, and doors should open inward.

■ Exterior doors should have at least two high-quality locks on them: one that cannot be opened without a key, like a dead bolt, and a police-rated chain lock or bar lock. Having two locks lends added security, giving you more time if one lock has already been breached.

■ Consider installing a peephole. That way you'll always know whether the person waiting for you on the front step is a friend or a stranger (or a door-to-door salesperson).

■ Make sure the back door of your house is as secure as the front door.

■ Have a kitchen entry that worries you? A poor-man's alarm can be created from readily available items. Hang a set of wind chimes from the ceiling near the door. Attach a length of cotton line to the chimes and tie a cup hook to the other end. At night, attach the cup hook to the door lock. Even the slightest tampering with the knob from outside will ring the chimes. A louder alternative is to rig the line to a bicycle alarm.

Windows

■ Ideally, all windows should have locks, but windows on the ground and basement levels and close to drainpipes need special attention, since they are highly accessible. These windows should be locked just as doors are when you leave the house.

■ Secure a double-hung window by drilling a hole through the top of the lower sash into the bottom of the upper one at each corner. Insert a large ($1/4$ inch or $3/8$ inch diameter) bolt with an eye on the end at each hole through the entire thickness of both sashes; the eye provides a handle that allows you to easily pull each bolt out enough to open the window. Black eyebolts look better than regular steel. Make sure

Burglar Alarms: Are They Worth It?

If you live in an area with a large amount of break-ins, or have many valuables in your home, you may want to invest in a private security system. Weigh all your options before buying a system: Make sure the company you choose is nationally certified and check with the Better Business Bureau and local police department for credentials. The National Burglar & Fire Alarm Association has an informative website at *www.alarm.org*.

Invest in "fake" valuables hiders, like hollow soup cans or other deceptive objects.

Home Protection

Before you get a high-tech security system or a menacing guard dog, start home protection with something as easy as introducing yourself to the neighborhood. Neighbors are more likely to notify police when they see suspicious activity around your premises if they are familiar with you and your schedule. Getting to know your neighbors also can make it easier to find someone to check on your house or apartment when you are away. Join your neighborhood watch or block association, if there is one.

that the hole you drill is slightly larger than it needs to be; you don't want to have to screw the bolts in, as unscrewing them would take too much time in case of fire. An alternative is to insert the bolts through only the thickness of the upper sash, about 9 inches above the lower sash. This allows the window to be opened only partially from the bottom, preventing an intruder from entering. Or you might invest in keyed sash locks.

Garages & Sheds

■ Burglars can easily gain entry to a house through an attached garage. Make sure garage doors are in good working condition, and that the door leading into your house from the garage has sturdy locks on it.

■ Sheds should be locked to deter thieves from stealing equipment or tools. A heavy padlock is the best bet, since combination locks can easily be picked. Always make sure ladders are locked up, not left where burglars can get to them.

Let There Be Light

Another way to deter would-be thieves is to keep your property well lit. Motion-activated lights are excellent. Consider the maximum amount of area the light can cover without becoming an annoyance to neighbors or turning you property into a beacon. Set lights on timers, giving the illusion you are home when you are away. Keep doors, steps, and pathways well lit. Even if thieves don't thank you, guests will.

Childproofing

To effectively childproof any room in the house, it is better to err by over-doing. You cannot underestimate how much mischief the most innocent child can get into quickly. View your house from a child's point of view. This means actually getting down and crawling on the floor. You might feel silly, but you'll be amazed at the hazards you'll discover.

General Tips

■ Use nightlights to illuminate floors and minimize nocturnal accidents. ■ A baby monitor in the bedroom will keep you alert to your young child's activities. ■ Remove all glass-topped furniture or, if you must keep it, make sure corners are padded and the item is made from shatterproof safety glass. ■ Use outlet covers on all unused electrical sockets. ■ Anchor all top-heavy furniture to the wall. This includes anything that can tip over under extra weight like a climbing child. ■ Get rid of any possibly poisonous houseplants. (*See page 147.*) Make sure harmless plants are out of reach of children. ■ Don't use long drapery cords or window curtains. Children can trip or even become entangled in them. ■ Don't put a crib next to a window, even if the glass is reinforced. ■ Install safety gates at the top and bottom of stairways. ■ Keep windows and outer doors locked at all times.

The Bathroom

An adult should supervise young children in the bathroom and bathtub at all times. ■ Dissemble the bathroom door lock in favor of a hook and eye installed higher up. Try one on each side of the door—one to keep baby from getting into the bathroom when no one is in there, and one to keep baby out when it is occupied. ■ Remove electrical appliances and fixtures. Unplug them after each use. Store them away, where they cannot be retrieved by a wee one. ■ Bring in a stepping stool to help a youngster reach the sink on his own. ■ Keep soaps and shampoos that are child-friendly obvious and within reach. ■ Replace glass drinking glasses with plastic ones. ■ Keep glass bottles and other breakables out of reach.

The Kitchen

■ Keep cleaning supplies in a high up location, like the top shelf of a closet. ■ Invest in cabinet locks. ■ Keep sharp utensils and appliances stored safely away. ■ Utilize back stove burners and turn pot handles away from the edge of the stove to make sure pots can't be pulled down. Likewise, try not to use a tablecloth around very young children. ■ Use plastic containers rather than glass. ■ Unplug all appliances and wind up cords when not in use.

Common Household Poisons

■ Adhesives and toxic glues ■ Bleach ■ Cleaners: oven, drain, toilet, tile, wood, and metal ■ Fixatives and solvents ■ Furniture stain ■ Insect spray ■ Mothballs ■ Mouse traps ■ Oil-based paint ■ Paint thinner, turpentine and furniture strippers

For a more complete listing, check the Environmental Protection Agency's website at *www.epa.gov.*

Accidental poisoning is one of the most frequent home accidents. Store medications securely. When disposing of medicine, flush tablets and liquid down the toilet, instead of placing them in a garbage can where they can be found.

For additional child safety tips:
■ *www.redcross.org* ■ *www.childsafetyexperts.com* ■ *www.safekids.org* ■ *www.homesafetycouncil.org*

Water Purity Systems

Health experts agree that you should drink about eight glasses of water a day to maintain health. But depending on how clean that water is, you could be doing more harm to your body than good. Various contaminants can seep into water supplies, causing bad taste, odor, and even health problems. Luckily, there are many water treatment options available to the public today. By understanding what's in your water, you can decide on the best solution, whether it's a full-house system or a pitcher water filter.

The NSF International Public Health and Safety Company has a useful database for choosing a certified water treatment product for your particular problem at their website, *www.nsf.org/Certified/DWTU*

Your local municipal water supplier filters out most hazardous elements, but some chemicals like chlorine, lead, nitrates, and even arsenic can find their way into your home water supply. Unless you receive water from a well, it is unlikely that your water is too contaminated, but you might feel more comfortable with a water treatment system that will refine the water further. Although you can conduct your own test at home using a water kit, the water utility company can easily provide you with a list of contaminants and the amounts present in your community's water. This information is usually posted on their website, or you can contact them directly and ask for an annual water-quality report. Once you know what kinds of contaminants are present and at what level, you can take steps to finding the best water treatment system for you.

Two Basic Types

Water treatment options are divided into point-of-entry and point-of-use systems:

POINT-OF-ENTRY SYSTEMS are designed for the whole house and treat most of the water coming into the home. An example of this system is a water-softening device.

POINT-OF-USE SYSTEMS treat only the water coming through a single household tap. These are good if your untreated water is okay for bathing and laundry. Point-of-use systems include faucet mounted drinking-water filters, plumbed-in filters (usually connected to an existing water pipe under the sink), and pitcher filters.

While point-of-use systems are generally cheaper, they don't provide as much coverage as point-of-entry setups. Decide how much treatment coverage you think your house needs and then focus on that particular system.

Water Treatment Systems

ADSORPTION FILTERING Carbon, charcoal, or ceramic filters cause contaminants to adhere to them, thus removing them from the water. Filters can usually remove chlorine problems and certain chemicals and

Well Warning

If you receive your water from a private well, it's advisable to have your water tested regularly by a professional, and seek advice about what treatment system will work best for you. Get more information at the Well Owner website (*www.wellowner.org*) and the Water Quality Association (*www.wqa.org*).

pesticides. Inexpensive, they need to be changed regularly.

DISTILLATION Water is heated to boiling, which turns it into a vapor. The vapor is then collected and condensed back to liquid, leaving many contaminants behind. Distilling works well for fighting bacteria, lead, and arsenic, but it uses a tremendous amount of energy.

REVERSE OSMOSIS Water is forced under pressure through a membrane to change it from a more concentrated form to a more diluted one. Although reverse osmosis is effective against arsenic, lead, and parasitic disease carriers called cysts, it needs a very large amount of water to work correctly.

ULTRAVIOLET TREATMENT Ultraviolet light is used to disinfect water. This is especially good for high levels of bacteria, like those found in well water.

WATER SOFTENING Using sodium or potassium chloride, these systems reduce the amount of hardness in the water caused by calcium or magnesium. Although this does not combat contaminants, it does improve quality.

No matter what treatment system you choose, always make sure that it is labeled to treat your particular water concerns and is certified by NSF International.

The Fluoride Controversy

Since the 1950s, fluoride has been added to many states' water supplies. Although fluoride was originally intended to help battle tooth decay in America, many medical organizations are now saying that it is no longer necessary (since fluoride can be provided through diet and hygiene) and may actually cause health problems, like fluorosis and bone damage. If you are concerned about fluoride in your drinking supply and want to review both sides of the argument, contact the American Dental Association at *www.ada.org*, and the Fluoride Action Network at *www.fluoridealert.org*.

Bottled vs. Tap Water

Bottled water is popular and convenient, but how much cleaner is it than what comes out of your faucet? Bottled water can come from various sources: groundwater, mineral water, springwater, well water, and even municipal suppliers. Although bottled-water companies may use more stringent treatment methods, the main difference between tap and its more expensive cousin is that tap water is usually treated with chlorine, which can leave an aftertaste. Bottled waters usually taste "cleaner" because they have been treated with ultraviolet light or ozone.

Clear Air

W aking up with itchy eyes, dry skin, chapped lips, and a scratchy throat may be how you picture starting your day with a case of the flu. But surprisingly, these symptoms could all be caused by the quality of air in your home. By identifying what your air is missing (or what it has too much of) you can decide if purchasing an appliance like a humidifier, dehumidifier, or air purifier is right for you.

Air Purifiers

trap pet dander, dust, smoke, and pollen particles. They usually come in two forms: the filter type and the electrostatic precipitator (which draws air in through an electrical field that attracts and holds foreign particles).

DRAWBACKS: Air cleaners do not reduce levels of carbon monoxide, dust mites, odors, or viruses, and may be beneficial only to people suffering from pre-existing respiratory problems (like asthma). Electrostatic precipitators contain levels of ozone. Some air purifiers make noise when running, which can be distracting. The EPA states that an air purifier should be used only if all other forms of indoor air-pollution prevention have failed.

ADVICE: If you find an air purifier is necessary and you have a forced air heating/cooling system, you might want to install a whole-house system. The costs are high, but this system is the most effective for attacking large particles in the air. Otherwise, choose a room air cleaner that's for an area slightly bigger. That way you can run it on the lowest setting and save money on utilities. Systems with HEPA filters are the most highly recommended for reducing air-borne allergens.

C heck the efficiency and performance ratings of air-purifying appliances at the Association of Home Appliance Manufacturers' website, www.aham.org.

Dehumidifiers

absorb excess moisture from the air. They can reduce the concentration of toxic mold (black mold that grows in insulation and on walls), which can aggravate allergies. If your window panes "sweat," the humidity in your house is too high and you are creating ideal living conditions for mildew and mold spores.

DRAWBACKS: Refrigeration coils are prone to attract dirt. Condensation pan needs to be emptied consistently.

ADVICE: Purchase one with auto-shutdown, automatic defrost, and humidistat controls. Keep windows and doors shut to maximize dehumidifying power. Disassemble and clean apparatus at least once per season.

Keep a humidifier working for you

- Empty water tray and clean humidifier daily, or at least weekly.

- Sanitize your tank weekly by filling the tank with a solution of a teaspoon of bleach to a gallon of water. Let it sit for 20 minutes, then wash it out thoroughly.

- Use distilled water to cut back on white-dust production.

- Sanitize and dry your machine before packing it away for the season.

Humidifiers add moisture to the air through evaporation, steam, warm/cool mist, or ultrasound (transformation of water droplets into fine mist through high-frequency vibration). These products minimize static electricity and make the air feel warmer in the winter. They may help relieve congestion in cold and allergy sufferers; some can even dispense a medicinal vapor.

DRAWBACKS: If not maintained, they can actually spread bacteria and mold, and encourage dust-mite growth through excessive moisture or dirty water solutions. Using tap water containing chemical elements can also cause humidifiers to disperse "white dust" film throughout your house.

ADVICE: Ultrasonic and steam humidifiers seem to be the safest, as the mist provided by these machines usually has little mold or bacteria present. Look for HEPA filters in portable room models. Avoid ozone generators, as they may produce a sharp chemical smell, and release unhealthy levels of ozone into the air. Purchase a humidifier with auto-shutdown and humidistat controls to allow you to monitor the level of humidity. This will minimize the risk of accumulating too much moisture in your house. A humidifier with a wide tank opening will be easier to clean. Make sure your house has "vapor barrier" insulation (a reflective layer of material on the room side of the type of insulation used in most homes since 1950); otherwise, humidity could be lost through your walls and the system won't be as effective.

The Bottom Line

Even if you're certain your home is too dry or too damp, or that you really need an air purifier, there are steps you can take to clean your home's air before you start shopping for an appliance:

1. Ventilate rooms and make sure ductwork and ventilation systems are clean and in working order. Exhaust fans can eliminate most damaging levels of moisture. Empty air-conditioner and refrigerator water trays, and clean, dry, or discard water-damaged rugs and carpet.

2. Keep your house well swept, dusted, and vacuumed. This doesn't mean becoming a slave to your cleaning schedule—just be sure to clean your house regularly, especially when you see dust building up.

3. Leave a pot or large bowl of water on your radiator or floor vent during the winter, and refill it daily. It could add just the amount of moisture that your house needs.

4. Houseplants work well to clean indoor air and release moisture.

5. Follow the steps given on page 196 to remove the dangers of indoor pollution caused by hazardous gases.

Hazardous Gases

It's easy to take precautions when dealing with a visible threat in your house—like faulty wall sockets or broken windows—but many hazards can go unseen by you for years and still affect the health and happiness of the members of your household.

ASBESTOS was used in building materials like sheetrock, roofing, insulation, tile, and ducts before 1985. When it deteriorates, it releases a cancer-causing dust.

■ If asbestos remains intact and in good condition, leave it alone. ■ If you notice broken linoleum, ripped insulation, or chipped exterior paint, consult a professional. ■ A professional can advise whether you must have asbestos removed or if it is possible to seal it over.

CARBON MONOXIDE can be present in your house in fuel emissions from un-vented leaky furnaces, fireplaces, gas stoves, kerosene lamps, and running cars.

■ Install a carbon-monoxide detector in your house near the central heating system. ■ Do not use kerosene lamps indoors. ■ Do not leave cars running in an enclosed garage. ■ Use exhaust hoods or fans above gas stoves. To determine if a stove is working properly, check the flame: It should be blue. ■ Have the fireplace and central heating system regularly cleaned by a professional. Repair all leaks.

FORMALDEHYDE fumes are released from pressed-wood items, like particleboard, and various household items, like carpeting, insulation, some paints, and permanent-press fabrics. It is also contained in cigarette smoke.

■ Testing can be expensive, so contact your local health department. ■ Remove older furniture you suspect of containing formaldehyde. ■ Seal up cracks around floors and electrical outlets to stop formaldehyde fumes from insulation from seeping in. ■ Coatings can partially block fumes, so consider using sealant or varnish on exposed suspected surfaces. ■ Combat high temperatures and humidity (since these aggravate fumes) with cooling devices. ■ For new construction, use exterior-grade plywood. ■ Recommend people smoke outside the house.

LEAD is most commonly found in pre-1980s house paint, especially on metal surfaces and around windows. Lead pipes are another source. When lead paint flakes and peels, it releases harmful, breathable dust into the air.

■ Conduct a lead test using a home kit purchased online or at a hardware store. For more precise results, have a professional check your house. You may need to test your water as well. ■ If you notice peeling paint, cover it with lead-free paint or wallpaper. ■ Mop up paint chips and dust. Don't vacuum, since this will just spread the particles through the house ■ Pick up lead chips with masking tape, not your bare hands. ■ Keep your house well ventilated. ■ Make sure children's areas are thoroughly swept and cleaned. Kids are highly susceptible to lead poisoning. ■ If you are renovating and need damaged lead paint removed, consult a professional.

Several common home hazards are actually odorless and invisible gases, usually given off as building materials decay or deteriorate. Lead contaminates over 20 percent of U.S. households. Radon is linked to over 30,000 deaths from lung cancer per year. The statistics are frightening, but by testing your home and keeping your house maintained, you can ensure a healthy and safe living environment.

Learn More

If you are still concerned about the invisible dangers in your house, consult these websites and hotlines:

www.epa.gov
(The Environmental Protection Agency)

www.nsc.org
(National Safety Council)

1-800-438-4318
(Indoor Air Quality Hotline)

RADON is a radioactive gas released when uranium, found in rocks and soil beneath house foundations, deteriorates. The gas seeps into the house through cracks in foundations and basements.

■ Two types of home radon kits are available: short-term and long-term. Short-term tests are inexpensive but can be inaccurate; long-term tests cost more but are more precise. ■ If you suspect radon in your house, do not allow anyone to sleep in your basement. ■ Caulk cracks and fissures in your foundation and basement. ■ Keep basements well ventilated. ■ You may need to invest in a duct system that allows trapped radon gas to safely leave your house. Consult a professional first. ■ Contact 1-800-SOS-RADON to get more information on detecting.

Recycling

Recycling is an outstanding way to reduce landfills and remake products that are constantly in demand. Did you know that for every ton of paper recycled, about seventeen trees are saved? Or that recycling one aluminum can saves enough energy to run your television for three hours? If each household chose to recycle, America would save billions of dollars in waste management and energy costs every year. And since most communities have either curbside pickup or a local recycling center, do your part in making the earth a cleaner place.

Products

that can be recycled break down to four categories. Some communities don't accept all four types, so check with your local recycling center.

GLASS All clean, unbroken glass containers can be recycled. Glass drink bottles may also be returnable to the supermarket for deposit.

METAL Metal lids; clean, flattened cans; and aluminum foil are all used in products that can be remade again and again.

PLASTIC Plastic containers stamped with a #1 or #2 and plastic grocery bags marked with a #2 or #4 can be safely recycled.

PAPER Stacked piles of newspapers, as well as mixed mail, magazines, and flattened cereal/product boxes are also collected. Make sure to remove all rubber bands, paper clips, staples, and tape. Check with your local recycling agency to see if newsprint must be tied with string or twine in bunches first, and whether cardboard can be recycled.

Although it would be nice to be able to re-use and remake everything, some stuff should be thrown in the trash:

■ Broken glass ■ Wet, dirty paper ■ Lightbulbs, windows, ceramics, mirrors ■ Aerosol spray cans, paint cans ■ Plastics that are of #3, #4, #5, #6, #7 type. Often, plastic caps. ■ Magnetic metal parts ■ Napkins, tissues, fast-food wraps, waxed milk cartons and drink boxes

Some items need special consideration when being disposed of:

■ Batteries Check to see if there is a place to drop off old batteries in your community. Find a rechargeable battery collection center by contacting 1-800-8BATTERY.

Some municipal waste departments provide residents with their own recycling receptacles. Contact your local sanitation department to find out if you are eligible to receive one.

The website www.earth911.org has invaluable recycling information, and can even direct you to local disposal centers based on your zip code.

■ **Eyeglasses, computers, electronics** Donate to a charity or a repair shop, or find out from your community where to dispose of unusable electronic parts— these have radioactive material inside and should not end up in landfills.

■ **Ink cartridges** Contact suppliers on how to send back. Some companies actually provide return-address envelopes for sending in spent cartridges.

■ **Motor oil/tires** Contact your local tire shop or call 1-800-MOTOROIL.

Other Ways to Re-use & Recycle

■ Start a compost heap in your backyard. Build or purchase an enclosed compost bin from a garden center. Alternate layers of dry dirt and leaves with decomposable waste products (like vegetables, lawn clippings, and even dryer lint). Keep the compost heap elevated and covered to make sure it doesn't attract pests. Composting cuts back on garbage and provides you with incredibly rich mulch for lawns and gardens.

■ Re-use scraps of paper and envelopes for jotting notes, taking messages, or making lists.

■ Re-use plastic shopping bags or better yet, carry your own reusable bags to the store when you shop.

■ Try to buy goods made from recycled materials, like toilet paper and paper towels made from recycled non–chlorine-bleached paper, which also cuts back on chemical pollution. The websites *www.Redjellyfish.com* and *www.portagebaygoods.com* offer directories of earth-friendly businesses that sell dozens of recycled goods.

Paper, Paper Everywhere

■ If everyone in America recycled one in ten newspapers, it would save approximately 25 million trees a year.

■ More than 40% of what American households throw out each year is paper, and paper is the biggest component of most landfills.

Energy Conservation

Every year, fossil fuels like coal and petroleum provide energy for the world, from powering air conditioners to running cars. But fossil fuels are not inexhaustible, and they are being used up at an alarming rate. In addition, the combustion of fossil fuels releases into the atmosphere large amounts of carbon dioxide (CO_2), a harmful gas that plays a major part in air pollution and global warming. Protecting our planet is a global priority, but many people think that billions of dollars need to be spent in order to fix our ecological problems. The truth of the matter is, saving the planet can start right in your home, and actually saves dollars.

Easy Ways to Conserve Energy

■ Open shades and curtains during the day to allow natural light into your house. In warmer climates, keep shades on the west and south sides of the house closed to block the sun and cut back on cooling costs.

■ Turn off lights you aren't using.

■ Plug home electronics into power strips and turn power strips off when equipment is not in use.

■ A covered pot will boil water faster and consume less energy.

■ Range-top burners should be kept clean, so they can reflect heat better.

■ Cook meals in microwaves, toaster ovens, and pressure cookers rather than the oven whenever possible. A toaster oven requires 30 percent less energy than a conventional oven.

■ Lower the thermostat on your water heater to 120° F, a comfortable temperature that could save you up to 20 percent on water heating bills. Also, it reduces the danger of scalding in households with children.

■ If you have a fireplace, keep the flue damper tightly closed when not in use.

■ Wash your clothes in cold or warm water, with cold-water detergents.

■ Fit outdoor lights with photocell units or timers.

■ Install exterior and interior storm windows—they can reduce heat loss by 30 percent.

Carbon dioxide emissions are a major cause of global warming. The amount of carbon dioxide in the atmosphere has increased by 28 percent in the last century. In the United States alone, 15,000 pounds of CO_2 is produced per person each year. Yet, even something as simple as caulking air leaks around windows can reduce this number by 1,000 pounds annually, by minimizing the amount of energy needed to heat or cool your house. Here are some other ways to reduce carbon dioxide output.

If each American would . . .	The amount of CO_2 (in pounds) in the atmosphere would decrease by...
Ride mass transportation, bike, or walk instead of drive	20 pounds for each gallon of gas
Set thermostats higher in the summer and lower in the winter	500 pounds for every 2° F
Replace standard light bulbs with more efficient compact fluorescent bulbs	500 pounds per bulb
Recycle and buy reusable products	1,000 pounds
Install energy-saving windows	10,000 pounds

For each degree your thermostat is lowered in the winter, you save around 3% on your heating bill.

Cool & Efficient

The refrigerator is one of the most important appliances in your home. Keeping it well maintained can save you a lot of money.

■ Keep your refrigerator and freezer at the recommended temperatures of 40° F for the fresh food compartment, 0° F for the freezer.

■ Remember to regularly defrost your fridge—frost increases the amount of energy needed to keep the refrigerator running.

■ Vacuum the condenser coils in back at least once a year. Clean coils allow the refrigerator to run more efficiently.

■ To make sure each door is airtight, close a dollar bill in it so that half hangs out. If you can pull the dollar out easily, the gasket seal needs to be inspected and possibly replaced.

Every Drop Counts

Energy conservation doesn't end with fossil fuels. Water is also a valuable resource. Most of the planet's drinking water comes from groundwater (water under the soil and from rivers). But water pollution and overuse are putting stress on this precious system. Make sure a drop doesn't get wasted:

■ Do keep drinking water in the refrigerator, rather than let the faucet run until water is cold enough.

■ Do make sure your dishwasher is full, but not overloaded.

■ Do bathe small children together—it saves water and adds to the fun!

■ Do repair leaky faucets immediately.

■ Don't run water while brushing your teeth or shaving.

■ Don't take baths as frequently. Shower and save up to 15 gallons of water.

■ Don't use water to defrost food. Thaw it overnight in the refrigerator.

■ Don't rinse dishes before loading them into dishwashers; simply scrape off excess food first.

Ready To Make the Planet More Efficient?

These websites offer invaluable advice on energy conservation:

■ *www.eere.energy.gov* (Office of Energy Efficiency and Renewable Energy)

■ *www.ase.org* (Alliance to Save Energy)

■ *www.aceee.org* (American Council for an Energy-Efficient Economy)

■ *www.energystar.gov* (Energy Star program)

■ *www.hes.lbl.gov* (Home Energy Saver)

■ *www.epa.gov* (U.S. Environmental Protection Agency)

Pest Control

No one wants to play host to a family of rodents or pests, but there's hardly a household that hasn't been plagued by one infestation or another. Take action before you're forced to move into your car.

Five Steps Toward a Pest-Free House

■ **ONE** Check your house and make sure all holes and vents are screened or blocked up. Pay careful attention to high-water areas, like under the sinks and toilet. ■ **TWO** Don't let water sit out for a long time. This means making sure your kitchen sink doesn't stay filled overnight, and water doesn't lie stagnant in your plant pots. ■ **THREE** Don't leave open food lying around. Try to keep all perishables in tightly sealed containers or in the refrigerator to deter pests. ■ **FOUR** Clean your pet's food and water dishes regularly. Keep the area swept. ■ **FIVE** Make sure your garbage can has a tightly fitting lid, and you take it out regularly. Don't let stacks of paper, cardboard boxes, or paper grocery bags accumulate. Recycle them or they'll turn into pest palaces.

These repellents are natural and work wonders on cutting back the most common infestations: ■ **Ants** Sprinkle chili powder, ground cinnamon, or boric acid across their paths. Wash counters in equal parts water and vinegar or citrus juice. To get rid of nests, mix Borax and confectioners' sugar. Then scatter over the nest. Outside, place coffee grounds or sprinkle mint leaves near the ants' entry point to keep them away. ■ **Cockroaches** Commercial roach baits work well, since they are contained, or you can use homemade roach bait (*see opposite page*). Fill cracks with boric acid. ■ **Fleas** Put brewer's yeast in pet food. Comb your pet regularly. Clean the pet's sleeping area thoroughly and sprinkle with rosemary. Let lemons steep over-night in a pot of boiling water. When the liquid cools, sponge onto pet's coat. ■ **Flies** Hang up lavender or mint (they can't stand the aroma). Keep your outdoor and indoor garbage cans clean and dry ■ **Fruit Flies** Grow a pot of basil in your kitchen, or place fresh basil among your fruit. To make a trap, put a piece of raw fruit in a jar. Pour vinegar over the fruit. Flies will become trapped when they fly in to get the fruit, and then drown. ■ **Mealworms** Place a few wrapped sticks of spearmint gum around packages in the pantry to keep them away from dried goods. ■ **Mosquitoes** Let lavender oil or rubbing alcohol air-dry on wrists and behind ears. ■ **Moths** Use lavender, cedar chips, or rosemary in place of moth-balls. ■ **Rodents** Seal up any holes with steel wool (they can't chew through it) or caulking. To find where they are entering, sprinkle baby powder where you've found droppings. When they revisit the area, their tracks will lead back to the nest. Position traps close to the wall. ■ **Termites** Keep lumber and woodpiles away from the house foundation. Remove wood debris and tree stumps. Regularly check decks, wooden outdoor furniture, and fences for damage. If termites are detected, contact an exterminator, as they can do a great amount of damage quickly.

Sprinkling bay leaves, as well as black pepper, in cupboards and empty storage containers is a great universal bug repellent.

If creepy-crawlies are still driving you up the wall, consult the National Pesticide Information Center at 1-800-858-7378 or call your local exterminator.

Homemade Roach Bait

Roach bait is safer to use than bombs, since the area of contact is much more controlled and there's less of a chance of becoming poisoned from pesticides. Here's a quick recipe to get rid of some very annoying visitors:

$1/2$ cup Borax
$1/4$ cup cornmeal
$1/4$ cup flour
$1/8$ cup confectioners' sugar

Combine ingredients and sprinkle on paper plates or jar lids. Let sit for about 10 days, then replace if necessary. Keep out of reach of children and pets. You should notice a drop-off in the roach population within two weeks.

Pets

A pet can bring joy and happiness to any household. But it can also be a lot of work dealing with allergies, odors, chewed-up couches, and fleas!

Keeping Your House Pet (and Human) Friendly

■ Pets can carry certain diseases and parasites. Always wash your hands well after petting or playing with them, and after cleaning litter boxes and pet beds.

■ Keep pets off counters, tables, beds, and furniture.

■ Wash pet dishes separately from yours, and wash them out before every refill.

■ Keep pet food and water dishes on a plastic/rubber tray to make sure food stays where it's supposed to.

■ Don't let pets beg for scraps. Try to keep them on their own diet—you might inadvertently make them sick, or at the least overweight, if you give them "human" food (check the American Animal Hospital Association's website at *www.healthypet.com* for more information about poisonous foods for pets).

■ Don't let pets track mud into your home. Make sure to wipe their paws down before they come in, or invest in paw coverings for wet days.

■ Pick off pet hair by winding tape around your hand sticky side up and using it on fur-strewn surfaces. Or rub a used fabric softener sheet over furniture.

■ Pets can't make a mess if you keep garbage cans and receptacles tightly sealed.

Pet Problems

Allergies

Contrary to popular belief, the fur of a pet is not to blame for allergies. Pet allergens are actually released into the air from dander, pet saliva, and even urine when it dries. Cat allergenic particles are very small and stay in the air for a long time (which might explain why more people appear to be more allergic to cats than to dogs).

■ **Bathing and Grooming** Bathe your dog monthly. Brush a pet's coat every day. Try to do this outdoors so allergens don't accumulate inside, and get someone who doesn't have allergies to do it. Prevent your pet's skin from drying out by adding a few drops of vegetable or canola oil to their food.

■ **Bedding** Always make sure your pet's bedding is clean, and vacuum around the area often. Keep pets out of your bedroom.

■ **Air Purifier** Consider investing in an air purifying system that contains a HEPA filter (*see page 194*).

Skunked! If your pet has been sprayed by a skunk, rub undiluted tomato juice or a vinegar-and-water solution directly on the affected areas. Wash it off and rinse well. This won't get rid of the smell, but it will diminish it.

Furniture Damage

■ Provide adequate exercise and chew toys if dogs are chewing on furniture. Be firm and consistent in commanding your dog not to chew.

■ You can rub oil of cloves on items as a deterrent or get a spray from the pet store that leaves a bad taste in dogs' mouths. If your pet persists, it might require professional training.

■ If cats are scratching furniture, make sure to trim their claws properly about every two weeks . Put double-sided sticky tape on commonly scratched spots—when claws meet the stickiness, cats usually back off. A sisal scratching post or pad can distract cats and the best way to prevent a new kitten from learning to scratch furniture is to have a good, tall scratching post in place BEFORE the cat arrives. Once kitty is home, feed him healthy treats for using his post.

■ To make sure cats and dogs don't jump on furniture, employ a little association. Place aluminum foil on furniture, and line up empty soda cans and cans filled with pennies near the edges of counters. When pets jump up, they will hear an unpleasant, loud noise and soon learn to keep off furniture and counters. Use positive reinforcement to designate where pets are allowed to go and provide them with alternate activities, rather than just punishing them for bad behavior.

Pet Odors

■ **Litter boxes** Change scoopable kitty litter at least once a week and scoop out solid waste daily. Keep the box in a well-ventilated area, away from food and cooking surfaces. Baking soda can take away some of the smell, but wash and disinfect the litter box regularly.

■ **Cages** To avoid smells in cages, clean them twice or more a week. Just be careful not to traumatize the pet by turning it out of its living quarters too frequently. Keep cages away from beds and cooking areas.

■ **Urine** Talk to your vet about habitual spraying. Make sure your dog is regularly walked and let outside. When a stain occurs, act fast to make sure it does not soak into surfaces or rugs. Absorb the urine with a cloth or clean up feces. If it is a carpet, rub some vinegar into the spot, and then sprinkle with baking soda. Let sit for a day and then vacuum up. If draperies or cushions have been soiled, immediately remove and isolate the items. Try the cleaning method described and follow up with an odor neutralizer. If you're still plagued by odors, try *www.planeturine.com* for some helpful tips.

Fleas and Ticks

■ Ask your veterinarian about anti-tick and -flea medications.

■ Regularly wash your pet (with an anti-pest shampoo, if necessary). Wash your pet's bedding with hot, soapy water and vacuum the area at least twice a week. Consider getting a flea collar.

■ Since ticks and fleas lay eggs in carpeting and upholstery, it's important to vacuum the floor and furniture regularly and throw out the vacuum bag every time you use it.

Although the Humane Society of America claims that technically there are no "hypo-allergenic breeds," some breeds might be a little easier to take care of for allergy sufferers. For example, Irish terriers, Chihuahuas, poodles, and bichon frises all shed very little and do not produce as much dander as most dog breeds. Some cats, like Siamese. Abyssinian, and Burmese, lack a woolly undercoat and tend to shed once a year; still others are hairless or almost hairless and are easy to groom.

When cleaning up cat stains, be careful with ammonia-based products: This smells like urine to a cat and may promote more spraying.

Chapter 5
Entertaining
& Etiquette

Entertaining

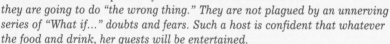
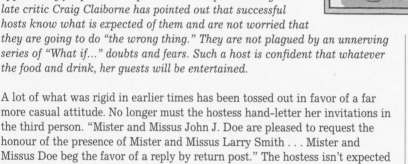

Hospitality should be a treat for everyone—hosts and guests. Planners, caterers, florists, and other people who work in the party business agree that there seem to be two types of hosts. One group relishes every moment of planning and holding a social occasion; the others dread even the thought of an informal gathering. We all wish we were in the first group and could be popular, gracious hosts. The good news is that entertaining has never been more relaxed and comfortable, and it has never offered so much opportunity for personal expression and experimenting. The late critic Craig Claiborne has pointed out that successful hosts know what is expected of them and are not worried that they are going to do "the wrong thing." They are not plagued by an unnerving series of "What if..." doubts and fears. Such a host is confident that whatever the food and drink, her guests will be entertained.

A lot of what was rigid in earlier times has been tossed out in favor of a far more casual attitude. No longer must the hostess hand-letter her invitations in the third person. "Mister and Missus John J. Doe are pleased to request the honour of the presence of Mister and Missus Larry Smith . . . Mister and Missus Doe beg the favor of a reply by return post." The hostess isn't expected to polish every piece of silver and beat each rug in her home. When you are the guest, you don't arrive at a party in a lab coat with a clipboard and white gloves. That's true for your guests, too—they come to your home in a spirit of enjoyment.

   Probably the most common fallacy about entertaining is that it requires lavish food and drink. There isn't any need for puttin' on the Ritz (which, ironically, is more likely to put guests on edge). Ordinary food, when it is well done, is the most delightful gesture. Great chefs know the value of comfort food, whether it's called Boeuf Bourguignon or beef stew. When you plan a party, build the menu around your own specialties. If you make terrific fried chicken,

Hiring Help

You're the host and it's up to you to bring in support, whether it is a bartender, a dishwasher, a caterer, or all three. Teenagers or college students enjoy the extra money that they can make helping you. (If they are serving, ask them to wear black trousers and white shirts; you can provide matching white cotton aprons.) When you hire help, review what you expect from each person, the basics of your event, and the hours of employment.

Theme parties might seem like they're for children, but who says that kids get to have all the fun? If you're tired of simply throwing the same old dinner or holiday parties, why not spice it up with one of these fun and fresh party ideas?

- Have a cocktail party with swanky drinks, smooth music, and lounge decorations. ■ Halloween in March can break up an otherwise un-festive month. ■ A night in paradise could find you sipping fruity concoctions and enjoying a tiki-torch lit barbecue in your backyard, surrounded by lei-strewn friends. ■ Celebrate Oscar night by getting decked out, munching on appetizers, and taking bets as to who will win the coveted award!

let that be the main course and add a few side dishes. If you don't cook, or never had the desire to learn, bring in food from a caterer or a restaurant and serve it in your own dishes. Either way, guests will be supremely satisfied.

Where to Begin?

Answers to why, what, and where will get the party ball rolling. Why is it in the works—a birthday or an anniversary, graduation or a promotion, engagement or wedding, bon voyage or welcome to our town, a fund raiser or a fun raiser. What is the event —a brunch, cocktails, or dinner. Lastly, decide where it is held—in the dining room, around the big-screen TV, or outdoors by the pool. Answer these questions and you can figure out the when and who.

Every party offers a menu from three different styles of food service:

BUFFET Guests serve and seat themselves. Food is arranged on platters placed on a table or sideboard. Stacks of plates, flatware, and napkins are also on the table.

FAMILY-STYLE A casual, informal gathering where guests are seated at a table. Courses are placed on the table or sideboard, where they remain during the entire meal, and guests serve themselves.

FORMAL A seated dinner consisting of five or more courses served by waiters. Serving dishes are never left on the table at a formal meal. When it is appropriate, the host signals servers to clear one course and begin serving another.

Earlier hours, from breakfasts to lunches and teas, inspire the simpler buffet and family-style meal. Formal service is restricted by realities of space and the demands on kitchen facilities. An intimate celebration, such as a wedding or an important anniversary, can be designed as a formal breakfast for eight or ten; the element of formality provides the event with flair.

Happy parties all share one quality: a host who's confident, relaxed, and excited for the company of the guests. That confidence is the heart of entertaining. Hosting skills can be acquired by anyone who enjoys sharing the hospitality of their home. A party begins with the invitations you send, the greeting you extend to guests, and the atmosphere you create. Who doesn't like to open the mailbox and find an invitation to a party? Even a most traditional family event, like the twins' birthday party, takes on much more excitement with a mailed invitation.

Who Will Come?

As host, it's your call. Family invitations include children and others who live in the household, like an adult sibling or a grandparent, unless you specifically name those included. ("Who's been invited?" can be a real hornets' nest. Some children are invited, others aren't; some boyfriends are in, others not—we've all been there. Consistency is your "get out of jail free" card here.) The invitation can be made by telephone, e-mail, face to face, or on a written card. If there is a theme for the party, tell guests in this initial contact. Give them the hours of the event as well as the date, and let them know when you will need their acceptance of the invitation. Do not assume that people who have not responded will attend; contact them individually.

Here's Your Hat; What's Your Hurry?

Do guests linger, reluctant to call it a night? It is a compliment that your party is good fun, but you're exhausted and not looking forward to the clean-up. One way to manage party time is to indicate the event's duration on the invitation: "Please join us for cocktails on Wednesday, from 6 to 8 P.M." Still one or two friends comfortably chatting away? Sum up the evening and wish them adieu: "This has been such fun; I'm so glad to have seen you." And, finally, you can refrain from serving alcoholic beverages and bring out the coffee.

Decorations

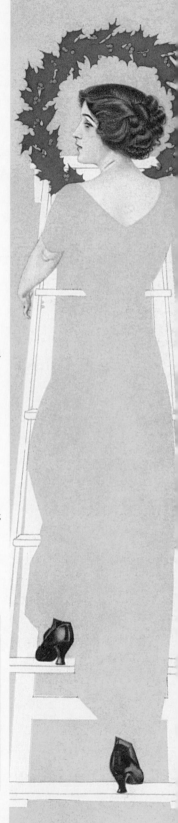

I t's pretty common to plan the party, pick a date, invite guests, and then skid to a full stop over "decorations." Actually, defining decorations can bring out a vigorous debate. Yes, decorations include how the table is set and how the napkins are folded, which dishes are chosen, and what flowers and vase will be the centerpiece. If you ask an accomplished hostess, you'll be told that decorations are everything she does to spread cheer and make guests welcome.

"Decorations set the stage" is a cliché now, because we know that parties start with the atmosphere you create. If you've ever kept a swatch book for interior decorating projects, consider one for party ideas. Magazines are filled with exquisite settings; if something appeals to you, pull the page and add it to your party book. Before your party, snap a set of photos before guests arrive to keep track of how everything looks. Note on each photo the details: how many and what kind of flowers were involved, who was the florist and if the price was reasonable. Also note anything that you'd change the next time around.

A Good First Impression

Your open door, a bouquet of flowers, and soft music all speak well of a party. Soft lighting is an important element, both for setting a mood and for flattering guests. Candles, so inexpensive and basic, are a proven way to light your rooms.

It's Summertime and The Living Room's Outside

H ere are a handful of time-tested outdoor party tricks that bring magic to the fun. High on the list is setting up interior furnishings for guests outside.

■ Relocating fine furnishings from inside the house is exciting for an outdoor party. Arrange a loveseat and chairs under the maple tree, or set an area rug right on the grass, and set up the buffet table on it.

■ Fill out the party area with buckets of cut branches: they are impressive and inexpensive.

■ Organize the beverage station in an ice-filled wheelbarrow.

Fantastic Funtak

F untak is a plastic material that can be the means for holding party decorations in position. Take small pieces of it from its package, knead it briefly, and then press it onto a wall or door to hold flowers or a sign.

■ Hang paper lanterns from trees and in a garland across the patio; line the driveway with luminaria.

■ If you've got a canvas party tent in your back garden, dress it with a carpet, a chandelier, or some great potted palms.

■ When children get together to celebrate, they are instinctively attracted to the outdoors. Their antics can be given free reign there if you've reserved an area where they can run about.

I Hear Music, Mighty Fine Music

When the first phonographs appeared, the vinyl recordings they accommodated played music for a few minutes, but then a different recording had to be set up on the turntable. Now music can be programmed within an audio system to last hours, so you can plan the soundtrack to your party well in advance. Some reliable recording artists are:

■ Louis Armstrong & Ella Fitzgerald ■ Frank Sinatra ■ John Coltrane & Johnny Hartman ■ The Modern Jazz Quartet ■ Sade ■ Diana Krall ■ John Pizzarelli ■ Sarah McLachlan ■ Norah Jones ■ Sheryl Crow

Any Time Is Party Time

Entertaining is often associated with dinner and evenings, but earlier hours offer excellent opportunities for celebration. A weekend or holiday brunch, a luncheon, and an afternoon tea are all good party premises, particularly as showers for women friends.

Setting your multiple CD-player to random will insure that your music set stays original the whole night, but if you have the time, consider making mix tapes and CDs showcasing your own favorite party music.

Candle Power

Luminaria is a Spanish word for the free-standing candlelights set out at night. In a garden or lining a driveway, luminaria provide festive light; what's more, they are quick and easy to make at home.

Clean sand
Paper bags with flat bottoms
White kitchen candles
Votive candle glasses

1. Pour two or three inches of sand into every paper bag.

2. Fix a candle in each votive glass. Nestle the votive securely in the sand.

3. Set the luminaria along pathways, around patios and on food and drink tables. Light the candles.

4. After the party, extinguish each candle and take the luminaria apart.

Food & Drink

When planning food and beverage for a party, a few considerations will narrow down the seemingly endless options to the point where you can conjure a wonderful repast. For instance, more than eight guests can be considered a large party, and you will be entertaining on a larger scale. More intimate lunches, brunches, teas, and suppers involve cooking in manageable quantities, and so there are many, many possibilities. Your own specialties, be they humble pot roast or a hearty Tuscan bean soup, do work wonderfully for guests, and it's fair to say that a family favorite is a good reliable choice.

Delicate, hands-on dishes, such as omelets to order or filet of sole, are best left to a lunch that you're making for yourself and a good friend. When your guest list is only three or four, a great pan of lasagna can be too much of a good thing. Menu planning is a bit like orchestral music: you do not want every course (or movement) to be a crescendo; you will have presented a dinner without subtlety, which gives no relief to the palate. A simple menu can be based on this formula: a starter, a main dish that usually includes meat, side dishes that should include vegetables and a starch, and a dessert. Be sure to choose a selection of foods that contrast each other; soft mashed potatoes are the perfect complement to crusty fried chicken.

At a spur of the moment gathering, pull a jar of olives or salted almonds from the pantry— arrange them in a lovely silver dish and voilà! That's entertaining.

Nut Brittles

Nut brittles are quick and easy to make at home, and sweet and satisfying to serve guests. Offer some with a dish of ice cream or sorbet.

3 cups sugar
3 cups unsalted almonds, cashews, macadamia nuts, or pistachios

1. In a heavy, medium-size saucepan, over medium-high heat, cook the sugar until it melts and turns golden; a candy thermometer will reach the HARD CRACK stage. Watch the pan closely to make sure the sugar doesn't burn. Meanwhile, arrange the nuts in an even layer on a baking sheet. As soon as the sugar has caramelized, pour it over the nuts. Spread the mixture with an offset spatula.

2. Allow the brittle to cool completely in a dry, well-ventilated area. At informal gatherings you can present it on the baking sheet and give each guest a tiny new hammer to break up the brittle.

Cooking in Quantity

Not every party requires the feast that a Super Bowl will, but the nagging question—Will there be enough? —does not need to arise with practical menu planning.

■ Choose main dishes that can vary in serving size, like stews, casseroles, and pasta dishes, rather than lamb chops or steaks.

■ Fill out a buffet table with great bowls of fresh green salad.

■ Offer plenty of bread and rolls, breadsticks, and toast.

■ Always make two additional servings, just to be sure!

"Does this have anything in it?"

So many of us live with dietary restrictions of one kind or another that you will want to make some allowances for guests. If you are hosting an intimate sit-down dinner, inquire in advance about allergies. When you expect folks for a buffet, post alongside each dish a card listing its ingredients. If you are worried that a cousin who's allergic to nuts or the guest of a guest who is a lactose-intolerant vegetarian will not have enough to eat, put out a tray of oven-roasted vegetables: beautiful and delicious.

The Essential Bar
■ wine ■ beer ■ vodka ■ gin ■ rum ■ whiskey ■ club soda ■ tonic ■ soft drinks ■ plenty of ice ■ liqueurs: Grand Marnier, Kalhua, and Amaretto

You Eat with Your Eyes

Presenting your food can be a challenge, but we are no longer expected to offer every dish on a platter. Use trays, baskets, or even new clean terracotta pots as serving pieces. Garnishing is not about intricately carving a tomato into flower, but accenting food to hint at what is inside; a simple dish of pasta in a butter-sage sauce looks wonderful with a spring of fresh sage alongside.

Cocktails at Seven

Invite friends to relax at the end of the day and catch up with each other. A cocktail party is more straightforward than a sit-down dinner, and every bit as much fun. For hors d'oeuvres? Forget the pâté and caviar; produce in season is colorful, succulent, inexpensive, and appealing. A case in point: the luscious cherry tomato. Let guests dip them first in vodka, then in sea salt.

Cocktail Party in a Box

A cocktail party needn't be an extravagant affair; martinis and cheesesticks can serve the purpose. In a box, pack a cocktail shaker, a small bottle of gin or vodka, a small bottle of vermouth, olives or cocktail onions, martini glasses, fun cocktail napkins, swizzle sticks, and cheesesticks. Step out to the backyard, surprise a friend, or send off as a gift.

Table Settings

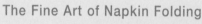

able settings might be associated with formal affairs, but simple arrangements of silverware, dishes, and napkins can make an ordinary dinner quite extraordinary. Turn a Wednesday night supper into something special or dress up your next party with impeccable dinner settings and interesting centerpieces.

Quick Centerpieces

■ Bowls of fresh artichokes, squash, or lemons bring lively color to the table.

■ A flowering plant (that's not too tall) is long-lasting; beware of any with intense fragrance.

■ Got an unframed mirror? Lay it at the center of the table and whatever you place on it—candles, tree branches, or a delicate bit of porcelain—will be reflected.

■ Gather a velvet throw, a paisley scarf, or a vintage textile and mass it at the center of the table to anchor a candelabra or two.

■ A precise parade line of fresh pineapples.

■ Unmatched silver pieces, sugar bowls, fruit bowls, candlesticks, a baby mug, or a tray all play well together. There's no need to polish them; their lovely patina is beautiful at a casual meal.

■ A hurricane glass with a candle or with glass balls or pine cones.

■ The game-winning soccer ball on a pedestal cake stand.

■ A tropical vacation, complete with clean sand, colorful drinks, umbrellas, and toy figures sunbathing.

■ A representation of a collection: half a dozen Steiff animals, snowglobes, or hat stands.

White linen has always been the traditional choice to dress party tables, but there are far more options. Cover each table with an undercloth; bedsheets will provide the long drop to the floor. A favorite fabric, a tapestry, or an Oriental rug will all look beautiful on the table.

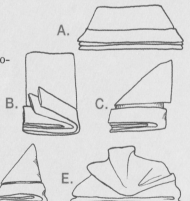

The Fine Art of Napkin Folding

1. Lay the napkin flat and fold in half so the fold is at the left.
2. Starting at the bottom, make accordion folds until about two-thirds of the way to the top (see figure A). Pleats should be about 1 inch wide.
3. Fold the napkin in half again, pleats out (see figure B).
4. To create stand for the fan, fold the top left corner down to it sticks out about 1 inch past the folded accordion part (see figure C).
5. Fold that one inch overlap under (see figure D).
6. Let go of the pleats and adjust folds (see figure E).

A.

B.

C.

D.

E.

Table Settings

Formal Dinner

Settings should be at least a foot apart, and one inch from the edge of the table. The rule of thumb is to set the table in the order the courses will be served, starting from the outside. For a course containing soup, fish, entrée, and dessert, set the table in this order, starting from the left: napkin, fish fork, dinner fork, salad fork, plate, soup bowl on top of plate, dinner knife, fish knife, soup spoon. The water glass should be placed above the tip of the knife, and wineglasses should be placed to the right of the water glass. The bread plate and butter knife should be to the upper left, with the knife's handle facing right. A dessert fork and spoon are positioned horizontally, one above the other facing opposite directions, above the dinner plate. (A variation is placing the bread plate to the far left, with the napkin and butter knife on top.)

Casual Dinner

Beginning from the left side: Salad plate, fork, dinner plate, napkin (placed on plate), dinner knife, teaspoon. The bread plate and butter knife are to the top left. The water glass is to the top right. (If there is soup, place the napkin to the far left, and place the soup bowl on the plate. Place the soup spoon to the right of the teaspoon.)

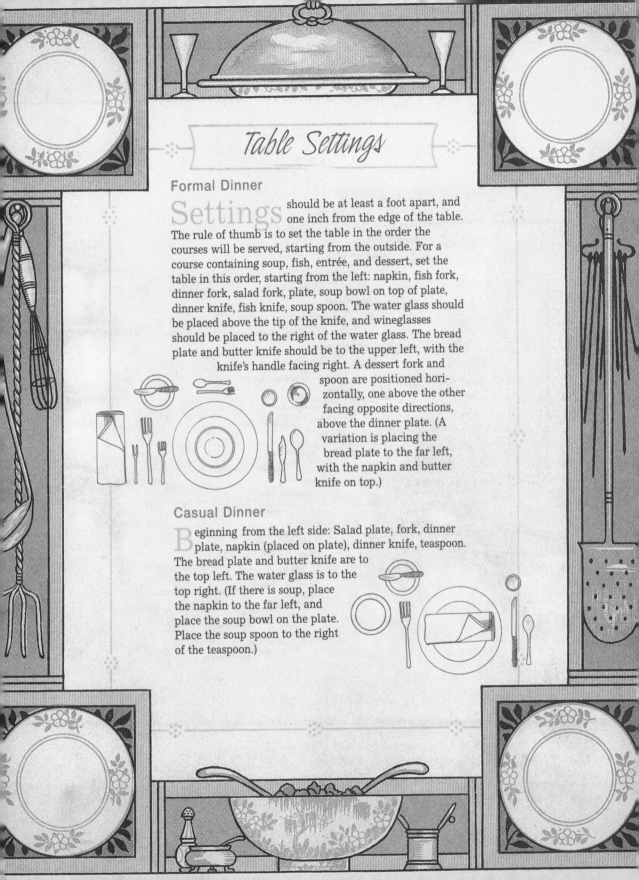

Great, Big Parties

A silver anniversary! A graduation! A wedding! These are the happiest of moments of life—times when family and friends gather to celebrate achievement. On life's scoreboard of success and disappointment, there are undeniable high-water marks and deserve every bit of celebration you can muster.

Here are some of the best tips we've found to keep the guest count up, the costs under control and the event memorable.

■ For flowers and produce, capitalize on the season; naturals at their peak are the most beautiful and the least costly.

■ Hire a musician. Live music immediately makes a gathering memorable. The local college can refer a student musician, a violinist, a harpist, or a soprano.

■ Gather your forces: Borrow friends' silver serving pieces, pitchers, and tablelinens.

■ Rent what you do not have. Many antique shops rent fine-quality side chairs and silver services, nurseries rent potted trees and statuary, and party companies offer outdoor tents of every size.

■ Provide good support systems. Have back-ups: icemakers, a dishwasher, and a refrigerator. If you expect a great crowd, rent outdoor toilets.

■ Check your house and property. Look for potential hazards like a tear in a carpet that could cause a fall. Have a septic inspection well before the event.

■ Play the party out in your head, from guests' arrival to clean-up.

■ Provide a platform for speakers. These happy milestones are something to wax eloquent about. Rent a microphone so that toasts can be made.

■ Alert your insurance carrier, the local police, and your neighbors beforehand.

■ Set-up a photography stage. Everyone wants to be photographed, and photographers will appreciate their own area. There you can control the light and the background. To facilitate posing, set a piano seat, a bench, a slipper chair, or a side chair where the camera angle is optimum.

Powder Room Pamper

A nticipate a guest's sudden need in the powder room. Set up a small basket with an emergency sewing kit, safety pins, a couple bandages, a small bottle of aspirin, and a small box of tampons. Counter the utilitarian feeling of the basket with a potted orchid or another flowering plant and a candle burning within a hurricane glass.

These Are Good Signs

When lots of folks are headed your way, you may want to think about crowd control. Paint up a half dozen signs to let guests know what's where. Number one is an indication where to park. Number two is the welcome. Add signs directing traffic to the coat station, the powder room, the telephone and, for a big group, a first aid station. At the exit from the parking area, post a sign of "Good-bye! Thanks for coming!"

Design signs in the spirit of your home. A country place might inspire worn wood board that is whitewashed, and lettered with brush and paint. In the city, a computer-generated message board can be the most sophisticated. The signs can be retrieved every time you entertain, so the effort invested in their style will be repaid over time.

The Wedding Planners' Warning

Do not choose a home wedding, wedding professionals advise, if your goal is to save money. Offering wedding cake and Champagne where the service is held will be far less expensive than the many incidental costs incurred with a home celebration.

The Guest of Honor

The bride and groom, the graduate, the new mom, and the retiree—they hold a position at their party that is neither guest nor host, but centerpiece. Acknowledge that by including them in choices that you would normally make as the host. Consult with the guest of honor on the major elements of the day like the time of the party, the guest list, the menu, and the music. At this party, your role is to slip into the background so that the guest of honor can luxuriate in the bliss of her day. Make it personal. Feature photographs of the guest of honor throughout the site—from her childhood to the big day.

Parties for Children

A youngster's birthday party is always the most thrilling day of the year. Having your child's friends and relatives come around to join the celebration is the stuff that memories are made of. For younger children, a party that lasts $1^{1}/_{2}$ to 2 hours is plenty long. Plan for games, cake cutting, present opening, and good-bye. Older children enjoy longer parties and creating their own entertainment, but they'll still rush up when it's time to cut the cake!

Children's Party Themes

- *Cinderella* ■ *Pool*
- *Finger paint* ■ *Bowling*
- *Circus* ■ *Dinosaurs*
- *Magic* ■ *Puppet*
- *Rodeo* ■ *Carnival*

Are You Registered?

Life's rites of passage—buying a house, getting married, having a baby—are celebrated now by registering for gifts. Like its ancestor, the hope chest, the registry is meant to provide you with the things you need to begin this new stage of your life.

Department stores were the first to volunteer as registries, and for good reason: they sold just about everything for every stage of life, from crystal champagne flutes to cribs and cotton diapers. Home furnishings stores are still popular, but the arc of registry has widened; it's just as valid to shop at a garden and landscape center or a home improvement chain.

Tradition dictates registries include silver, china, and linens. Today's registries are more inclusive with everything from small soaps to big ticket items like antique candlestick holders. Register for a wide range of prices; this will ensure everyone will be able to find a gift for you.

The most popular places to register are still the major department stores. Choose a store that is accessible to all your guests; a good choice is one with a website, where people can view your registry and purchase gifts to be delivered to you.

When it comes time to register, the happy couple should decide what they need and their style before they go. Once in the store you can become overwhelmed with choices. Select the store you plan to register at and call them to make an appointment with a consultant who will take down all your information and be your contact whenever you have questions. Bring your list and wear comfortable shoes!

To register for a wedding, or any event, ask for the help of a friend whose opinion you value. Choosing so many items in a short time can lead to "buyer's remorse." The store will provide you with a list of all the items on your registry. Check that each model and color choice is correct, as well as the delivery addresses. Let family and friends spread the word; it is not appropriate to send registry information yourself.

If you are registering, feel free to mix it up with home improvement centers, plant nurseries, and furniture shops. Sadly, you cannot register for money. When the down payment on your dream house is your greatest imperative, put the word out through friends and family that you're eagerly saving, saving, saving.

All-purpose Newlywed Registry

- Dinnerware, 8- to 12-piece setting, formal and everyday
- Crystal, formal and everyday
- Flatware, silver and everyday
- Serving Pieces
- Cookware
- Tablelinens
- Bathlinens
- Bedlinens
- Framed mirrors, lamps, candelabra

Off-Beat Gift Registries

There are so many wonderful reasons to give presents, and the trend is moving toward registering for more occasions than the traditional bridal and baby. If you're going to give a present, why not be sure it's just what would be on that wish list!

TRAVEL REGISTRIES Tossing aside life as it's known and taking a year off for travel requires well-thought-out support systems, and you might register for powerful cell phones, good mapbooks, cameras, and such.

HOBBY REGISTRY For the passionate quilter or sailboat enthusiast.

EMPTY NEST REGISTRY No more Power Rangers sheets! It's time for linen and luxury, and everything Harley-Davidson.

Baby Registry

- Crib ■ Crib mattress ■ Crib bedding sets ■ Baby quilt or blankets ■ Musical mobile ■ Changing table ■ Chest of drawers ■ Bookshelf ■ Rocking chair ■ Baby swing ■ Bouncing chair ■ Baby monitor ■ Night light ■ High chair ■ Mini food processor ■ Sling ■ Car seat ■ Carriage/stroller ■ Jogging stroller ■ Diaper bag with changing mat

Gifts & Wrapping

" It's the thought that counts" is absolutely true. A gift that reflects consideration, however unconventional the item may be, is always welcome.
A toddler will be captivated with an ordinary flashlight; the proud
owner of a new house will appreciate spanking fresh deluxe trashcans.

If the recipient is a person close to you, chances are that you will have a good
idea of what he wants. Build a theme: if he is desperate for tickets to see his
favorite sports team, tuck the tickets into a jacket from the team's sports store.
Dad's official retirement is coming up? Think of his favorite activity and share
it; show up at his house with your fishing pole and a cooler full of sandwiches
and beer.

Presents of Pride

Children learn the joy of giving by example. A child old
enough to appreciate getting a present can begin
to understand the pleasures of thinking of a good gift, spending some
time crafting it, and wrapping it. A boy or girl whose name is attached
to a present selected by an elder on their behalf is being short-changed.

Encourage a child to observe family members' likes and dislikes.
Does dad love one particular brand of salsa? Is mom really fond
of a certain magazine? The extravagance is in the consideration,
not the cost. Once the gift has been purchased and brought home,
a personalized wrapping will demonstrate another part of the
equation—the drama of concealing the gift within colored paper,
adding some outstanding decorations (white glue will hold
uncooked macaroni, some coins, little dog biscuits, or puffy
cereals), and writing the important card that expresses love.

Great Housewarming Presents

It's a fact: Americans move far more frequently now than before there was
television. Residential choices are wider ranging than that home on the
range or city apartment, too. And many moves are prompted by life pas-
sages—families adding children, job transfers, or an empty nest. When your
friends move for the third time in a few years, it's only natural to think "I
mustn't send anything bulky or heavy; they'll likely be moving again." Still,
some gifts never fail to delight the new homeowner:

■ Elegant social stationery printed with their name and new address.

■ A photograph (or drawing) of the new home in a silver frame engraved
with the date of the move.

■ A pair of miniature sterling silver pineapples; pineapples are the symbol
of hospitality.

Going, Going, Gone
Online auction sites
are an invaluable
resource for finding gifts.
Use a site that is rep-
utable, one that provides
feedback about sellers,
and has a secure server
for purchasing. When pur-
chasing an item, be sure
you know the return
policy, what the shipping
and handling cost will be,
and, most importantly,
when you will get it. Some
of the best categories to
browse through include
antiques, entertainment
and sports memorabilia,
stamps, and pottery.

Favorite Favors

Favors are wonderful keepsakes that will remind guests of your fabulous parties.

- A small box filled with homemade spiced nuts
- A tiny terra-cotta pot with a sprig of English ivy
- A nightlight with a cus-tom-made shade
- Customized pencils with the date of the party

- A painted tin tray or a colorful cotton tablecloth painted in the souvenir fashion of their location.
- A vintage engraved street map, matted and framed.
- A weathervane representing their special interest, for instance, race horses or sailboats.
- A red birdfeeder to mount near the kitchen window. The color red attracts hummingbirds.
- A gourmet gift basket filled with local specialties: for someone moving to the Chesapeake Bay area, it would have crabcakes and chowders.
- A virtual dinner. A gift certificate for delivery of a dinner from the old neighborhood tells them they're missed.
- A welcome mat!

Wrapsody

When you give a gift, presentation is all. Your present is even more mean-ingful when you take time to make it look intriguing and fun. Add more magic to your gift:

Alternatives to traditional wrapping paper:

- Kraft paper ■ Fabric, especially tablecloths and silk scarves ■ Maps ■ Foreign-language newspaper ■ Wallpaper

Wrapping accents:

- Beads strung onto ribbon ■ Copper wire in place of ribbon ■ Acorns and pinecones ■ A miniature toy car ■ A photograph of you both as a gift card

Holiday Wrapping Station

During the holidays, put together a gift-wrap station where you can stash packages. You'll need a good flat surface that's well lit and can accommodate paper for large items. A heavy-duty holder/cut-ter for rolls of brown Kraft paper and white butcher paper, available at office supply stores, will hold thick rolls of wrapping paper too. Other necessities:

- Cellophane tape in sturdy dispensers ■ Double-sided sticky tape ■ A glue gun ■ Kitchen cord and cotton string ■ Scissors and pinking shears ■ Single-edge razors or a utility knife ■ Funtak ■ Paint pens ■ Rubber stamps and ink pads ■ Assorted wrapping papers and ribbons ■ Rulers ■ Tissue paper

Etiquette

Mind Your Manners

E tiquette is one of the most contentious parts of human behavior, responsible for high emotions between family and friends. At its simplest, etiquette is equal parts common sense and the Golden Rule—do unto others as you would have them do unto you. As life adapts to telephones, computers, and technology, our etiquette also shifts. A woman does not wait in the passenger seat for the male to spring from the driver's side, trot around to open the door, and usher her safely from the vehicle. Men are not expected to walk closer to the road along sidewalks, shielding their women from mud thrown up by horse-drawn carriages. And some graces have been around long enough to rise in popularity again: one should not light a cigarette without asking permission of companions. Some basic hot-button etiquette will see us through most situations.

Thank-you Note

W hen you've received a gift, send a note of thanks to the giver, even if it is someone you see every day and have thanked them in person. There is no need to write a long letter, simply:

- Acknowledge the present with a brief description ■ Share how you will use it or why you so like it ■ Express gratitude for the thoughtfulness

If the gift was monetary, it is not necessary to repeat the amount in your note; it would be better to share what you plan to do with it. If you've registered, a

The Handwritten Note

W e can thank the rigid and often humorless Victorians for a lot of today's etiquette. At the beginning of the last century, handwritten notes and letters were the linch-pins of social activity—the means for arranging events, agreeing upon meetings, and exchanging news (and gossip). Rare was the person who did not spend some part of each day writing and receiving letters from family and friends. Of course there was still no telephone, and it's interesting to speculate what these stuffy folks would have done if they had been confronted with electronic switchboards, call-waiting, and busy signals. So quickly do the "rules of etiquette" change that no one is really an expert anymore.

WHEN TO WRITE A NOTE: Graduation ■ Marriage ■ New address ■ Baby ■ Death ■ Acknowledgement of a gift

thank-you note lets your benefactor know the present has arrived, that it is the correct size and color, and it is indeed what was wanted.

Thank-you notes for calendar occasions like holidays and birthdays should be mailed within two weeks of getting the gift. When the happy occasion is marriage and there are many, many notes to write, they should be done within a month. Men and women are expected to express gratitude, whether they are fiancées, grooms, or new fathers.

Invitations

A casual invitation is fine for informal events, during a conversation, a telephone call, or an e-mail note. A sit-down dinner or more formal affair like a wedding does rate written invitations (engraving is only an option; handwritten cards are always acceptable):

You are cordially invited to join us for dinner on Saturday, February 30th, at 8:00 o'clock. RSVP 555.555.555 or e-mail host@pleasecome.com.

RSVP represents the letters for *Répondez, s'il vous plaît*, the French phrase that means "please respond."

Be precise in addressing the invitation: if you are hoping to host the whole family, list them. Spouses (life partners and couples living together) should be invited, even if they are unknown to you. Never assume an invitation is intended to include someone not mentioned.

The Home Telephone Answering Machine

A good outgoing message is formulaic: state your name or your number to confirm the caller has reached the intended home, ask the caller to leave a name and number, and promise to return the call. If you are not the only person in your household, answer on behalf of others—name adults, then children. For peace of mind, you may want to leave your cell number or an emergency contact. It is not appropriate to ask a child to record your message, include music or other sound effects, speak simultaneously with another person on the tape, or record your message after enjoying cocktails. Call your number periodically to ensure that the quality of your message is still good.

Chatiquette (electronic correspondence)

E-mail is a part of our daily lives, but this wonderful invention has also made a contribution to the erosion of manners. The speed of e-mail can be a blessing or a curse. Many believable stories circulate about angry messages sent by mistake, to an unintended recipient, or even to an entire address book—that means grandma, the pastor, and members of your book club! The basic etiquette of e-mail: Every one should have a greeting and signature; it should be re-read for mistakes before being sent; should not be all capital letters (this can be misinterpreted as anger); and, even though it is so obvious that it hurts us to say it, there should be no foul language.

In correspondence with friends and family, some shorthand is acceptable:

■ **AKA:** also known as ■ **ASAP:** as soon as possible
■ **EMSG:** e-mail message ■ **FYI:** for your information ■ **GTG:** got to go
■ **IM:** instant message ■ **LOL:** laugh out loud ■ **PM:** private message
■ **TX (THNX):** thanks ■ **UIN:** user identification number

Chapter 6
Resources

Sources and Agencies

Alliance to Save Energy
Energy conservation strategies for the planet and home

1200 18th Street NW, Suite 900
Washington, DC 20036
1-202-857-0666; www.ase.org

American Association of Poison Control Centers
Provides resources for local centers and gives general tips on poison prevention

3201 New Mexico Avenue, Suite 310
Washington, DC 20016
1-202-362-7217; www.aapcc.org
(Emergency hotline: 1-800-222-1222)

American Automobile Association (AAA)
Reference for travel safety, maps, and automobile tips

www.aaa.com

American Consumer Credit Counseling, Inc.
Advice on budgeting and credit consultations

1-800-769-3571; www.consumercredit.com

American Feng Shui Institute
Provides online courses and seminars on the practice of feng shui

108 North Ynez Avenue, Suite 202
Monterey Park, CA 91754
1-626-571-2757; www.amfengshui.com

American Gas Association
Information on natural gas utilities and appliances

400 North Capitol Street NW
Washington, DC 20001
1-202-824-7115; www.aga.org

American Homeowners Foundation
Collection of sources for home buying, selling, and renovating

6776 Little Falls Road
Arlington, VA 22213
1-800-489-7776; www.americanhomeowners.org

American Lighting Association
Provides information on choosing lighting and fan options for the home

P.O. Box 420288, Dallas, TX 75342
1-800-274-4484
www.americanlightingassoc.com

American Lung Association
Tips on improving indoor air quality

61 Broadway, 6th Floor, NY, NY 10006
1-800-LUNGUSA; www.lungusa.org

American Red Cross Foundation
Provides first aid tips, safety procedures, and preparation for emergencies

Public Inquiry Office
1621 Kent North Kent Street, 11th Floor
Arlington, VA 22209
1-800-HELPNOW; www.redcross.org

American Society of Interior Designers
Presents tips on finding a designer, gives basic interior design information, and also lists events

608 Massachusetts Avenue NE
Washington, DC 20002
1-800-775-2743; www.asid.org

American Society for the Prevention of Cruelty To Animals (ASPCA)
Information on pet care and nutrition; behavior tips

424 E. 92nd Street
New York, NY 10128-6804
1-212-876-7700; www.aspca.org

Arm & Hammer
Cleaning tips and product information

469 North Harrison Street
Princeton, NJ 08543
1-800-524-1328; www.armhammer.com

Association of Home Appliance Manufacturers
Consumer section provides expert advice on everything from major appliance to indoor air quality

Suite 402, 111 19th Street, NW
Washington, DC 20036
1-202-872-5955; www.aham.org

Asthma and Allergy Foundation of America
Improving indoor air quality and allergy prevention tips

1233 20th Street NW, Suite 402
Washington, DC 20036
1-800-7-ASTHMA; www.aafa.org

Better Sleep Council
Tips on finding good beds and caring for mattresses

501 Wythe Street, Alexandria, VA 22314-1917
www.bettersleep.org

Carpet and Rug Institute
Carpet care and stain removal tips

310 Holiday Avenue, Dalton, GA 30720
1-800-882-8846; www.carpet-rug.com

Centers for Disease Control and Prevention
Tips on food safety, sanitation, and health standards

1600 Clifton Road NE, Atlanta, GA 30333
1-404-639-3311; www.cdc.gov

Chimney Safety Institute of America
Tips on choosing a care specialist, avoiding fire hazards, and maintaining your chimney properly

2155 Commercial Drive, Plainfield, IN 46168
1-317-837-5362; www.csia.org/homeowners.htm

Color Restorations
Tips on carpet care and maintenance, including a spot removal guide

PO Box 771461, Winter Garden, Florida 34777
1-888-472-7500; www.carpetexpert.com

Consumer Federation of America
Information on product and child safety, as well as indoor air and water quality

1424 16th Street NW, Suite 604
Washington, DC 20036
1-202-387-6121; www.consumerfed.org

Consumer Product Safety Commission
Product information, safety guidelines, and recall updates

Washington, DC 20207
1-800-638-CPSC; www.cpsc.gov

Consumers Union
Produces Consumer Reports *magazine and website (www.consumerreports.org); reports and rates a wide array of products; also has helpful home tips*

101 Truman Avenue, Yonkers, NY 10703-1057
1-914-378-2000; www.consumersunion.org

Cotton Incorporated World Headquarters
Information on cotton products

6399 Weston Parkway, Cary, NC 27513
1-919-678-2220; www.cottoninc.com

Council of Better Business Bureaus
Reports on businesses and charities; addresses consumer complaints; provides a directory of local bureaus

4200 Wilson Boulevard
Arlington, VA 22203
1-703-276-0100; www.bbb.org

Energy Conservation Center
Provides professional advice on appliance efficiency and home energy programs

P.O. Box 1258, Newark, NJ 07101
1-800-854-4444
www.pseg.com/customer/home/welcome/
    conservation.html

Energy Efficiency and Renewable Energy Clearinghouse
U.S. Department of Energy guidelines for energy efficiency and conservation

P.O. Box 3048, Merrifield, VA 22116
1-800-363-3732; www.eren.doe.gov

Energy Star Program
Product information and energy conservation tips

US EPA
Climate Protection Partnerships Division
ENERGY STAR Programs Hotline
& Distribution (MS-6202J)
1200 Pennsylvania Ave NW
Washington, DC 20460
1-888-STAR-YES; www.energystar.gov

Environmental Defense Fund
Energy conservation, pollution reduction and air quality improvement

257 Park Avenue South
New York, NY 10010
1-212-505-2100
www.environmentaldefense.org

Environmental Protection Agency
Recycling and conservation tips; ways to protect the environment; improve water and air systems

Public Information Service
401 M Street, Washington, DC 20460
1-202-272-0167; www.epa.gov
EPA Safe Drinking Water Hotline: 1-800-426-4791

Federal Emergency Management Agency
Preparation information for emergencies, disasters, and home safety

Federal Center Plaza, 500 C. Street S.W.
Washington, D.C. 20472; www.fema.gov

Federal Home Loan Mortgage Corporation
Federally chartered corporation gives information on buying and owning a home, acquiring a mortgage, and lists property sales

8200 Jones Branch Drive, McLean, VA 22102
1-703-903-2039; www.freddiemac.com

Federal Trade Commission
Information for consumer safety and awareness, mortgages and loans, and energy efficiency.

600 Pennsylvania Avenue, NW
Washington, D.C. 20580
1-877-FTC-HELP; www.ftc.gov

Feng Shui Help
Provides basic background information and free hints

www.fengshuihelp.com

Fight Bac!
Kid-friendly website for food safety guidelines and sanitation tips

www.fightbac.org

FirstGov for Consumers
Offers federal information on everything from getting off mailing lists and filing consumer complaints to product recalls and food safety

www.consumer.gov

Food and Drug Administration
Tips on food preparation and kitchen sanitation

HFE-88, 5600 Fishers Lane
Rockville, MD 20857
1-888-463-6332; www.fda.gov

GE Answer Center
Tips on appliance troubleshooting and maintenance

1-800-626-2000; www.geappliances.com/geac/

Homestore
Provides extensive household information on everything from finding a house to interior decorating

www.homestore.com

Home Safety Council
Non-profit organization supplies guidelines for keeping homes secure and safe

1725 Eye Street NW, Suite 300
Washington, DC 20006
1-202-349-1100 ; www.homesafetycouncil.org

Home Ventilating Institute
Information on indoor air quality and ventilation

1000 N Rand Road, Suite 214, Wauconda, IL 60084
1-847-526-2010; www.hvi.org

Indoor Air Quality Hotline
Information on improving air quality in the home

1-800-438-4318

International Association for Child Safety
Promotes safety awareness and accident prevention for children; also allows consumers to locate a childproofing professional for the home

P.O. Box 801 , Summit, NJ 07902
1-888-677-IACS; www.iafcs.com

International Fabricare Institute
Information on dry-cleaning and fabric care

12251 Tech Road, Silver Spring, MD 20904
1-800-638-2627; www.ifi.org

Internal Revenue Service
Federal tax and financial information

1-800-829-1040; www.irs.gov

Major Appliance Consumer Action Panel (MACAP)
Provides solutions to appliance problems

20 North Wacker Drive, Chicago, IL 60606

Marble Institute of America
Information on the care and restoration of marble surfaces for consumers and professionals

28901 Clemens Road, Suite 100
Westlake, OH 44145
1-440-250-9222; www.marble-institute.com

National Association of Homebuilders
Information on renovating and finding a contractor

1201 15th Street NW, Washington, DC 20005
1-800-368-5242; www.nahb.com

National Association of Professional Organizers
Locates and contacts organizers; online seminars are also available

4700 W. Lake Avenue, Glenview, Illinois 60025
1-847-375-4746; www.napo.net

National Association of the Remodeling Industry
Tips on finding a remodeling professional; has a home owner guide on the remodeling process

780 Lee Street, Suite 200, Des Plaines, IL 60016
1-800-611-NARI; www.remodeltoday.com

National Audubon Society
Provides gardening and landscaping tips

700 Broadway, New York, NY 10003
1-212-979-3000; www.audubon.org

National Center for Health Statistics
Reference for a large amount of national health and safety statistics

U.S. Department of Health and Human Services
Centers for Disease Control and Prevention
National Center for Health Statistics
Hyattsville, MD 20782
1-866-441-NCHS; www.cdc.gov/nchs/

National Crime Prevention Council
Home safety tips on everything from burglary to identity theft

1000 Connecticut Avenue NW, 13th Floor
Washington, DC 20036
1-202-466-6272; www.ncpc.org

National Electrical Safety Foundation
Information and tips on maintaining electricity safely in the home

1300 North 17th Street, Suite 1847
Rosslyn, VA 22209
1-703-841-3211; www.esfi.org

National Fire Protection Association
Has a wide array of information about fire and home safety, including a special section for kids

1 Batterymarch Park, Quincy, MA 02169-7471
1-617-770-3000; www.nfpa.org

National Gardening Association
Sponsored by Burpee, this site provides tips on growing gardens and landscaping

W. Atlee Burpee & Co.
300 Park Avenue, Warminster, PA 18974
1-800-333-5808; www.garden.com

National Glass Association
Consumers section supplies information on home decorating with glass and how to choose a glass specialist

8200 Greensboro Drive, Suite 302
McLean, VA 22102-3881
1-866-DIAL NGA; www.glass.org

National Insurance Consumer Hotline
Information on home and life insurance policies, and a directory to state insurance departments

1-800-942-4242: Mon-Fri 8:00-8:00 EST

National Kitchen and Bath Association
Information on planning and maintaining new kitchens and bathrooms

687 Willow Grove Street, Hackettstown, NY 07840
1-877-NKBA-PRO; www.nkba.org

National Lead Information Center
Tips on preventing lead poisoning and testing for lead in the home; also provides order forms for lead testing kits

1121 Spring Lake Drive
Itasca, IL 60143-3201
1-800-424-5323; www.nsc.org/issues/lead/

National Paint & Coatings Association
Provides hints on painting and suggestions for troubleshooting; also has resources on lead paint

1500 Rhode Island Avenue, NW
Washington, DC 20005
1-202-462-6272; www.paint.org

National Pest Management
Invaluable information about pest control and preventing infestations of specific pests; also has a children's section and professional referral service

8100 Oak Street, Dunn Loring, VA 22027
1-703-573-8330; www.pestworld.org

National Radon Information Hotline
Tips on detecting and treating radon in the home

1-800-767-7236

National Safe Kids Campaign
Child safety and accident-prevention tips

1301 Pennsylvania Avenue NW, Suite 1000
Washington, DC 20004
1-202-662-0600; www.safekids.org

National Safety Council
Safety statistics and accident prevention resources

1121 Spring Lake Drive, Itasca, IL 60143-3201
1-630-285-1121; www.nsc.org

National Wood Flooring Association
Tips on the care and maintenance of wood flooring

16388 Westwoods Business Park
Ellisville, MO 63021
1-800-422-4556; www.woodfloors.org

Porcelain Enamel Institute
Showcases porcelain enamel products, gives cleaning suggestions, and provides consumer information

3700 Mansell Road, Suite 220, Alpharetta, GA 30022
1-770-281-8980; www.porcelainenamel.com

Rand McNally
Maps, driving instructions, and travel itineraries

P.O. Box 7600, Chicago, IL 60680-7600
1-847-329-8100; www.randmcnally.com

Scrapbooking.com
Tips on creating scrapbooks and photograph storage

www.scrapbooking.com

Shopsmith, Inc.
Woodworking tips and project ideas

6530 Poe Avenue, Dayton, Ohio 45414-2591
1-800-762-7555; www.shopsmith.com

Soap and Detergent Association
Cleaning and laundry tips and product information

1500 K Street NW, Suite 300, Washington, DC 20005
1-202-347-2900; www.sdahq.org

Tile Council of America
Mostly geared towards professionals, but has some information on new tile products and maintenance

100 Clemson Research Blvd., Anderson, SC 29625
1-864-646-8453; www.tileusa.com

Underwriters Laboratories Inc.
Product safety standards and home safety tips

333 Pfingsten Road, Northbrook, IL 60062
1-847-272-8800; www.ul.com

United States Department of Agriculture (USDA)
Consumer information on food safety and health

Food and Consumer Services (FCS)
USDA, Personnel Division, Room 623
3101 Park Center, Alexandria, VA 22303
www.usda.gov

United States Department of Labor
(Occupational Safety and Health Administration)
Information on the chemical hazards of dry cleaning

Occupational Safety & Health Administration
200 Constitution Avenue, NW
Washington, DC 20210
1-800-321-6742; www.osha.gov/SLTC/drycleaning

United States Government's Official Web Portal
Web directory for information from countless sources: from tax matters to home security to property auction dates

www.firstgov.gov

United States Postal Service
Information on moving and relocating

Washington, DC 20260-6720
1-800-ASK-USPS; www.usps.com

United Way of America
Information on volunteering and ways to build community within states and neighborhoods

701 North Fairfax Street, Alexandria, VA 22314
1-703-836-7112; www.unitedway.org

The Weather Channel
Reference for forecasts, weather advisories, as well as information on weatherproofing, home maintenance, and gardening

www.weather.com

Best Home Web sites
www.marthastewart.com
www.houseandhome.msn.com
www.doityourself.com
www.gardenandhearth.com
www.organizedhome.com
www.housenet.com
www.newhomemaker.com
www.digsmagazine.com
www.about.com/homegarden/
www.bhg.com
www.homeportfolio.com

Top 10 Home Magazines
Better Homes & Gardens
Budget Living
Country Home
Family Circle
Good Housekeeping
Home Magazine
House & Garden
Martha Stewart Living
Real Simple
Traditional Home

Top 10 Design Magazines
American Style
Architectural Digest
Classic Home
Elle Décor
Fine Homebuilding
House Beautiful
Metropolitan Home
Southern Accents
This Old House
Town & Country

Consumer Reports

For the most accurate information on appliances and other purchases for the home, *Consumer Reports* is your best bet. Started in 1936 by the Consumers Union, the publication is committed to testing and evaluating thousands of goods available to the public each year. The monthly magazine showcases new products, provides tips on what to look for when shopping, and rates which product is most worth your money. No longer resigned to magazine form, *Consumer Reports* is also available online at *www.consumerreports.org*. Although a fee is required to access some information and the archives, there is a wealth of free product data available for everything from the best automobiles to which air conditioner cools the fastest. Several publications also give recommendations for those looking to purchase, including the annual "Best Buys for Your Home." In addition to product ratings, helpful articles are provided on how to improve your home and maintain appliances.

Escaping Telephone Solicitor Lists and Reducing Junk Mail

You may not realize it, but each time you provide your name and address for a purchase or service, you could be added to a mailing list. Junk mail is not only an annoyance, but it also wastes paper and could be stolen by identity thieves. Here are some steps you can take to reduce your mountain of mail:

1. If you get excessive amounts of junk mail, you are probably on a list of one of the major distribution companies: Direct Marketing Association (DMA) or Abacus. Contact DMA at *www.the-dma.org/consumers/offmailinglist.html*

or by mail at Mail Preference Service, P.O. Box 643, Carmel NY 10512. Simply send them a message saying that you would like to be removed from their lists and provide your complete name and address. For Abacus, write to them at P.O. Box 1478, Broomfield, CO 80083.

2. If you are still receiving a lot of mail after a few months, you'll have to contact companies directly by calling their customer service departments.

3. To reduce mail from credit bureaus, call 1-888-OPTOUT to have your name removed from the list of three major credit bureaus (Equifax, Experian, and TransUnion.)

4. Consider using an unlisted telephone number. This won't take care of all your calls, but it may reduce them.

5. Contact the Direct Marketing Association at DMA Telephone Preference Service, P.O. Box 9014, Farmingdale, NY 11735 to be removed from some telemarketing lists for a period of up to five years.

6. When you do receive a telemarketing call, tell them to remove you from their list. They are obligated to then place your name on a "do not call" list for a period of ten years.

7. You can also register online at the Federal Trade Commission's Do Not Call Registry. This free service is available at www.donotcall.gov, and is good for up to five years. If a telemarketer continues to contact you, you will be able to file a formal complaint.

Protecting Against Identity Theft

Identity thieves steal pieces of your personal information and use them for financial gain. Often times people are not even aware their information has been used until they receive a bill, or are financially rejected due to a poor credit record. At best, identity theft can be an annoyance; at worst, it can permanently scar your credit history, making it impossible to be accepted for loans, rentals, or insurance. Although there is no foolproof method to preventing identity theft, there are several steps you can take to protect yourself.

■ Order credit reports from the three major credit bureaus annually and check for any inconsistencies.

■ When choosing a password, don't pick easily guessed words, like your birth date, Social Security number, or mother's maiden name.

■ Secure personal documents in your home and office. When discarding paperwork with personal information on it, make sure to shred or cut it up and disperse the pieces in three different garbage cans.

■ Don't give out personal information over the telephone or Internet until you've verified the authenticity of the solicitation.

■ Identity thieves can confiscate mail, so check your mailbox and collect mail as soon as you can. If you will be away from your house for awhile, contact the post office and have a hold put on your mail. When moving, always fill out a change of address form.

■ Don't keep your Social Security card on you. Secure it in a safe location in your home.

■ Pay attention to your billing cycles, and immediately alert companies if you do not receive a notice on time.

■ If you do fall victim to identity theft, contact the FTC at 1-877-IDTHEFT (438-4338). You'll be able to speak to a financial counselor and receive tips on what to do next.

Getting a Mortgage

■ **Assess your financial situation before you consider a mortgage.** This means making sure you are on a budget and your financial status is relatively stable. The annual cost of a home should not be more than 25 percent of your gross income, so figure out if you can manage a monthly payment of 25 percent of your monthly income. Take note: it's beneficial to put an additional 10 percent of your annual income aside for yearly unseen expenses.

■ **Get preapproved.** More involved and trustworthy than loan prequalification, preapproval involves finding a potential lender, and basically providing all of the information that you would provide in a real loan application, but before you find a house.

■ **Decide what loan is best for you.** Loans usually fall into two classes: fixed-rate and adjustable rate. Fixed-rate mortgages have a steady monthly payment which usually does not change over the course of the 15-30 year mortgage period (this does not guarantee taxes or insurance). Adjustable rate mortgages (or ARMs) will fluctuate according to government interest rates, so your interest and principal payments will also change. This may be beneficial when dealing with a shorter-term loan, since interest rates usually start lower. But be warned that interest rates can increase.

- **Find and compare different lender programs to discover the best loan**. Once you've selected a group of lenders to consider, take the time to interview each one and see how their approval process works, what kind of loans they specialize in, how competitive are their rates, and, very importantly, if they give you this information in a clear, understandable manner.
- **Complete all applications and stick to your schedule of monthly payments.**

Mortgage Websites

www.hsh.com (HSH Associates)
www.eloan.com (an online mortgage broker)
www.hud.gov (U.S. Department of Housing and Urban Development)
www.mortgagequotes.com (from monster.com)
www.fanniemae.com (Federal National Home Mortgage Association)
www.freddiemac.com (Federal Home Loan Mortgage Corporation)
www.va.gov/vas/loan/index/htm (U.S. Veteran Affairs)

Preparing Your Home for Sale

- Pay attention to the outside—it's the first thing potential buyers will see when they drive up. If your house trim or front looks bad, you should repaint.
- Fix any broken or cracked windows.
- Keep the landscape neat and repair your driveway. It doesn't have to look like a botanical garden, but a clean, uncluttered lawn, trim hedges, and clear pathways can do wonders for a house's image. You might even consider planting some flowers if the season is right.
- Take care of any minor indoor repairs, like loose fixture and boards.
- Replace worn cabinetry, towel racks, and shower curtains.
- Buy new bathroom rugs and throw towels.
- Get rid of unwanted furniture and promote spaciousness. You're trying to create a feeling of space from the moment buyers walk in the door. This will allow them to picture the house with their own furniture inside.
- Although it's probably a good idea to paint walls or clean wallpaper in every room, this is especially necessary for the kitchen, bathroom, and master bedroom. All other rooms can usually get away with just a cleaning, if they've been repainted recently.
- Wash windows and lights.
- Clean or replace carpets with a neutral color (like gray).
- Consider undertaking major renovation, like roof, plumbing, landscape, or wall repair, if it is really necessary. Be careful about assessing how much the work will cost in comparison to how much your home is actually worth.
- Photograph your house without your car in the driveway in the best possible light exposure. These photos can be given to your listing agent for promotion.
- When it's time for an open house, keep all pets out of the area, and make sure your house is tidy, presentable, and well aired.

Home selling websites Websites

www.homegain.com
www.realtor.com
www.owners.com (For those selling by owner)

Published in 2004 by Welcome Books®
An imprint of Welcome Enterprises, Inc.
6 West 18th Street, New York, NY 10011
(212) 989-3200; Fax (212) 989-3205
www.welcomebooks.com

Publisher: Lena Tabori
Project Director: Alice Wong
Designers: Timothy Shaner and Christopher Measom
Text by Ella Stewart, Sarah Zwiebach and Deidra Garcia,
with contributions by Julia Kilmer, Clark Wakabayashi, Franco Rehor, and Marsha Heckman
Project Assistants: Deidra Garcia, Bethany Cassin Beckerlegge, Kathryn Shaw, and Naomi Irie
Line Illustrations on pages 22, 115, 116, 119, 161, 162-163, 174-177, 182-183, 216-217 by Kathryn Shaw

Distributed to the trade in the U.S. and Canada by Andrews McMeel Distribution Services
U.S. Order Department and Customer Service Toll-free: (800) 943-9839
U.S. Orders-only Fax: (800) 943-9831
PUBNET S&S San Number: 200-2442
Canada Orders Toll-free: (800) 268-3216
Canada Order-only Fax: (888) 849-8151

Library of Congress Cataloging-in-Publication Data on file.

ISBN 1-932183-26-4

Printed in Hong Kong

FIRST EDITION

1 3 5 7 9 10 8 6 4 2

ILLUSTRATION CREDITS: **pages 2-3:** F. William Haemmel; **12:** Grace M. Rahming; **1, 14, 17, 24, 31, 100, 114, 117,
191, 216, 217:** J.G. Sowerby and Walter Crane; **21, 32:** C. Coles Phillips; **30:** M'alaga Grenet; **37:** Kurtner; **42:** Whitney Darrow;
56, 113: Henriette Willebeek Le Mair; **61:** C. Twelvetrees; **63:** Janet Laura Scott; **72:** Frances Tipton Hunter; **75, 85:** Clare Victor
Dwiggins (Dwig); **86:** Edouard Halouze; **89:** Adolph Treidler; **99:** John Newton Howitt; **111:** Helen Dryden; **119:** Ruth M. Hallack;
123: Maxfield Parrish; **135:** McClelland Barclay; **147:** Alice Wanke; **156:** Bomelmann; **158:** Elizabeth Gordon; **159:** Jessie Willcox
Smith; **160:** L. Jansen; **161, 192:** Maud & Miska Petersham; **163:** Walter Beach Humphrey; **168:** Maurice Day; **182:** M. Morris;
193: Kate Greenaway; **203:** Joseph Morgan; **207:** Edward L. Chase; **211:** May Wilson Preston; **214:** Oliver Herford;
221: Lucile Patterson Marsh; **222:** John Herold; **223:** Pauli Ebner